MW00461829

Alternative Universities

Alternative Universities

Speculative Design for Innovation
in Higher Education

David J. Staley

 JOHNS HOPKINS UNIVERSITY PRESS, BALTIMORE

© 2019 Johns Hopkins University Press
All rights reserved. Published 2019
Printed in the United States of America on acid-free paper
9 8 7 6 5 4 3 2

Johns Hopkins University Press
2715 North Charles Street
Baltimore, Maryland 21218-4363
www.press.jhu.edu

Library of Congress Cataloging-in-Publication Data

Names: Staley, David J., 1963– author.
Title: Alternative universities : speculative design for innovation in higher
    education / David J. Staley.
Description: Baltimore, Maryland : Johns Hopkins University Press, 2019. |
    Includes bibliographical references and index.
Identifiers: LCCN 2018027565 | ISBN 9781421427416 (hardcover : acid-free
    paper) | ISBN 1421427419 (hardcover : acid-free paper) | ISBN
    9781421427423 (electronic) | ISBN 1421427427 (electronic)
Subjects: LCSH: Education, Higher—Aims and objectives—United States. |
    Alternative education—United States. | Educational change—United
    States. | Universities and colleges—United States—Planning.
Classification: LCC LA227.4 .S76 2019 | DDC 378.73—dc23
LC record available at https://lccn.loc.gov/2018027565

A catalog record for this book is available from the British Library.

All illustrations are by Hemalatha Venkataraman.

*Special discounts are available for bulk purchases of this book. For more information,
please contact Special Sales at 410-516-6936 or specialsales@press.jhu.edu.*

Johns Hopkins University Press uses environmentally friendly book materials,
including recycled text paper that is composed of at least 30 percent post-con-
sumer waste, whenever possible.

In memory of my father

Contents

Acknowledgments

Twenty years ago I began serious and sustained work on foresight and futuring: first, publishing on futures methodologies in academic journals and, later, writing more general pieces on future trends. My consulting work in this area was with a wide range of industries, including insurance, architecture, commercial construction, and publishing. About a decade ago, I turned my attention toward the future of higher education. I was delighted to convene some faculty at Ohio State around the theme "The Future of the University," and we continue to be engaged in deep conversation about the trends affecting higher education. I have benefited greatly from the ideas generated by this group, which has included Robert Holub, Frank Donoghue, Angela Brintlinger, Mark Rudoff, Miriam Shenkar, Stuart Hobbs, John Heimaster, Sarah Iler Pfeffer, and Laura Fathauer. With them, I first started exploring alternatives to the form and organization of the university.

The present book began as an article in *Educause Review*, where I introduced five of the alternative universities presented here. For this book, I wanted to flesh out and expand the ideas sketched in that article, and so I invited a group of designers, historians, and scholars of educational studies to help me conduct a thought experiment for each of the alternative universities. What would this university look like? How would it function? What would it be like to be a student or a faculty member? Participants in this monthly charette included Sapna Singh, David McKenzie, Richard Voithofer, Joshua Harraman, Jessica Mercerhill, Jackie Blount, Hemalatha Venkataraman, Trisha Shah, Laura Fathauer, Marcia Ham, Patrick Potyondy, Sarah Iler Pfeffer, Adam Fromme, Joshua Morrow, and Darwin Moljono. Each helped me to visualize these speculative designs.

Stephen Millett and Michael Hogan read the entire manuscript and offered thoughtful observations that I hope I have addressed. The anonymous reviewer for Johns Hopkins University Press similarly offered cogent suggestions for rethinking many of my assumptions. At the press, Greg Britton was an early and enthusiastic supporter of this project. The copyediting by Merryl Sloane was meticulous.

For each of the chapters, I wanted to include some sort of visualization to give solidity to what might read as abstract ideas. The artist/designer/poet Hemalatha Venkataraman listened to my description of each alternative university, watched me draw ideas in the air and on paper, and translated these into the striking illustrations found at the beginning of each chapter.

I presented early ideas for the Liberal Arts College at Educause Connect in 2014, and I thank the audience for their ideas and suggestions. Members of Columbus Futurists similarly heard presentations on the Liberal Arts College and Interface University, and I have benefited from their observations and suggestions. My Ohio State colleagues Barry Shank, Zeb Larson, Mark Lubbe, Rick Livingston, Susan Williams, and Peter Hahn each read and commented on the Humanities Think Tank chapter, and they suggested not only organizational changes but concrete ideas about how to actualize this speculative design.

Katherine Prince, a fellow futurist, always finds time in her busy schedule to meet for coffee to share ideas about the future of education. It was Katherine in particular who introduced me to the idea of a microschool. Katherine also invited me to present at the "Making Sense of the Future of Learning" symposium in May 2016 hosted by the KnowledgeWorks Foundation, where I explored some of these alternative universities with an audience that included educators, futurists, and education entrepreneurs.

One day over coffee, I shared the idea for the Liberal Arts College with Reese Neader, the CEO of Forge Columbus, a social entrepreneurship incubator. Reese immediately grasped the implications of this new kind of collegiate experience and worked with me on a business plan for realizing it, even beginning the process of securing funding.

Indeed, some of the ideas Reese brought to this business plan made their way into chapter 5. Reese tragically died in December 2016 at only thirty-four years of age, before we could launch the Liberal Arts College as an actual institution. I am certain that one day I will found such a college, organized around many of his ideas, and when that day comes I will name it the Reese Neader School in his honor.

I introduced some of the ideas presented as Platform University in the article "Managing the Platform: Higher Education and the Logic of Wikinomics," again published in *Educause Review*. Parts of chapter 6 on Interface University were originally published as "The Future of Higher Education in the Age of Synthetic Intelligence" in *Southeast Education Network* magazine.

It was my hope that I could complete this book in time for my father, Joseph Emmett Staley, to place a copy on the living room coffee table along with other books by his son, which he proudly displayed. This book is dedicated to him.

Introduction

On Innovation in Higher Education

Teresa Sullivan was the first victim of the "Big One."

In 2012, Sullivan was forced to resign as president of the University of Virginia by the board of visitors, specifically by Rector Helen Dragas and Vice Rector Mark Kington. The public reason for the dismissal stated, "The Board feels the need for a bold leader who can help develop, articulate and implement a concrete and achievable strategic plan to re-elevate the university to its highest potential. We need a leader with a great willingness to adapt the way we deliver our teaching, research and patient care to *the realities of the external environment*" (emphasis mine).[1] The "external environment" here meant the sudden rise in online education made possible by MOOCs (massive open online courses). Sullivan was moving too slowly—"deliberately" was the term she preferred—and the board of visitors felt that Virginia simply did not have the time to wait: UVA was facing an "existential crisis." Online education had been a reality for at least two decades, but it was usually associated with community colleges, for-profit education companies, and other lower-tier colleges and universities.

MOOCs, on the other hand, were developed at prestigious schools, such as Stanford and Harvard Universities. Sebastian Thrun, one of the first Stanford professors to develop a massive open online course in computer science, suddenly found that tens of thousands of students signed up for his course. Venture capitalists saw enormous potential in this model of delivery, and soon Thrun left Stanford to start a new company, Udacity, that would deliver MOOCs in a wide number of subjects. At about the same time, Harvard and the Massachusetts Institute of Technology (MIT) launched a similar initiative, edX, which featured open online courses that also drew thousands of eager students from around the globe.

Several University of Virginia Board of Visitors members expressed alarm at the changes to the higher education landscape that MOOCs apparently represented. Sullivan was urged to watch a video by Thrun about Udacity, which was "a signal that the on-line learning world has now reached the top of the line universities and they [Virginia] need[ed] to have strategies or [would] be left behind."[2] An email that circulated among the board of visitors asked, "How are we thinking about [online learning] at UVA? How might it lower our costs, improve productivity and link us to a group of students we couldn't afford to serve (maybe more kids from the state to please the legislature) . . . maybe more second career grads?"[3]

Sullivan was moving too slowly, and the MOOC revolution would soon leave many higher education institutions in its wake if immediate strategic action was not taken. Online education posed no challenge to UVA as long as only the University of Phoenix was delivering it. But once Stanford, MIT, and other upper-tier institutions were leading in this area, Virginia had little choice but to join in. An editorial in the *Wall Street Journal* pronounced, "The nation, and the world, are in the early stages of a historic transformation in how students learn, teachers teach, and schools and school systems are organized."[4] "What happened to the newspaper and magazine business," observed David Brooks in a *New York Times* op-ed, "is about to happen to higher education: a rescrambling around the Web." Brooks said that a "campus tsunami" was engulfing higher education.[5]

Many in higher education had been anticipating the Big One to strike for well over a decade. The "Big One" is a reference to the massive earthquake that is destined to hit California and lead to unimaginable levels of destruction. Residents await every tremor and wonder, "Is this it? Is this the Big One?" Higher education has its threatened Big One as well. In 1997, management guru Peter Drucker told *Forbes* interviewers that higher education as currently organized was unsustainable. "Do you realize that the cost of higher education has risen as fast as the cost of health care?" Drucker observed. "And for the middle-class family, college education for their children is as much of a necessity as is medical care—without it the kids have no future. Such totally uncontrollable expenditures, without any visible improvement in either the content or the quality of education, means that the system is rapidly becoming untenable. Higher education is in deep crisis." Technology would help usher in a new model, a new way of delivering higher education. "Already we are beginning to deliver more lectures and classes off campus via satellite or two-way video at a fraction of the cost. The college won't survive as a residential institution. Today's buildings are hopelessly unsuited and totally unneeded. . . . It took more than 200 years (1440 to the late 1600s) for the printed book to create the modern school. It won't take nearly that long for the big change." These observations led to Drucker's big announcement:

> Thirty years from now the big university campuses will be relics. Universities won't survive. It's as large a change as when we first got the printed book.[6]

Part of what made Drucker's reputation as a management guru was that he had been proven right about so many changes to the modern world. His pronouncements about the next thirty years, therefore, were noted by many in higher education, who waited with heightened expectation for the Big One that was finally going to disrupt higher education. Every technological tremor led observers to wonder whether Drucker's Big One had finally arrived.

Also in 1997, Clayton Christensen published *The Innovator's Dilemma*, which quickly became required reading among technology entrepreneurs. Mature industries and incumbent businesses in those industries are capable of continuing success via incremental innovations. "Existing institutions find [major] innovation difficult because their structures and norms are oriented around doing, and even improving, what they already do," writes Johann N. Neem. "Agile new institutions can enter the market because there is demand for more suppliers and they are not beholden to the past."[7] Mature industries are ripe for what Christensen termed "disruptive innovation": new advances, usually at the lower end of the market, that nevertheless transform whole industries. Those successful firms no longer appear so successful since they cannot match the industry-upending innovations of the newcomers.

The 2006 Spellings Report (policy recommendations from the Commission on the Future of Higher Education led by US secretary of education Margaret Spellings) announced, "American higher education has become what, in the business world, would be called a mature enterprise: increasingly risk averse, at times self-satisfied, and unduly expensive. It is an enterprise that has yet to address the fundamental issues of how academic programs and institutions must be transformed to serve the changing educational needs of a knowledge economy. It has yet to successfully confront the impact of globalization, rapidly evolving technologies, an increasingly diverse and aging population, and an evolving marketplace characterized by new needs and new paradigms."[8] By 2013, Christensen was similarly proclaiming that higher education was one of those mature industries that was ready to be upended by disruptive innovation.[9] "I think higher education is just on the edge of the crevasse," he told *Wired* magazine. "Generally, universities are doing very well financially, so they don't feel from the data that their world is going to collapse. But I think even five years from now these enterprises are going to be in real trouble." Online education was the source of this disruption. "It will take root in its simplest applications, then just get better and better. You know, Harvard Business School doesn't teach accounting anymore, because there's a guy out of BYU whose online accounting course is so good. He is extraordinary, and our accounting faculty, on average, is average." Some universities would no doubt survive the disruption that was heading their way. "Most [universities] will evolve hybrid models, in which universities license some courses from an online provider like Coursera but then provide more-specialized courses in person."[10] The language of disruptive innovation began to swirl around higher education. Mark Cuban was among the celebrity entrepreneurs who began investing in higher education start-ups, a further signal that disruptive innovation was about to be unleashed.[11]

Richard DeMillo was among those observers who anticipated technology having disruptive effects on the landscape of higher education.

"The rush to define the twenty-first-century university is driven by a combination of political and economic factors. It is fueled, above all, by *enabling technology curves*, the growth-driven law of the Internet era that describes the annual doubling of capability and capacity for equal costs. Paradoxically, mainstream universities—where much of the technology originated—have been slow to embrace these technologies, even as they became ubiquitous in other sectors of the economy."[12] DeMillo wrote these words a year before Sullivan resigned from UVA, but he could have been voicing the concerns of the board of visitors. However, DeMillo did not believe that institutions like UVA would be most affected by the enabling technology curves. DeMillo argued that universities in the United States stratified into three levels. At the top are elite universities, which "are at a tremendous advantage as they compete for students, money, and global prestige." At the bottom are for-profit universities, which DeMillo believed (in 2011) were primed to be the disruptive force: the lower-end market of higher education, if you will, that would unleash disruptive innovation. "Most colleges and universities," concluded DeMillo, "lie in the *Middle*, a land where the resources of a top-ranked school are just out of reach, a region where they find themselves unable [to] find better ways of using what money they have to become more competitive. In American higher education, wealth flows to the top and bottom strata, but not the Middle."[13]

Universities in the middle were the most at risk of disruption in the higher education marketplace, and it was the rise of the for-profits—especially their effective use of technology—that was the main threat. "With their ability to scale to match demand, deliver consistent value for market process, and place graduates in attractive first jobs," argued DeMillo, "For-Profits are clearly poised to attract what [University of Phoenix president Bill] Peppicello sees as a large number of capable students—not only the nontraditional students who are shopping for part-time degree programs, but the increasing numbers of applicants for traditional institutions who prefer the learning experience, price, and employment prospects of an institution that is run like a business."[14] Again, this was written in 2011, when the for-profits were on the rise and seeing enormous increases in their enrollments. These predictions seem incorrect today, as for-profit enrollments have plummeted, largely as a result of increased regulation by the Obama administration. It is very likely the for-profits will rise again, since we can expect a relaxation of these regulations under the Trump administration and a Republican-controlled Congress. But DeMillo's point was that not all universities would be so impacted by technological disruption. "In short, the overlap between the Middle and the For-Profits should concern leaders of traditional universities. . . . Colleges and universities in the Middle are completely exposed to the threat of proprietary universities. . . . In order to compete for these students, an institution in the Middle needs two things: an equally compelling value proposition and a way to deliver it at a reasonable cost."[15] Lower-cost delivery was to come, presumably, via technology. DeMillo and many other observers believed that technological disruption in higher education was only a matter of time.

And then MOOCs hit the scene.

Surely, this was the Big One that Drucker had anticipated. Indeed, for a time it seemed that MOOCs were going to fundamentally change higher education in the way Drucker had predicted. A few prestigious universities would make their courses available free for anyone—and why not: their professors were tops in their field. Why would students want to take a class with a second- or third-class professor when they could learn from the best in the world? Some observers noted that MOOCs might be adopted by smaller institutions or institutions in the developing world; the video lectures would be supplemented by local faculty, who would lead discussions and manage classes taught by an MIT luminary. Maybe some universities would survive—Harvard, MIT, Stanford—but many other institutions of higher education would not be able to compete in such an environment.

■   ■   ■

It is debatable whether MOOCs have had the transformative, disruptive, tsunami- or earthquake-like effects that so many expected. We still have MOOCs, of course: Georgia Tech, for example, teamed up with Udacity and AT&T to develop an online master's degree program in computer science that is dependent on MOOCs and seems to be successful.[16] But many of the MOOCs today are neither massive nor open, and they have not turned traditional campuses into relics. At the height of MOOC hysteria, I was invited to give presentations on the meaning of the MOOC phenomenon. I suggested that the idea of upper-tier universities giving away all of their courses for free via MOOCs simply was not a sustainable model, a lesson the newspapers learned in the 2000s, when many of them gave away all of their content for free and then determined there was no way to monetize that practice. Universities would not give away courses, no matter how disruptive the practice might be.[17] I often concluded these presentations with a prediction: in ten years, we would not even be talking about MOOCs—and certainly not in a way to suggest that MOOCs had disrupted higher education.[18] Indeed, Sebastian Thrun himself seemed to be walking back the disruptive power of MOOCs by 2013. "We were on the front pages of newspapers and magazines, and at the same time, I was realizing, we don't educate people as others wished, or as I wished. We have a lousy product," Thrun told *Fast Company*. Indeed, the magazine wondered whether "Thrun might be giving up the moon—free education for all! Harvard on a piece of glass!—in favor of something far more pedestrian. It will be, Thrun admits, 'the biggest shift in the history of the company,' a pivot that involves charging money for classes and abandoning academic disciplines in favor of more vocational-focused learning."[19] Udacity remains a thriving company, but traditional, incumbent universities remain standing in great numbers.

■ ■ ■

Two weeks after she was forced to resign—after howls of protest from faculty, students, and alumni—Teresa Sullivan was reinstated as president of UVA. What did the Sullivan affair teach us about disruptive innovation in higher education?

In the first place, MOOCs were not the Big One. Online education is certainly having an effect on higher education outside of the for-profits. Nonprofit institutions, such as Western Governors University and Southern New Hampshire University, have thriving online programs, and for many other institutions online programs are an important feature of their offerings. But traditional campuses lying in ruins simply has not come to pass (although we still have eight years left in Drucker's prediction). The for-profits have not disrupted higher education in the manner DeMillo predicted, although a new kind of for-profit entity—the prehire training company—might just have that effect. But Harvard, Stanford, and a few other elite institutions providing MOOCs for everyone is a model that shows little sign of appearing. A more pertinent question in the wake of the Sullivan affair might be "Will there be a Big One at all?" Christensen's theory of disruptive innovation has come under criticism,[20] and perhaps there is in fact no Big One to be anticipating.

Even if MOOCs have not rescrambled the higher education landscape and even if disruptive innovation has not yet occurred, there are challenges facing higher education. Responding to these challenges (and not to the assumption that technology will disrupt) may well prove a source of disruptive innovation in higher education. Perhaps innovation will arrive from other sources in response to other external threats whose answer is not technologically determined?

■ ■ ■

In describing higher education as a "mature" industry, one ripe for disruption, there is a presumption that institutions of higher education in the United States are lumbering dinosaurs, slow to change and reluctant to innovate. The history of higher education would suggest otherwise: innovation has occurred at several junctures, some examples of which might even be described as disruptive. In the mid-nineteenth century, the land-grant universities represented a significant innovation in higher education, from their source of support to the populations they served to the content of their curricula. In the early twentieth century, experimental institutions, such as Deep Springs College, Bennington College, Black Mountain College, and St. John's University, proliferated. By the mid-twentieth century, the development of the community college similarly represented an innovation in accessibility and affordability. "In the 1960s and early 1970s," writes Joy Rosen-zweig Kliewer, "academic planners, reformers, countercultural gurus, faculty members, and students converged upon mountaintops, held retreats in the woods, and occupied classrooms and board rooms for days at a time, to give life to new and radically different institutions of higher education. Scores of innovative or experimental colleges and subcolleges burst onto the scene against a backdrop of social and polit-ical turbulence, heated and passionate student demonstration, rapid enrollment growth, economic upswings, and countercultural lifestyle exploration."[21] While many of these experimental institutions had short lives, there are a number that remain today, such as the College of the Atlantic, the New College of Florida, and the University of California, Santa Cruz.[22] All were the product of a particular moment when the external environment placed demands on the university, demands that were met with innovative ideas.

The innovation that was the German research university similarly developed in the context of significant changes in the external envi-ronment. The crisis of the university of the eighteenth century—the external disruption that helped to birth the research university—was information overload. By the end of the eighteenth century, so many books had been printed that one scholar could not possibly master all the knowledge they contained. The eighteenth-century university was the home of the erudite, who "constituted a distinct social class or a traditional estate . . . which included university professors, as well as university-trained professionals. . . . Membership was based not on birth but primarily on knowledge of Latin and, usually, a university education."[23] Indeed, German erudites tended to cluster in universities, where encyclopedic knowledge of the range of printed books was the expectation. An information explosion of printed materials challenged the ethos of erudition. "What was the purpose of the university in an age where print had reached a saturation point?" asks Chad Wellmon. "If universities continued to present students 'the entire world of books, which already lies printed before everyone's eyes,' warned Fichte, they would soon become redundant. Universities had not figured out how to respond to technological change, and if they could not distinguish themselves from printed books, they would fail."[24] Technological change was threatening a crisis in the idea of the university, a parallel to our own digital moment not unnoticed by Wellmon.

The university as imagined by Kant and other philosophers and as put into practice by Wilhelm von Humboldt was to produce a new kind of scholar, a new "subject" in Wellmon's terms. "The story of the German research university," he writes, "has given us not just the ideals of academic freedom and the unity of teaching and research," innovations in and of themselves, "it has also lent us the logic of intellectual specialization that continues to form the contemporary university."[25] The ethos of erudition was replaced by the ethos of *Wissenschaft*. By the end of the eighteenth century, the term "science" had shifted its connotation from an individual mental trait to a body of objectively shared knowledge. "Once the unity of knowledge was grounded not in mental faculties common to all but in objectified systems of knowledge," says Wellmon, "general access could not be presumed." The new university enacted by von Humboldt would not be a place for the polymath or the erudite scholar who traversed any discipline across the encyclopedia of knowledge. "Instead, [knowledge] had to be cultivated through institutionalized habits, practices, and disciplines. Particular scientific cultures emerged that distinguished between [the] expert and the layman. Disciplinarity gradually arose in this context as a system for managing the distinct sciences and the people who labored within those sciences."[26] The innovative German university existed as a way not only to manage objective knowledge, but to form a specific kind of student: this was a shift from the erudite to the "disciplined" subject.

The German university's new raison d'être highlights the degree to which universities are sites for transformative experiences. What that transformation is can vary, but at its heart a university exists to transform subjects—be they students or faculty—such that they leave the institution a different person than when they arrived. This is not the same thing as saying the same person plus a new skill set, an attitude that seemingly defines the nature and purpose of higher education today. I quote at length the computer scientist Joseph Weizenbaum on the university as a transformative experience:

> The function of a university cannot be to simply offer prospective students a catalogue of "skills" from which to choose. For, were that its function, then the university would have to assume that the students who come to it have already become whatever it is they are to become. The university would then be quite correct in seeing the student as a sort of market basket, to be filled with goods from among the university's intellectual inventory. It would be correct, in other words, in seeing the student as an object very much like a computer whose storage banks are forever hungry for more "data." But surely that cannot be a proper characterization of what a university is or ought to be about. Surely the university should look upon each of its citizens, students and faculty alike, first of all as human beings in search of—what else to call it?—truth, and hence in search of themselves. Something should constantly be happening to every citizen of the university; each should leave its halls having become someone other than he who entered in the morning. The mere teaching of craft cannot fulfill this high function of the university.[27]

For Weizenbaum, the search for truth is the mission of the university, but a more fundamental role for the university is ensuring that everyone who enters "become[s] someone other than he who entered." That person might be searching for truth, for erudition, or for a disciplined mind.

The university is more—much more—than simply a transactional exchange: I pay you tuition, you certify my skills. In the German university as enacted by von Humboldt, one left the university a different person, transformed into a disciplined subject. The threat posed by the external environment in the German case was indeed an existential one: Could the university continue to exist in its present form given the changes occurring in the external environment? That is, of course, the same question posed by the board of visitors at UVA, but its response was not to innovate around a new kind of transformational experience, but rather to innovate around a transactional exchange.

■   ■   ■

I would submit that truly disruptive innovation in higher education comes with changes in the nature and purpose of those transformative experiences. Too many examples of what passes for innovation in the twenty-first century—MOOCs especially—focus on transactions, on questions of delivery.[28] Anyone seeking innovation in higher education today should concentrate on the kind of transformational experience it enacts.

The problem is not that universities are lacking in innovation, but rather that they suffer from a poverty of imagination of what that innovation might be. "This is an existential moment for universities," writes the philosopher of higher education Ronald Barnett, who invokes language similar to that of the board of visitors. But Barnett sees a very different existential moment. Will institutions evolve into technologicalized, market-driven "entrepreneurial universities"?[29] Or are there other possibilities for the university beyond what Drucker and others have predicted? "All systems of higher education across the world are moving inexorably in the direction of the marketised university," claims Barnett. "Consequently, the pool of ideas through which the university is comprehended is shrinking."[30] Indeed, the main existential crisis facing the university is a poverty of ideas about what universities can become. Keri Facer laments, "The educational imagination of the last two decades has been dominated by one particular vision of the future, a vision of a global knowledge economy fuelled by international competition and sustained by digital networks. This vision has driven investment in new technologies, new approaches to teaching and learning, new education industries and massive school rebuilding programmes around the world. This vision has promised students and nations that with enough education, creativity and new technology, their futures will be secure." That vision, in Facer's opinion, "can no longer be considered either robust or desirable enough to act as a reliable guide for education."[31] We must look elsewhere, more broadly and with greater imagination, for potential sources of innovation.

"Ideas of the university in the public domain are hopelessly impoverished," Barnett emphasizes, echoing Facer.

> "Impoverished" because they are unduly confined to a small range of possible conceptions of the university; and "hopelessly" because they are too often without hope, taking the form of either a hand-wringing over the current state of the university or merely offering a defence of the emerging nature of "the entrepreneurial university." Against this background, the questions arise as to what, if any, are the prospects for imagining the university anew? What role might the imagination play here? What are its limits and what might be its potential for bringing forward new forms of the university? This then is the problem before us: the problem of the place of the imagination in developing the idea—*and* the institutional form—of the university.[32]

Part of the hopelessness of our current ideas about the future of universities is not only because of the paucity of fresh ideas, but because the ideas that are publicly discussed "are being driven forward with such determination that it may appear that 'there is no alternative.' "[33] For Barnett, there are indeed alternatives, if we only imagine the possibilities. "The entrepreneurial university is not the end-point of the unfolding university," he concludes. "There are choices before it."[34]

To envision those choices, Barnett urges us to employ our imaginations productively to generate "a proliferation of ideas of the university."[35] Using our imaginations allows us "to open up a gap, a gulf or even a chasm between what is and what might be. . . . In turn, [imagination] can show that the corporate university, the entrepreneurial university, the marketised and the bureaucratic university are not the only available representations of the university."[36] While Barnett is not directly addressing Drucker or others who have predicted disruptive innovation to higher education, his observations highlight the degree to which the presumptive MOOCification of higher education represents only one future path, one direction that disruptive innovation might—or must?—take. Barnett, instead, asks us to consider multiple possibilities. There is a wide variety of possible innovations, especially around reimagining the purpose of the university itself.

The products of our imaginative ideas about the future of the university are what Barnett terms "feasible utopias."

> [Feasible utopias] have four significant features. First, they are utopias. They are almost certainly not going fully to be realised. Second, they are *feasible*: that is, in being utopian, they are not fanciful. There are sufficient exemplars *already present* that show that these utopias *could* be reached. Third, they contain both optimism and pessimism: they reveal positive possibilities in our present situation but they are confronted with forces in the world such that their coming into being is extremely unlikely. Lastly, utopias are not necessarily all to the good, even if they were realised. As utopias, they look forward to situations that would be mostly beneficial but, as utopias, they often harbour extreme hopes. Dystopias lurk within utopias.[37]

■   ■   ■

In this book, I have taken up Barnett's challenge and employed my imagination to generate ideas about future forms of the university, alternatives both to our current practices and to the narrowly defined, technologically delivered university. What follows are ten feasible utopias; I believe that each has the potential to be enacted. (Indeed, I was approached by a social entrepreneurship organization to develop one of these alternative universities.) Each of my descriptions of these feasible utopias may be read as an initial blueprint or an early stage of a business plan—to borrow the language of entrepreneurship—that I hope to one day put into practice. I fully expect to found all of these as fully realized, actual universities.

Each chapter describes one alternative university, including a description of its broad contours and main features. The ten alternative universities are organized into four parts.

Part I: Organization. The three alternative universities proposed here are distinguished by their organizational forms—specifically, the way that knowledge is categorized and ordered—and by their differences from the way most universities are organized today. **Platform University** is structured like a multisided platform. In business, a platform is an organization that does not sell or produce anything but instead exists only to connect buyers and sellers. A platform is also a social form that facilitates interactions between people; it is agnostic about the nature of those interactions. (The Athenian agora would be an example of this kind of platform.) Since it does not have an overarching administrative hierarchy, Platform University is organized and managed organically, with decisions arrived at through the unregulated interactions of teachers and students.

Chapter 2 describes a system of higher education made up of thousands of small **Microcolleges**. A Microcollege consists of one professor and twenty students. The curriculum and pedagogical philosophy of each Microcollege is as unique as the professor who leads it: an architect, a poet, an entrepreneur. Faculty leaders establish their Microcolleges in a range of settings: urban, rural, office parks, cultural institutions. Each specific location helps to shape the underlying pedagogical and research philosophy.

Unlike the typical policy institute, which brings together social scientists and scholars of business and international relations, the **Humanities Think Tank** is staffed and led by scholars from the humanities disciplines: literature, history, religious studies, art history, philosophy, and so on. The researchers at the Humanities Think Tank ask questions of interest to a wider public and contribute to a broader public discourse, but unlike the traditional public intellectualism of humanists, the knowledge produced is intended to influence policy-making: its audience is a very specific kind of "public." The knowledge produced at the Humanities Think Tank is not meant to be contemplative—it is not art for art's sake—but is intended to produce change in the world. The audience for the think tank's work includes humanities scholars, government officials, policy-makers, corporations, nongovernmental organizations (NGOs), and the military.

Part II: Apprenticeship. Both of these alternative universities are based on the idea of substituting classroom instruction with experiences in real-world settings, led by practitioners. Students learn by doing, but they also receive a broad, liberal education that develops a wide set of intellective skills. Chapter 4 describes a scenario where work is no longer tied to location, and so **Nomad University** is not grounded in a single site. Indeed, the physical location shifts around the world from course to course, from year to year. This university is organized like a series of gap-year experiences, but rather than seeing these as preparatory to a university experience, students engage in a series of eight to ten gap-year courses *as* the university experience. Students arrive at a site and work under the guidance of a faculty member on a specific problem, while immersing themselves in the local culture. Then, after a six- to eight-month stay, the students disperse, heading off to other experiences with other faculty in other locations with new sets of students. In addition to acquiring a broad set of skills, students gain an "education in place."

The **Liberal Arts College** is centered on skills rather than subjects, specifically concentrating on what is necessary to participate in the modern economy. The curriculum of the Liberal Arts College is organized around seven broad intellective skills: (1) complex problem solving, (2) sense-making, (3) making, (4) imagination, (5) multimodal communication, (6) cross-cultural competency, and (7) leadership. Students demonstrate mastery of each skill as a condition of matriculation. Instead of focusing on classroom-based coursework, students are placed in apprenticeships with local companies or organizations to develop each intellective skill. For example, one student might intern for six months with a nonprofit and work on a project that develops her imagination. She then might engage in an eight-month apprenticeship with an engineering firm to work on making. In addition to providing the students' training, the organizations that work with the Liberal Arts College also employ the graduates. These organizations can be confident that they are hiring people with the kinds of skills they have identified as necessary for the modern workplace.

Part III: Technology. In both of the alternative universities described in this part, technology plays a key role in education, but not as a system of delivery. Students learn how to interact with technology to engage in cognition. **Interface University** is based on the idea that the future of cognition will be a hybrid between artificial intelligence and human intelligence. Thinking will be a process of humans and machines working together to achieve cognitive feats neither could achieve alone. At this university, students take standard courses in standard majors, but in every case they learn to partner with algorithms. Students learn how to think *with* computers, using them not simply as a tool but as an extension of human cognition.

The **University of the Body** exists in a world of external media: information has moved off electronic screens and into the surrounding environment. The symbols and information in such a world come to us via all of our senses. We might manipulate information by great gestures or by small disciplined movements of our bodies. Information might come in the form of distinct smells or via sensations on our skin. Students develop the capacity to take in more and more information compared to what they can absorb from their eyes and ears alone: information arrives via all of the body's senses. The University of the Body develops in students the literacy skills necessary to decode and to compose in a world of externalized media.

Part IV: Attributes. The alternative universities explored in the first three parts of this book assume a particular kind of transformative experience. The three speculative designs in this part are focused on producing a certain kind of graduate; they are institutions that are transformative in specific ways. If some universities are about the preservation and transmission of knowledge, and research universities are about the discovery of knowledge, then the **Institute for Advanced Play** is about the generation of new and novel knowledge. Indeed, imagination is valued higher than knowledge. Play is a sophisticated cognitive activity, an important source of creativity and innovation, but adults allow themselves little occasion to play. Play is typically associated with the activities of children, yet the benefits of play extend to adults as well. The Institute for Advanced Play is a kind of playground where adults can engage in serious play, where unplanned and unexpected insights are the results.

Every student at **Polymath University** majors in three very different disciplines. In addition to imparting a body of knowledge, a major is designed to teach the habits of mind of that particular discipline. Students are thus required to demonstrate mastery of three distinct habits of mind: they major in one of the sciences, one of the arts or humanities, and one of the professional disciplines. Innovative and creative ideas emerge at the boundaries between different fields, and students learn to negotiate those boundaries.

Just as the case study is the central feature of a business school education, the future scenario is the basis of study at **Future University**. A scenario is a plausible narrative of how the future might unfold; it is a description of the potential state of a complex system at some point in the future. Students at Future University live in the future, visualizing it in order to better design and build that future. The curriculum is balanced between pure futuring (exploring the future for no other reason than curiosity about what is next) and applied futuring, where the future is studied in order to anticipate change so that what is next might be managed or designed.

■   ■   ■

This book is an exercise in imagining alternative universities, an example of what Anthony Dunne and Fiona Raby refer to as speculative design: "to use design as a means of speculating how things could be." Design can play a role in "facilitating alternative visions" and in "[opening] up all sorts of possibilities that can be discussed, debated, and used to collectively define a preferable future for a given group of people." They point to the concept car as a kind of speculative design: designers promote new ways of thinking by presenting an alternative vision, even if the car itself never goes into production. In a way, then, what I present here are ten "concept universities."[38] I present alternatives to the existing institutional forms of the university as a way to critique our current practices. Indeed, Dunne and Raby insist that one goal of speculative design is to "unsettle the present rather than predict the future."[39] Historically, utopias have often been as much about commenting on the present as they are about envisioning the future, and the ten designs presented here—whether they are unsettling or not—should also be viewed in that context.

But this project is also utopian in that, given our present circumstances, it will be a significant challenge to realize any of them. The current system of accreditation, for instance, would prove to be an insurmountable brake on most of these ideas. Polymath University, to take one case, has no provisions for general education courses. No regulator in the country would permit a university to receive accreditation without general education. Thus, to make Polymath University a reality would require a significant change in what an accreditor would permit. The Institute for Advanced Play eschews the idea of career preparation as an outcome. Given our current environment, where job preparation is widely viewed as the sole purpose of higher education, an institution devoted strictly to serious play would be an anomaly. Many faculty would refuse to work at Platform University because of its lack of tenure. "It will not be easy to transform the university from the inside," predicts Cathy Davidson. "Many academics are traditionalists, and many institutions revere their traditions and are rewarded for them. They often reject innovation simply because it represents a departure from how things are done."[40] In order for any of the designs proposed in this book to be actualized, I suspect we would very likely need to create a new institution, rather than expect to redesign or reorganize an existing organization, since resistance to change is endemic in higher education.

Another obstacle in the realization of these speculative designs is that there seems to be little appetite for developing universities that deviate so dramatically from the norm. "The similarity of college curricula comes from the twin power of competition and regulation," observes John Lombardi. "Competition ensures that each college and university offers much the same curriculum to a common marketplace of students and parents seeking equivalent products. In competing for students, most institutions focus on minor forms of product differentiation, image and presentation. Regulation reinforces this standardization of content through accreditation, a process that encourages or coerces colleges and universities to deliver remarkably similar undergraduate programs."[41] Institutions of higher education are keen to benchmark other universities, emulate their peer institutions, and, as a result, all look alike. Each has the same offerings, each has the same goal, and their mission statements read very much the same. "The strategy of most schools is one of imitation, not innovation," say Clayton Christensen and Henry Eyring. "Little-known and smaller institutions try to move up in the ranks by adding students, majors, and graduate programs, so as to look more like the large universities,"[42] a process derisively called "Carnegie climbing," referring to the organization that classifies institutions of higher education. In the end, all institutions strive to emulate Harvard, and in so doing look the same. In such an environment, innovation that seeks to create new transformative experiences appears risky and quixotic.

Barnett calls for nothing less than a new poetics of the university. Poets "imaginatively [bring] into being new worlds," chiefly by employing metaphor. "The creation of new metaphors through which to comprehend universities, therefore, is one of the most powerful acts of the imagination."[43] Each of the alternative universities in this book should be read as metaphors, and I hope that I have found "the conceptual and linguistic wherewithal . . . to describe the scene picked out in the imagination, so as to reveal it adequately to others, such that they in turn might find in the scene a situation of personal meaning and potential action." Barnett asks, "Can we develop a *practical poetry* . . . of the university?"[44]

I have taken up the challenge that Barnett has announced to university presidents, vice chancellors, and other higher education leaders: they "should become poets of the university, coming forward with new languages, new metaphors for understanding the possibilities for the university."[45] Faculty are not excluded, of course, inasmuch as they are able to exercise some control and influence over the future direction of the university. But "the rise of university strategy as a field of inquiry and a zone of construction raises the question of the locus of creativity," notes Simon Marginson. "Has it shifted from the academic disciplines to the institutional agency of the university, and from the research professorate to the university executives? Are very bright people increasingly drawn to quasi-entrepreneurial roles at the head of these organizations?"[46] This book specifically addresses the "very bright people" engaged in university strategy, for that group is involved in what Marginson calls "university making." "University making and space making have become creative activities in their own right, practiced by multi-performing university leaders who draw on a portfolio of qualities and roles, from business entrepreneur to scientific boffin to patron of the arts. Sometimes they are artists themselves of a kind. Most are timid. Some are bold. A few make changes that reverberate through the university world. These university leaders are supported by teams with an assemblage of specialized skills. Yet much rests on their own 'animal spirits' and visioning."[47] Michael Crow is one such university-maker,[48] but my sense is that Barnett's call for more "practical poets" is aimed at the university presidents, higher education policy experts, corporate executives, and entrepreneurs whose university building has been imaginatively impoverished and imitative.

The speculative designs presented here are in the spirit of the great university-makers of the past, such as von Humboldt, John Andrew Rice (the founder of Black Mountain College), and Lucien L. Nunn (the founder of Deep Springs College). These ten alternative universities might be understood as practical poems about the future of the university.

I ORGANIZATION

1

Platform University

This university is organized like a multisided platform, which is defined as an organization that exists solely to connect producers and consumers. An example of a multisided platform is a shopping mall. The mall itself is not providing a particular product but, rather, provides the space that connects businesses and customers. Like a Middle Eastern bazaar or a medieval fair, Platform University is a physical space that facilitates the interactions between teachers and students. The space itself is agnostic about the kinds of intellectual exchanges or academic activities that may occur. Platform University mirrors early medieval universities, which were self-organizing associations of teachers and students. Platform University is a physical location that provides teachers with spaces to profess and students with spaces to learn. Like at an unconference or an Open Space gathering, teachers enter the space with ideas to teach, and they seek out students eager to learn. At the same time, students have learning needs and seek out professors whose interests match their own.

Platform University is permeable, meaning there are no hard and fast boundaries separating the space for learning from the outside world. There are no formal admission processes, or to state it another way, anyone is permitted to enter the space of Platform University. There are no guarantees they will remain: students are free to leave when they wish (or may be invited to leave). The faculty also treat Platform University as permeable. There are no permanent or tenured faculty members. At Platform University, a "professor" is defined as someone who has expertise/qualifications sanctioned by the world outside the university who then enters the university as a teacher, attracting interested students to share her knowledge. If she chooses, that professor can then return to her professional life, or she can move back and forth across the permeable boundary of the university. Platform University has no tenure, but nevertheless has long-standing faculty. This longevity comes from reputation: a successful, popular, or revered teacher remains within the platform by community consent.

As a self-organizing, permeable organization, Platform University is protean, although a core of semipermanent regulars will emerge: the teachers most prized by the community and the students who continually return. Surrounding this core is a cloud of students and teachers who pass through the platform teaching and learning when there is the need to do so. Platform University is amorphous in organizational form; without a fixed shape, it shifts and evolves based on the changing composition of teachers and students and their changing interests.

As a space that facilitates self-organization, Platform University does not begin with a course catalog, a series of required courses, or even a curriculum. The unplanned interactions of teachers and students allow for the emergence of courses, and departments or schools may form. A course is formed when a teacher and a critical mass of students coalesce around a particular subject. Teachers may announce a subject and draw in students such that a course is formed. Or students may make known that they wish to explore a certain subject, and a professor steps forward to teach the agreed-upon class. The university has a fluid temporal structure; there are no semesters: teaching and learning are ongoing activities.

After a number of courses are created in this fashion, clusters of teachers and students can decide to create a department or school. The curriculum is the macro level product of this open, self-organizing system, and it too is epistemologically fluid, an emergent property of this self-organizing network.

Platform University does not have a formal administrative hierarchy that must approve each course or the formation of a department. The agreement among teachers and learners to cluster together for mutual benefit is approval enough. But as easily as courses, schools, departments, and curricula can form, they can just as easily unform as student interest or faculty availability wanes. A course might prove very successful and be a staple of Platform University, but it is just as likely that a course disappears after only a few times of being taught. Some courses might not be formed at all. Courses and schools are just as likely to fail as they are to succeed. Student interest and faculty ability determine the success of any course or curriculum.

As with other kinds of multisided platforms, this self-governing university achieves its stability and coherence through protocols based on community values and voluntary regulation rather than through administrative rules and fiats. As a consequence, there is a very light administrative structure at Platform University. Reputation within the community of faculty and students—rather than an appointment from above—determines who is an academic leader. Administrators lead via cultivation and care, not command and control, redefining the distribution and exercise of power in the university. Because Platform University is a self-organizing, self-governing institution, administrators act as catalysts, cultivating the organization and facilitating and maintaining the conditions for teaching, learning, and research to emerge. Administrators serve only for a brief time and then either return to teaching roles or leave the platform entirely to resume their professional lives in the world.

Platform University is agnostic as to what kind of institution it will be. The academic orientation of Platform University is only determined after enough students and teachers coalesce and after they are interacting with each other. Further, that academic orientation will change and transform based on the decisions made by students and teachers. Perhaps at first Platform University's orientation is toward technology and engineering, but after five years, based on the composition of the student body and the faculty, the orientation might shift toward the arts and humanities.

■ ■ ■

In 1999, Sugata Mitra placed rudimentary computers in poor areas around New Delhi. Encased within walls, the internet-enabled computers came with no instructions on how to use them, nor were there any adults or teachers nearby to provide guidance. Groups of children gathered around the "holes in the wall," as they were called, and within a few months these children had taught themselves how to use the computer, surf the web, and perform a number of operations. Mitra announced that this was an experiment in "self-education," that, absent an administrative infrastructure or the compulsion to enter formal schooling, children could self-organize and learn together if a space was provided for them. Richard DeMillo proclaimed: "The Mitra experiments are remarkable because they document the power of spontaneous, self-organizing learning communities."[1] Indeed, DeMillo saw in the Mitra experiments the seeds of a new way of thinking about open education."It is a small step from open software to open systems," said DeMillo, "an approach to information sharing that enables anyone to plug into a simple, easily understood interface: no hassle, no restrictive standards, and—best of all—no guard at the door to check credentials and turn away those who do not satisfy the admissions criteria. The open system concept—the ability for a community to manage the distribution and growth of systems without a centralized authority"—is one way we might think about organizing a university.[2] The children of the hole-in-the-wall experiment had demonstrated the kind of effective learning outcomes that might result when school is deinstitutionalized: "On a small scale, Mitra discovered that learning communities apparently form spontaneously around leaders independent of any top-down direction or formal authority figure."[3] Platform University is more than simply a computer in a wall, but it is similarly a physical space that invites groups to spontaneously gather, to self-organize into teaching-learning communities.

Mitra had established a kind of platform, a new kind of business organization. Multisided platforms are defined as "technologies, products or services that create value primarily by enabling direct interactions between two or more customer or participant groups."[4] There are any number of modern businesses that act as platforms, such as

Airbnb (which connects owners of dwellings with short-term renters) and Lyft (which connects those needing a ride with drivers willing to shuttle them). Neither of those companies is in the business of providing shelter or transportation: they are instead in the business of facilitating exchanges between producers or service providers and consumers. "A platform is a business based on enabling value-creating interactions between external producers and consumers. The platform provides an open, participative infrastructure for these interactions and sets governance conditions for them. The platform's overarching purpose: to consummate matches among users and facilitate the exchange of goods, services, or social currency, thereby enabling value creation for all participants."[5] Platform University facilitates interactions between teachers and learners without a guard at the door.

The types of activities that occur within a platform "cannot be entirely planned; they also emerge. Remember that one of the key characteristics that distinguishes a platform from a traditional business is that most of the activity is controlled by users, not by the owners or managers of the platform. It's inevitable that participants will use the platform in ways you never anticipated or planned."[6] Thus, the kind of classes taught, the kind of research undertaken, and the curriculum itself are all unplanned, emerging from the interactions of teachers and learners.

■　■　■

Contemporary platforms are often virtual spaces. Wikipedia might be the most successful of such digital platforms: a virtual space that allows thousands of writers to contribute and edit encyclopedia articles. There is a "management" layer to Wikipedia, but this group emerges from among the many contributors; they are editors who maintain the community's standards. Platform University, in contrast to Airbnb and Wikipedia, will be a physical space in the way a shopping mall is a physical space for businesses and consumers. Platform University could also look like an artist collective or a co-working space.[7] In that physical space, artists rent studios and carry out any type of work they wish. The artist collective, or the entity that provides the space, is in the business of providing a place of exchange. A co-working space offers a location for workers to plug in their laptops, and it may provide business equipment, meeting rooms, and the like. Similarly, advocates for deschooling suggest that preexisting spaces could be easily repurposed as sites for teaching and learning. Mary Hamilton, professor emerita in the Department of Educational Research at Lancaster University, asserts, "We should increase physical spaces for people and groups to meet and exchange ideas, and as access points for information (libraries, cyber cafes, bookshops, advice centers, Internet buses, community halls) so that citizens can engage in virtual or actual meetings with each other and with experts."[8] Paul Goodman says, "There is no technical reason why a city neighborhood should not be a campus with the physics building replaced by a factory for light manufacture and the library by the local movie [theater]."[9] That is, a preexisting physical space can become a site for Platform University simply by opening it up to teachers and students. Co-working spaces, maker spaces, libraries, museums, and even office buildings are potential sites for Platform University; the only criterion is that the space is open. The space would be designed to act as a magnet, attracting teachers and learners and inviting them to cluster.

Platform University will derive its energy and direction from self-organization and the emergent properties thereof. By self-organizing, I mean that this institution will be directed by the interactions of the users, not determined by leadership decisions at the top.[10] The self-organizing activities of teachers and students will be like jazz improvisation, where "neither the flow of notes nor the musicians are passive: they are engaged, instead, in a process of spontaneous self-organization, in which a unique musical coherence emerges contingently, a coherence that is not imposed by an orchestra conductor nor by a precomposed score but arises immanently from the creative activity of the group. The jazz band follows immanent rules (*nomoi*) that remain implicit, instead of obeying explicit laws (*logoi*) formulated or imposed by a transcendent instance of command such as a composer or conductor."[11]

Platform University will not be anarchic, however. As I detail below, the interactions between teachers and students will be governed more by nomoi than by logoi. "Responsible autonomy" is the management principle at Platform University, where "a group decides what to do, but is accountable for the outcome. Accountability is what makes responsible autonomy different from anarchy."[12]

But some anarchy might actually be welcomed by and beneficial to the university, says David J. Siegel:

> Everyday anarchism . . . restores human agency and calls us to do more than submissively await and execute the commands of machine programmers. This is not about tossing Molotov cocktails down the corridors of the ivory tower; rather, it is about what James C. Scott, in *Two Cheers for Anarchism*, describes as the crux of Pierre-Joseph Proudhon's original conception of anarchism: "*Cooperation without hierarchy or state rule.*" It has to do with the care and feeding of cultural values through autonomous organizing based on principles of mutuality, sociality, and solidarity. . . . After all, one of the competencies squandered in our citadels of teaching and learning is the capacity to self-organize to solve the problems that vex us. The spread of specialized administrative duties has promoted a learned helplessness among the rank and file, an overdependence on formal structures and schemes to accomplish the work that many of us in small groups know—or knew before we were systematically devitalized and deskilled—perfectly well how to perform. We have become habituated to infrastructure and incentives that encourage interdisciplinary projects, for instance, but that support is not necessary. Bottom-up initiatives of similarly inclined scholars forging ties across departmental lines to advance the cause of interdisciplinary inquiry can be just as, if not more, effective.[13]

Ivan Illich referred to self-organizing entities as "convivial or spontaneous institutions," in contrast to "manipulative institutions," which include the schools he wished to "deschool."[14] Platform University will be such a convivial institution, with an anarchic disposition that would please Paul Goodman, who writes, "It is impossible to consider our universities in America without being powerfully persuaded of the principle of anarchy, that the most useful arrangement is free association and federation rather than top-down management and administration."[15]

The unplanned interactions between teachers and students produce the individual courses at Platform University. For example, teachers announce their intention to teach a course and then draw in a number of interested students. Alternatively, a group of students find they have a common interest, announce their desire for a course, and seek out a teacher to enter Platform University to satisfy their demand. An online form organizes these announcements and calls for courses; the actual courses, however, occur in a physical location. Like early universities, students directly compensate the professor for the courses she teaches.

The curriculum of Platform University is also an emergent property of this self-organizing network. The "emergent curriculum" developed out of children's education, based on the idea that a curriculum should be built around children's interests, with teachers observing and nimbly and flexibly responding to those interests. This approach "treats curriculum not as a product for imposition but as a process of emergence and interaction. It is forward-looking in that it embraces the contingency and uncertainty of educational outcomes. . . . The curriculum, from a complexity perspective, is an open system of constant flux and complex interactions rather than a closed system of prescriptions and linear progressions."[16] Similarly, at Platform University, courses emerge out of the interactions between student interests and faculty abilities. As closely related courses are developed, these are organized into a larger curriculum. The initial exchange yields courses, and a constellation of courses yields a curriculum. Think of the way articles are published on Wikipedia via the collective decision of the participants rather than being handed down by tradition or enforced by a higher authority. Platform University looks very much like an unconference, where the agenda (curriculum) emerges as a result of the interactions of the participants (teachers and students). Platform University is permeable and open, and its curriculum will develop in the same manner.

When enough teachers and students coalesce around a particular curriculum of interest, they may form their own school. Or a critical mass of teachers and students may form around the subject of sociology or computer science and thus create a department. The university —in the form of a dean or some other figure in an administrative hierarchy—need not approve the formation of departments and schools. If anything, the university merely affirms decisions that teachers and students have made via their act of clustering together. But the ease with which they are formed also means that departments and schools can just as easily unform as students and teachers lose interest. This is a fundamental characteristic of platforms: groups are just as likely to fail as they are to thrive. Clay Shirky describes this process with regard to the online organizer Meetup:

> The most basic service that Meetup provides is to let its users propose groups and to let other users vote with their feet, like the apocryphal university that lets the students wear useful paths through the grass before it lays any walkways. Most proposed Meetup groups fail. . . . This distribution—lots of failure, some modest success, a few extremely popular—is the same pattern (the power law distribution) that we have seen elsewhere. The advantage of having a system where failure is normal and significant success rare is that, by its very existence, Meetup continually readjusts to its current context. . . . The rise of new groups and the retiring of old ones is not a business decision, it's a by-product of user behavior.[17]

Indeed, many courses "fail" at Platform University: there is not enough of a critical mass to sustain a class; a class is taught once or twice before interest wanes; a course that has been taught a number of times loses its popularity and then is no longer taught. At a macro level, a circle of teachers and learners might form a department that thrives for some time, but this, too, might end as interest declines or attention shifts to a new discipline. The distribution of "successful" courses and departments will likely also follow a power law relationship, including a long tail of failed or seldom-taught courses, as we see in many open, self-organizing systems.

The academic orientation of Platform University is based on the shifting configurations of faculty-student interaction. The curriculum changes as new students arrive and as new faculty are drawn into the university. Today, Platform University may be an engineering school, but in five years it may transform into a technical school, and in another five years it may transform into a liberal arts college with a focus on the arts and humanities. Platform University, in providing only the space for exchange, is academically agnostic and protean.

Platform University has no hard and fast boundaries separating the space for learning from the outside world. Douglas Hague once described a future university as being "permeable," by which he meant that it was in exchange with the larger world outside its boundaries, in particular with the wide world of intellect in the ever-growing knowledge industries and with a larger pool of learners.

> The more the universities are permeable and the more the knowledge industries and all citizens who embrace intellectual pursuits and causes come within them, the more successful they will be. The best universities of the 21st century will bring together brain power *where it is*, not where it can be institutionalised. The aim must be to create a republic of the intellect open to all, whose natural constituency will be those who keep themselves intellectually aware throughout their lives. That constituency must be heavily represented in the knowledge industries. The successful university of the 21st century cannot be an academic bunker; it will have to be permeable.[18]

Hague observes that intellect and creativity can be found just as readily in the world outside the university; similarly, there are growing numbers of "nontraditional" students who seek to learn but whose conditions and expectations are different from those of eighteen- to twenty-two-year-old full-time students. Thus, there is no formal admission process in the permeable structure of Platform University: anyone is permitted to enter the space of the university. Whether someone remains is determined by the quality of her performance in the various courses. Students may find they wish to leave or may be discouraged from returning.

Faculty as well treat Platform University as a permeable structure. Professors enter the platform when they want to teach and when they are able to draw sufficient numbers of learners around them. But they are just as likely to have occupations and avocations outside of the platform, practice their craft in the world, and enter the space to teach about that avocation. A faculty member may leave the platform to resume her professional life or might engage in teaching on a part-time basis. In effect, professors toggle between the university and the professional world, just as many students toggle between the platform and the world beyond. There are some faculty members who encamp permanently at Platform University because they are popular or revered by cohorts of students. This is not the same, however, as a formal guarantee of tenure.

Because it is a permeable institution, because teachers and students enter and leave with ease, and because the curriculum is self-organizing and malleable, Platform University is protean. Michael Malone defines a protean corporation as one "that features: (1) [a cloud,] an amorphous external form that uses technology to rapidly adapt to changing situations with regard to market, customers, competition, finance, and even ownership; and (2) [a core,] a slowly evolving internal center that uses interpretive tools to maintain the identity and continuity of the enterprise over time." The protean corporation is not without shape or form, "but rather . . . it will have no *fixed* shape, transforming itself to meet the changing marketplace."[19]

Platform University is a protean institution. There will be large groups of students and teachers that enter and exit the university on a regular basis, an ever-changing cloud that surrounds a more stable core of teachers and students who remain for longer periods of time. It is from this more stable group of teachers, especially, that the administrators of Platform University emerge, similar to the way the editors of Wikipedia emerge from among the regular contributors. Platform University will be without a fixed shape, shifting and evolving based on the changing composition of teachers and students and their changing interests. As a self-organizing, permeable organization, the shape and form of Platform University will reflect these centrifugal and centripetal forces: it will evolve and change while being balanced by forces of stability and stasis.

■   ■   ■

A common complaint from faculty is that the modern university functions too much like a corporation, with administrators driven more by business values and the bottom line or making decisions in a command-and-control fashion. A colleague recently complained that "the university was forcing" him to do something against his will. In this instance, the university is an entity above the professor and the learner, a fictional person with interests and demands forced on teachers and students. John V. Lombardi identifies the "administrative shell" of the research university, which helps to create the conditions for learning and research. Research universities—a similar model might be found across a variety of institutions—are organized around "two related, closely linked, but operationally relatively independent structures. The first is an academic core, composed of a group of faculty guilds that have primary responsibility for the academic content and quality of the enterprise. The second is an administrative shell, responsible for the acquisition and distribution of resources and for the management of the enterprises that support the faculty guilds as well as the interaction with external governance of boards and political institutions."[20]

Lombardi views the administrative shell as supporting the work of the faculty guilds: "The shell mobilizes and distributes resources that support the work of the guilds, and it protects the guilds from harmful external forces. The shell manages the interactions among the guilds. Most important, the shell manages the university's money and creates the incentives that motivate guild behavior. . . . The shell organizes structures and systems to raise private endowments and gifts, to lobby for public funds, to compete for federal dollars, to seek foundation revenue, and to create a hospitable and supportive academic and cultural environment."[21] There are a number of faculty today who might dispute the degree to which administrators support faculty work, and at Platform University these administrative roles are given to the professors. The tasks of managing money and seeking external sources of funds largely fall to individual faculty members. Groups of faculty and students who have organized together into schools and departments manage their own affairs, something like the responsibility-centered management employed by some universities. "The key principle here," writes Lombardi,

> is that if the university makes each significant unit within the institution responsible for earning its own income and controlling its own expenses, the university at large will be most efficient. . . . This system has a beautiful simplicity and the appearance of tough, no-nonsense management. It appeals because it appears to put the authority for success into the hands of the local responsibility center managers. An additional advantage is that it appears to remove the conversation about values from the upper administration to the responsibility centers and perhaps to let the invisible hand of economic determinism and the market adjust the budget and, in the process, determine values.[22]

Ori Brafman and Rod A. Beckstrom similarly identify the way a decentralized organization manages funds. "Because they are autonomous, the units of a decentralized organization are almost always self-funding. In open organizations, there is often no central well of money. Individual units might receive funding from outside sources, but they are largely responsible for acquiring and managing those funds."[23] Faculty seek out their own sources of funding for lab equipment or other tools needed for teaching and research. In effect, Platform University houses groups organized and funded the way scientific laboratories are in contemporary universities.

This is not to say that there are no administrators or academic leaders at Platform University. The leaders tend to emerge from among the faculty, not unlike the way editors at Wikipedia emerge from among the many contributors. Reputation within the community, rather than an appointment from above, determines who is an academic leader.[24] Paul Goodman imagines that his community of scholars "seems to require only a handful of unpretentious administrators—a rector unwillingly elevated from the faculty for a short term, a typist, and a couple of janitors."[25] These leaders practice a management style that looks less like command-and-control than coordinate-and-cultivate. Thomas Malone expands on this style of leadership:

> Rather than just telling people what to do, managers will increasingly cultivate their organizations and the people in them. To cultivate something successfully—whether it's your farm, your garden, your child, or your organization—you need to understand and respect its natural tendencies at the same time you try to shape it in ways you value. More specifically, you try to discover and encourage its positive potential and limit the harm caused by negative tendencies. Rather than just trying to impose your will on the system, you try to balance the right kinds of control with the right kinds of letting go.[26]

Self-organizing, open, protean institutions tend to be led by catalysts. Brafman and Beckstrom identify a "catalyst" as a "person who initiates a circle [or group] and then fades away into the background. . . . a catalyst gets a decentralized organization going and then cedes control to the members. . . . [A catalyst] makes the introductions, helps people connect, and then, in typical catalyst fashion, gets out of the way."[27] The president of Platform University, the provost, and the deans do not act like CEOs or other corporate executives, but rather like gardeners, cultivating the organization and creating and maintaining the conditions for teaching, learning, and research to emerge. "Managing a decentralized network," conclude Brafman and Beckstrom, "requires someone who can be a cross between an architect, a cheerleader, and an awestruck observer."[28] Administrators at Platform University function as catalysts, not managers.

■ ■ ■

A common feature of multisided platforms is that they are regulated by community standards by which all agree to abide. As Parker, Van Alstyne, and Choudary say, a platform "sets governance conditions" for those who enter it. Platforms—or "matchmakers," according to David S. Evans and Richard Schmalensee—"often facilitate interactions by organizing participants around a standard that they all agree to use."[29] "Because circles don't have hierarchy and structure, it's hard to maintain rules within them," say Brafman and Beckstrom, and so a hierarchy of administrators whose job is to enforce rules does not seem to work well with self-organizing platforms. "No one really has the power to enforce them. But circles aren't lawless. Instead of rules, they depend on norms."[30] Norms and standards might also be defined as "protocols," which Alexander Galloway says are present in many open, distributed, networked systems. "Protocol is not a new word," he notes.

> Prior to its usage in computing, protocol referred to any type of correct or proper behavior within a specific system of conventions. It is an important concept in the area of social etiquette as well as in the fields of diplomacy and international relations. . . . However, with the advent of digital computing, the term has taken on a slightly different meaning. Now, protocols refer specifically to standards governing the implementation of specific technologies. Like their diplomatic predecessors, computer protocols establish the essential points necessary to enact an agreed-upon standard of action. . . . [A] protocol is a technique for achieving *voluntary regulation* within a contingent environment. (emphasis mine)[31]

Community members serve as control mechanisms, holding other members to the protocols agreed upon by those entering the platform. A layer of bureaucracy dedicated to rule enforcement is therefore not present in a platform. Again, this is not to suggest that there are no administrators or academic leaders. Their role, their task, however, is very different: catalyzing interactions, maintaining the platform, and ensuring protocols (which the community is just as likely to enforce).

Platform University will resemble Burning Man, a yearly, self-organized gathering of tens of thousands of artists and free spirits in the Nevada desert. "Open systems [like Burning Man] can't rely on a police force," say Brafman and Beckstrom. "On the one hand, there's freedom to do what you want, but on the other hand, you have added responsibility: because there are no police walking around maintaining law and order, everyone becomes a guardian of sorts. You become responsible for your own welfare and that of those around you. In open systems, the concept of 'neighbor' takes on more meaning than just the person next door."[32] Platform University is administered by faculty and student "neighbors."

■   ■   ■

The first universities were formed in order to more efficiently bring together students and teachers, knowledge seekers and knowledge producers. As teachers and students gathered in the twelfth century, European universities emerged to formalize and legalize these gatherings. That is, the university was born to provide a structure to govern the student-teacher relationship. Paul Goodman sees the formation of universities as "the spontaneous product of that *instinct of association* which swept over the towns of Europe in the course of the eleventh and twelfth centuries" (emphasis mine). Thus, he looks back to the medieval foundation of the university for his model of self-organizing association going forward, and so can we. "It is remarkable how from the beginning were perfected the only two possible types of schooling: Either a youth says Show me How, and finds a teacher who will show him—this is in principle the professional school of Bologna; or a thinker professes a truth he knows and a fascinated youth latches on to him and asks What and Why—this is in principle the school of liberal arts in Paris. Ever since, the thousands of *studia generalia* have combined both principles."[33]

Platform University has as its core function the creation of a space that facilitates students finding teachers and teachers finding students. As Goodman observes, "If a teacher wants to teach something, he must think it worthwhile; and students want either to learn something particular or to find out what it is they want to learn. This is enough for a school."[34] This is also enough for Platform University.

2

Microcollege

This system of higher education is made up of thousands of small Microcolleges, each with one professor and twenty students. Microcolleges are established in a wide range of settings. Some are located in rural farmhouses and concentrate on agriculture, biology, or ecology. Others are established in urban environments, affording students the opportunity to work with cultural institutions and at the same time to be confronted with the challenges of navigating that environment, including participating with the community to solve problems and networking with civic leaders. The location of each Microcollege helps to shape its central pedagogical and research foundations. Some Microcolleges are located within existing institutions such as public libraries, architect's offices, or scientific laboratories. The pedagogical focus of each Microcollege is a reflection of the mission of the institution in which it is housed.

The curriculum and concentration of the Microcollege is a manifestation of the mind and personality of the professor. Like at early American colleges, the professor is at once president, teacher, instructional designer, and mentor to students. In the ecosystem composed of thousands of Microcolleges, there are as many curricular and educational missions as there are individual professors. The professor designs the overall learning experience for each student by monitoring their progress through various self-paced courses, identifying and pairing students in mentor-mentee relationships, delivering a weekly lecture attended by the entire community, and engaging in research involving all students. The professor has an area of concentration—engineering, humanities, finance—but within her discipline takes a broad, polymathic perspective. The Microcollege that has Judith Butler as the professor puts feminist, queer, and gender theories at the center of its educational mission. The Microcollege led by

Daniel Libeskind concentrates on architecture, space, and design. At one Microcollege, the educational mission is the apprehension of beauty; at another, the mission is the meaning and practice of justice. A Microcollege is led by Roger Schank, whose curriculum is based on developing twelve cognitive skills: prediction, modeling, experimentation, evaluation, diagnosis, planning, causation, judgment, influence, teamwork, negotiation, and describing. While having an educational focus, the professor is not a narrow specialist. He does not teach every course but instead demonstrates a broad understanding of his particular field, designing and implementing an academic plan that exhibits a particular philosophy of education. An artist, for example, might lead a Microcollege that focuses not only on sculpture, oil painting, and installations, but also on physics and social advocacy. Each professor establishes the philosophical and pedagogical orientation of the Microcollege.

The entire community works together on common research projects as directed by the professor. Some Microcolleges are organized like a scientific laboratory, with the twenty students serving in various roles in the overall hierarchy of the lab. At a Microcollege based on art, the professor organizes students in a studio workshop. Each Microcollege is a collaborative research project.

The professors have met stringent criteria as established by a regional accreditor, for it is only those so recognized who may start a Microcollege. Professors wishing to lead a Microcollege must first demonstrate their reputation in a particular field, determined by a record of scholarly production or recognition as a thoughtful practitioner. A Man Booker Prize–winning novelist or a former diplomat could be accredited to establish a Microcollege.

Students work at their own pace under the supervision of the professor. Because a single professor cannot be expected to know an entire college curriculum, a significant part of the curriculum is delivered via computer-mediated courses. Students move through them at a time they choose and at their own pace. A student with a facility for languages might complete a computerized course on Arabic in six weeks, while another student might take six months. The individualized courses are designed such that students move to higher-order problems after completing a specified level; if they fail a number of problems, the courseware drops the student down a level until they demonstrate mastery. To succeed in a course means that competence has been demonstrated. Technology also monitors students' progress across all of their courses, data that the professor assesses in order to make adjustments to the students' learning journey as needed. Because students are asked to spend significant amounts of time at self-paced learning, the Microcollege attracts people who are autonomous learners, autodidacts who are able to learn within the structure and organization of the Microcollege.

Analysis of the data collected from students also yields cognitive feedback that enhances learning. The Microcollege features sensors embedded in the learning environment to capture spoken language, thus assessing students on the fly without the need for quizzes or other interruptions to the learning process. Data from sensors and wearable technology indicate how well students are persevering through distractions or how vigorously they are participating in discussions. Data analytics both aid in the personalization of student learning and provide assessment information to the professor about how each individual student is progressing through the curriculum.

Since there is only one faculty member, students are called upon to assist in the administration of the college. They are asked to make decisions regarding applications, finance, and other issues. They are also invited to participate in conversations with the professor about philosophical and strategic questions concerning the Microcollege. This experience with academic self-governance is itself a learning outcome of each Microcollege.

Students at a Microcollege also engage in peer learning, where they simultaneously teach and learn from other students. Older, more experienced students are paired with younger students, serving as semiformal mentors. A student working through a computer-mediated course may call upon their peer mentor for support and guidance. The professor assesses the quality of that informal teaching as part of the overall assessment of the older student.

There is a weekly lecture delivered by the professor, which is a focal point of the community's activities; the totality of these weekly lectures is itself a kind of metacourse, a central feature of the curriculum. Nineteenth-century American college presidents taught a course in moral philosophy that was required of all students. At a Microcollege, the professor's weekly lecture performs a similar function, although the lecture is not about moral philosophy or character building but about the larger educational mission of the Microcollege.

Students also engage in weekly tutorials with the professor, usually in groups of three or four. Students prepare a project, engage in reading, write essays, solve mathematical problems, or otherwise concentrate on a single issue for that week. Then they present, argue, debate, and discuss with the professor and the other students. Students further along in the curriculum serve as teachers to less experienced students in such settings. The professor learns as much from these encounters as the students do.

Each Microcollege is a complex learning system. In any given week, students and the professor learn from online courses, a community-wide lecture, faculty research, Oxbridge-style tutorials, peer mentoring, and the administrative maintenance of the Microcollege.

■   ■   ■

Enrollment at the University of Central Florida has expanded over the past twenty years, and in 2018 it had more than 60,000 students. Arizona State University, with its new strategy of broadening access to higher education, had a student population of more than 70,000 in 2017, and this is expected to continue to climb. The rise of these mega-universities has been a key feature of the post–GI Bill landscape, and it is now possible to talk about the massification of higher education. But as Derek Bok reminds us, "It is only within the past 50 years that universities have come to boast the huge enrollments, the elaborately equipped research laboratories, and the legions of faculty members and other instructors that fill their campuses today."[1] Before the start of the twentieth century, there were much lower enrollments across all of higher education. Both private and public institutions were comparatively small; some had only a few hundred students. Indeed, the first colleges in the United States were the equivalent of the one-room schoolhouses that similarly dotted the landscape. In many of these early colleges, there were only a handful of students and one faculty member: the president, who taught all the classes, aided perhaps by one or two tutors.[2] The Microcollege is an echo of this colonial pattern: one faculty member—aided by computerized "tutors"—teaches all the classes, that single professor serving at once as president, teacher, instructional designer, and mentor to students.[3]

Microcollege is modeled after the "microschool," a current trend in K–12 education that has emerged out of the homeschooling movement, largely among Silicon Valley executives who want a top education for their children. There is no hard and fast definition of a microschool, although the most common feature is an enrollment of no more than about 150 students across all grades. Indeed, some Silicon Valley schools have only a dozen or so students. Advocates point to the research of Robin Dunbar, who argued that humans generally cannot manage relationships of more than 150 people.[4] Similarly, "when a school gets beyond about 150 kids," says Matt Candler, "it becomes very difficult for adults to keep track of individual students."[5] As a small community rather than a large, impersonal school with hundreds and even thousands of students, a microschool encourages interpersonal relationships between teacher and student and between students. The advocates for "human scale education" assert that "relationships matter and our experience tells us that in big schools it is difficult to establish the kind of human relationships that lead to good educational outcomes. By 'good educational outcomes' we mean not only academic achievement but student well-being." The community and human relations encouraged by the size of the microschool are themselves a learning outcome, whatever subjects are taught in such a school. "The key to small learning communities," these advocates continue, "is that students interact with a defined group of peers with whom they can develop a sense of belonging and community. This, rather than leaving them at sea to find their own identity in an institution of 1,000 plus students, would be a huge step towards overcoming the anonymity that is too often created by vertical organisational structures and the sheer size of many schools."[6] By "vertical organisational structures," they are referring to a school based around disciplines and subjects, meaning that in large schools students are parceled by subjects, and subject-based teachers are unable to see and come to understand students holistically. Thus, personalized teaching and learning is enabled and encouraged when the size of the entire school is small. The Microcollege is based on a similar principle: the small scale of the enterprise encourages interpersonal communication and community building as central pedagogical outcomes.

■　■　■

In order to establish a Microcollege, a potential professor must meet certain criteria as established by a regional accreditor. That is, not just anyone can start a Microcollege. At a minimum, the professor needs to demonstrate their reputation in a particular field. This might be determined by a record of scholarly production, but a professor might also be a well-regarded practitioner. A Tony Award–winning actor or a world-renowned architect might apply to establish a Microcollege. The professor cannot be a narrow specialist, however. Although she will not be teaching all the courses, she has to demonstrate broad competence in her particular field such that she can design and implement an academic plan that exhibits the particular philosophy of education that animates the Microcollege. An engineer, for instance, might develop a curriculum focused on making and building, on mathematics and design. The professor establishes the philosophical and pedagogical orientation of the Microcollege.

The Microcollege need not be oriented toward the liberal arts: a curriculum can focus on a particular discipline or area. Thus, a Microcollege led by an electrical engineer might have a formal curriculum that has students take classes in chemistry, mathematics, physics, and systems engineering as well as concentrations in electrical engineering. The professor might not have a deep knowledge of physics, systems engineering, or chemistry, but he needs to have a well-articulated understanding of what an electrical engineer must know in order to design an appropriate curriculum. For instance, the professor might think it is valuable for engineers to also understand history and sociology, the larger context in which the engineer's work is embedded. That concern for the social and cultural context of engineering is what makes this professor distinctive, what will attract students to his college, and what will meet with the approval of the accreditors.

■ ■ ■

The Microcollege looks similar to Deep Springs College in California, whose current bylaws restrict enrollment to only twenty-six students, not many more than in 1917, when there were twenty.[7] Deep Springs is located in the Sierra Nevada range, and a key part of the education involves working outdoors on a number of tasks: "cooking, cleaning, gardening, milking cows, saddling horses, herding cattle, moving hay, butchering chickens, wiring cables, sorting library books, fixing vehicles." This learning by doing is part of what makes Deep Springs so distinctive. The academic curriculum includes "ancient Greek, genetics, biology, music, philosophy, political science, mathematics, literature and international relations."[8] The Microcollege would be a four-year degree-granting institution, but students at Deep Springs stay only a year or two before transferring to other schools to complete their degrees. "Medieval Italian universities such as Bologna and Padua began eight centuries ago when students formed self-governing guilds and hired master scholars to teach them," writes L. Jackson Newell, former president of Deep Springs. "Deep Springs is, in a sense, a re-creation of these radical beginnings. . . . The college works, sometimes brilliantly, because students are at the center of things again."[9] Students don't technically select the professor of the Microcollege, but they nevertheless have a great deal of responsibility both for their learning and for the administration of the college.

Deep Springs has a small administrative infrastructure: a president (and philosophy professor), a dean of the faculty, and two chairs: one each for the natural sciences and the humanities. These four make up the long-term faculty. There is also a small number of visiting or short-term faculty. At the Microcollege, there is only one faculty member, who is aided by artificially intelligent "tutors," another echo of the antebellum American college. Furthermore, students at Deep Springs play a key role in the administration of the college. Organized as the "Student Body," they meet each week to discuss and act on matters pertaining to the college. Students are also divided into three committees: applications, curriculum, and review and reinvitations.[10] In addition to these administrative roles, students "require themselves to engage in regular discussions of philosophical questions concerning tenets of the Deep Springs education."[11] The Microcollege similarly asks students to engage in administrative responsibilities; the experience of self-government itself is a key part of the curriculum.

■   ■   ■

The Microcollege also echoes the gurukulas of India, which were the chief educational form before the arrival of the British. Students would gather around a master teacher (guru), who would instruct them for between nine and twelve years. (Students are not in residence for that long at the Microcollege.) In effect, students would join the guru's household and, like at Deep Springs College, would perform chores.[12] Indeed, the Microcollege is analogous to the preindustrial household, which was at once a familial unit and a location of production—although students at the Microcollege are not necessarily asked to perform manual tasks. Learners at gurukulas studied "the Vedas and other subjects, such as Śikshā (Phonetics), Vyākarana (Grammar) and Jyotisha (Astronomy), and sciences like Arthaśāstra (Economics), Dharmaśāstra (Laws), Śastravidyā (Art of Warfare), Kalā (Fine Arts)."[13] The total number of students at a gurukula was small, no more than two dozen or so. More important, "the Guru identified the capability of his students and accordingly imparted knowledge."[14] "There was a healthy interaction between the teacher and the student and the teacher was able to understand the student completely and mould him into a man with profound knowledge and wisdom of this world."[15]

Education at a human scale encourages this kind of individual attention to student development, a key feature of the Microcollege. It should also be said that "the students in the Gurukula were subjected to rigorous discipline. They had to live in a very austere environment, observe complete celibacy, practice yoga and meditation under the supervision of the Guru and perform many menial jobs for the Guru's household. The fundamental spirit of Āshram is shram (labour) and tapas (austerity)."[16] There is a similar austerity at Deep Springs College, in that students are forbidden to have alcohol or access to television. The Microcollege is not so disciplined and austere, but by engaging in administrative tasks and other duties necessary to keep the college functioning, students' education extends beyond what is presented in the formal curriculum.

■ ■ ■

The Microcollege is also reminiscent of the fifteenth-century Florentine bottegas (workshops) of the Renaissance.[17] A master artist would lead each workshop, which would draw a range of talent: artists, engineers, architects, mathematicians, sculptors, scientists, and craftspeople. While they worked separately, this disparate group of talented people also worked together under the coordination of the master artist. "For example," writes Piero Formica, "Andrea del Verrocchio . . . was a sculptor, painter, and goldsmith, but his pupils weren't limited to following his preferred pursuits. In his workshop, younger artists might pursue engineering, architecture, or various business or scientific ventures. . . . In Renaissance workshops, specialists communicated with each other consistently and fluidly, facilitating mutual understanding. The coexistence of and collision among these diverse talents helped make the workshops lively places where dialogue allowed conflicts to flourish in a constructive way. The clash and confrontation of opposing views removed cognitive boundaries, mitigated errors, and helped artists question truths taken for granted."[18] The Microcollege mimics the bottega, in that one "master artist" coordinates the education of a small number of apprentices who pursue their own interests—circumscribed by the professor's interests—while simultaneously working with the rest of the community. While students are encouraged to explore their own interests, they do so within the boundaries established by the "master artist," who has her own particular interests and aims in educating this community.

Bottegas, gurukulas, a college hidden in the Sierra Nevada: far from being an oddity, the combination of a single teacher and a small number of students is a timeless form of education. Multiversities with tens of thousands of students are the historical outliers. The Microcollege represents a return to an ancient educational form.

■   ■   ■

The professor cannot be expected to teach everything in the curriculum, and so artificially intelligent "tutors" teach a number of classes. These tutorials permit personalized learning.[19] The founder of 4.0 Schools observes, "What makes a modern micro-school different from a 19th century, one-room schoolhouse is that old school schools only had a few ways to teach—certainly no software, no tutors, and probably less structure around student to student learning. In a modern micro-school, there are ways to get good data from each of these venues. And the great micro-school of the future will lean on well-designed software to help adults evaluate where each kid is learning."[20] Thus, technology partners with teachers to serve as tutors, not unlike in the antebellum college. Microschool advocates refer to the curricula of their schools as "playlists," as when an eleven-year-old student at the Khan Lab School says, "Here it's different from my old school because you're doing your own playlist and you have more projects."[21] Given their smaller size and aided by data analytics, microschools are able to personalize learning, and indeed, the ability to craft individualized lessons is a key feature of the Microcollege.

■   ■   ■

Students at the Microcollege have a great deal of control over the time and pace of their work.[22] Because a fair amount of coursework is delivered via online tutors, students determine the time of day they are engaged in a particular class. These online tutorials are designed such that students move through them at their own pace.[23] "In 2013 QuantumCamp introduced language arts courses. Each academic class meets once a week for an activity-based exploration of big ideas and then offers out-of-class content that includes videos, readings, problem sets, podcasts, and other activities to enable students to continue exploring concepts at their own pace."[24] That is, students move through the curriculum at a pace determined by their fluency with the material. Take the case of learning a language. Today, Rosetta Stone offers university-level courses based on its highly effective language learning curriculum. In the digital version, a student answers a series of queries. With each correct response, the queries become more challenging; as the student falters, the queries are scaled back until the student reaches understanding and can then proceed with the more challenging material. This is something like leveling up in a video game, and with this pedagogical approach, a student can move through a course at a speed determined by their ability and grit. For example, one student might complete an introductory course in French in six weeks, while another student might require six months. Both would be certified as competent at the end of the course, even though they arrived at that competency at different rates. At the Microcollege, students similarly work with artificially intelligent "tutors" on many of their courses, especially the general education courses outside of the domain expertise of the professor.[25]

Computer-mediated courses also collect data from students, the analysis of which produces cognitive feedback that enhances individual student learning. Indeed, personalized, at-your-own-pace learning is made possible by such data analytics. The AltSchool microschool is planning to include sensors throughout the learning environment "that would be able to capture students' spoken grammar, obviating the need for a formal quiz or test. From there, the possibilities keep expanding— measuring how well students persevere in the face of distractions, or making sure boys and girls participate equally in discussions—through the use of data extrapolated from sensors, wearables, and other background methods."[26] Students at the Microcollege similarly wear tracking devices and are surrounded by other tools that capture large amounts of data.

There are some early indications that technologically mediated learning is having positive effects on student outcomes. One application, Teach to One: Math, has been used by some microschools. A report from Teachers College at Columbia University indicated that "Teach to One students gained 1.2 years worth of growth in math over the course of the school year, compared to the national average. Moreover, students who started the farthest behind made the greatest gains."[27] Data analytics and other forms of cognitive feedback not only aid in the personalization of student learning but also provide information to the professor about how an individual student is progressing. But to be clear: such technological assessment is not the sole form of assessment at the Microcollege. The professor also evaluates progress in a qualitative way via their personal interactions with the student. Students at the Microcollege are autonomous learners, autodidacts within a structured setting, even as they are at the same time members of a learning community led by the professor.

■   ■   ■

Computer-mediated tutorials form only one part of the overall pedagogical structure of the Microcollege. The professor delivers a weekly lecture to the entire college, a highlight of the week's activities. The accumulation of these weekly lectures/demonstrations is a kind of metacourse for all students. The professor also holds weekly Oxbridge-style tutorials: hour-long, concentrated conversations with three or four students at a time on a specific topic. The weekly meetings feature students producing some sort of work to be analyzed and critiqued by the professor, anything from an essay to a scientific problem set. A typical student has a dozen or so tutorials per academic year; the professor conducts enough of these tutorials that she sees and interacts with all twenty students at least once a week.[28] Paul Ashwin, a professor of higher education at Lancaster University, concludes that when tutorials work well,

> topics are opened up for debate, tutors admit to gaps in their own knowledge, and students are treated as academic equals. But Ashwin's interviews also highlight that many students, fresh from the prescriptive approaches and high-stakes testing of secondary education, are uncertain about their

role. Some felt the purpose of the tutorial was to clarify misunderstandings, while others felt it was to gain new knowledge. . . . His findings show that the best tutorials remain demanding, stimulating and thought-provoking, for student and tutor alike. The weekly discussions feed into the learning that takes place for the next essay, and the tutorial becomes one link in a chain of learning, dialogue, feedback and academic development.[29]

It is during tutorials that the professor personally assesses student learning, beyond what the data are able to tell her. Matriculation is more than simply demonstrating mastery of computer-assisted courses. Performances in the tutorials, regular attendance at the weekly lectures, the qualities of the interactions with the rest of the learning community, and a final evaluation by the professor all determine whether and when a student matriculates from the Microcollege.

■ ■ ■

Microschools also feature peer learning—students teaching and learning from other students—and the Microcollege includes this pedagogical feature as well. At the Microcollege, the professor matches an older student with a younger student to serve as a semiformal mentor. As students work through their online courses, their peer mentors offer support and guidance. The quality of that informal teaching is assessed by the professor and forms part of the overall assessment of the older student. This informal learning among students is part of the pedagogical infrastructure of the Microcollege.

■ ■ ■

The professor is not only a teacher but a researcher, and the entire community works together on research projects directed by the professor. A Microcollege might be organized like a scientific laboratory, with all twenty students serving in various roles in the lab. Older students take on managerial roles, overseeing the work of younger students. At a Microcollege based on art, the students are organized in a studio, working with the professor on projects and installations. A historian might have students in small groups researching in the archives. A digital humanist might be engaged in a large project requiring programmers, designers, and researchers, and the students fill these various roles. Each Microcollege acts as a collaborative research project.

■   ■   ■

A Microcollege does not need to be physically large, occupying one floor of a high-rise office building, for example. It needs to be large enough to contain workstations or other places for students to engage in digital coursework, but not so large that any student or the professor cannot see the entire community at once. There need to be spaces for student collaboration and the tutorials, as well as a space large enough for the entire community to gather for the professor's weekly lectures. There also needs to be space for research activities, although the size of this space depends on the scale of the research. Although it is not necessary in all cases, some Microcolleges might include space for student residences as well as a residence for the professor. Living and working together has obvious pedagogical advantages but is not required to forge community spirit.

A Microcollege could be established in a preexisting location, such as a maker space for a professor focused on engineering. A Microcollege could be in a house in the country, similar to the way Black Mountain College was established. The location of the Microcollege forms an important part of the pedagogical and research infrastructure: a Microcollege at a rural house probably concentrates on agriculture, biology, ecology, or another area that benefits from connections to nature. A Microcollege in an urban environment similarly affords students the chance to work with museums and other cultural institutions, or work with local community organizers on specific problems. Indeed, a Microcollege could be embedded within an existing institution: it could be located in a city's public library, at an architect's office, in a museum, or in a scientific laboratory. Indeed, such institutions might develop their own Microcolleges as part of their missions. An art museum, for example, might found a Microcollege and hire an artist or appoint a curator as the professor; the Microcollege then serves as an important expression of the mission of the institution. A city government might establish a Microcollege and house it at city hall, led by a former mayor, a ward alderman, or the chair of the city council. In each case, the pedagogical focus of the Microcollege is a reflection of the institution in which it is located.

There can be thousands of Microcolleges, each with its own unique pedagogical focus, an expression of the individual professor. The massification of higher education would then be achieved not with the growing of a few enormous multiversities but through the decentralization of higher education via thousands of small-scale enterprises.

Each Microcollege is a complex pedagogical system. It is far too simplistic to say that a Microcollege is only an online college. Students learn a great deal from online courses, but they also learn in the community-wide lectures, in the personal interactions in the tutorials, by participation in faculty research, from peer mentors and as peer mentors, and in the administrative roles they undertake on behalf of the Microcollege.

3

The Humanities Think Tank

The Humanities Think Tank is a policy institute that is staffed entirely with scholars from the humanities disciplines. It is a policy actor, providing information intended for an audience of government officials, policy-makers, corporations, NGOs, and the military. Most scholars at the think tank focus their research on pragmatic, present-day issues and solutions, while some look at future trends and provide strategic foresight. The Humanities Think Tank is action-oriented: the knowledge it produces is intended to provoke change in the real world. Fellows and scholars engage in public intellectualism; the audience for this knowledge is located outside of the academy. Humanists at traditional universities typically produce research intended for other humanists in a scholarly conversation between academics. The function of the Humanities Think Tank is to get "new [humanistic] ideas into the public sphere [and shape] the way that policymakers and the public understand issues."[1]

The Humanities Think Tank is an exercise in translational humanities: "the application of humanities expertise in domains beyond higher education and cultural heritage institutions."[2] Apart from their subject-matter concerns, the humanities disciplines (like history, philosophy, English, and women's studies) are distinguished by their specific methods. Those methods include ethnographic and archival research, textual analysis, sense-making, pattern analysis, and drawing larger conclusions from qualitative data through narrative. Humanities disciplines are about meaning-making and interpretation, and thus the policy briefs generated by the Humanities Think Tank are aimed at discerning meaning, drawing attention, framing new questions, and identifying policy alternatives. While the research fellows might draw insights from Matthew Arnold's "best that has been thought" from the past, the research concerns of the think tank focus on the present and future. The Humanities Think Tank engages in research projects that rely on the particular methods and habits of mind of humanists: meaning-making intended to influence and lead public policy.

The Humanities Think Tank is led by a president, who serves as the public face of the organization, connecting with governments, the media, clients, donors, and funding agencies. This person is a distinguished humanist, determined not only by publications and service to the academy, but also by a record of public service in government or with an NGO; she may also have experience as a management consultant or executive in a private firm. The president is at once a scholar, a public servant, and an accomplished executive with media experience.

A number of research directors report to the president. There is a research director for each of the core areas of interest of the Humanities Think Tank, for example, culture, religion, health, gender, technology, political economy, and the environment, although the range of interests expands and grows according to the interactions of social forces and cultural changes. The work of the think tank is organized around projects and questions; a principal investigator (senior fellow) leads a working group of four to six staff, postdocs, graduate students, or nonacademic expert consultants. There are a number of working groups operating at any given time. Each working group is constituted around a specific policy-oriented, humanities-grounded topic, like "Generation Z" or "the world is flat" or "democracy is imperiled" or "Islam." The senior fellow determines the question to be examined, but does so in consultation with the research director, who is mindful of contemporary issues and trends and the strategic goals established by the think tank. In some cases, the Humanities Think Tank works on a contract basis with firms, governments, or NGOs on a specific problem, and those research results are not disseminated publicly but are the intellectual property of the client (although there is often occasion for this work to be publicly shared). Typically, the research director works with the senior fellow to identify a target audience and a topic question. The working group then meets weekly to discuss/brainstorm responses to the topic question. Members of the working group locate appropriate texts to be interpreted to facilitate discussion. Working collaboratively under the leadership of the senior fellow, they achieve consensus around the results of their research.

The results of the working groups take several forms. Some research is presented in academic journals and as scholarly monographs, which may be published by outside academic presses but are just as often published by the Humanities Think Tank Press. The typical working group remains active for four months, after which the results of its research are disseminated via a policy brief, media appearances, social media, op-eds and articles, and public forums. The fifteen-page policy brief—with executive summary—concisely represents the group's work on the topic question and offers various policy positions. The research directors sponsor regular public forums that center on the results of the various working groups. These forums invite the policy-making community, other think tanks, and the interested public to hear presentations and discussions by the senior fellow and external experts. C-SPAN frequently airs these public forums, allowing them to reach a wider audience beyond those in the conference room. The research produced by the Humanities Think Tank always operates on the time frame and at the speed of policy-makers.

Like the president and the research directors, the senior fellows and other humanists employed by the Humanities Think Tank have broad experience not only in academia but in politics, business, and the media/public relations. Humanists possess the skills and academic attributes of scholars, while they are also skilled in addressing the issues and concerns among the policy-making community and other opinion leaders. They understand that ideas must be sold to customers, and they have some experience as intellectual entrepreneurs. They write influential opinion pieces for leading news organizations; it is very likely that a senior fellow has spent time writing for the *New Yorker* or for little magazines, such as *Jacobin* and *n+1*, or served as a staff writer for the *New York Times* or the *Wall Street Journal*.

The training of policy-oriented humanists has gone beyond what is offered in traditional PhD programs. As apprentice humanists, they spend time interning in government and business. The Humanities Think Tank relies on graduates of traditional programs, but also engages in its own training and its own graduate program in applied humanities, granting PhDs to future policy experts who have been broadly trained across all of these sectors.

■ ■ ■

There is an extensive literature lamenting the "crisis of the humanities." By many measures—enrollments, the job prospects for humanities graduates, the supposed relevance of humanistic scholarship—the place and prestige of the humanities within the traditional university have been diminished. James Turner has imagined the future of the human-ities in the university: "Contemporary pressures will more likely push them into a new shape, even ultimately a healthier one. . . . Budget cuts and shrinking enrollments will accelerate the blending of disciplines, as humanistic learning shifts its shape once again. There will be much pain, and diminishing support will force change. At many colleges and universities, adjunct and assistant professors will be fired, with tenured faculty members pushed into multidisciplinary units. Historians, art historians, classicists, and even literary scholars may find themselves sharing the same department."[3] Turner contends that the humanities existed and even thrived outside of the university for centuries, and the disciplines were only brought into the university around 1800.[4] If the humanities are struggling to assert their place within the university, then perhaps they should seek better fortune once again outside it. What might the constellation of disciplines called the humanities look like were they to once again locate themselves outside of the university?

Public intellectuals were prominent before the Second World War. New York provided an inexpensive and hospitable place for these in-tellectuals to live and work, and many of them wrote for little maga-zines and other organs of public discourse. As New York became more expensive in the 1960s, many of these public intellectuals moved to the relative stability of the university. "Careerism and specialization gradually opened up a gulf between intellectuals and the public. The sturdy prose of Edmund Wilson and Irving Howe gave way, by the mid-90s, to the knotted gender theorizing of Judith Butler and the cult-studies musings of Andrew Ross."[5] A result of this movement to the university, so goes this argument, was that the audience for humanistic knowledge was truncated to only other humanists, any influence confined to other scholars.

One of the effects of the so-called jobs crisis in the humanities—the relative lack of tenure-track university positions—is that some humanists have returned to the world of freelance writing, to the life of the public intellectual, whom the *Chronicle of Higher Education* calls "the new intellectuals." "This is a generation that refuses the vocation of mere scholar," says Harvard professor Samuel Moyn. "Evan Kindley[, a senior editor at the *Los Angeles Review of Books*, argues] that the hiring crisis has weakened incentives to produce peer-reviewed scholarship. Intellectual energy that in a previous era went toward filling a CV and trying to land a tenure-track job is now, for a small but influential clique, being channeled toward public debate."[6]

Many of the new intellectuals identified by the *Chronicle* are left-leaning or Marxist, writing to challenge, even subvert, the established order. That is certainly a valid standpoint from which to situate the humanities outside of the university—and it has a long pedigree—but this is only one model for the future institutionalization of the humanities. What if humanists engaged as public intellectuals in an advisory—in addition to an adversarial—role to decision-makers? "We urge the next president to establish a White House Council of Historical Advisers," Graham Allison and Niall Ferguson recommend.[7] While historians have certainly been invited to the White House to share their advice—and, of course, historian Arthur Schlesinger served directly in the Kennedy administration—there has yet to be a permanently established group of historians who would advise the president. "Operationally, the Council of Historical Advisers would mirror the Council of Economic Advisers," assert Allison and Ferguson. "A chair and two additional members would be appointed by the president to full-time positions, and respond to assignments from him or her. They would be supported by a small professional staff and would be part of the Executive Office of the President."[8]

To play this role, historians would not need to reorient their methods, but their raison d'être. "For too long, history has been disparaged as a 'soft' subject by social scientists offering spurious certainty. We believe it is time for a new and rigorous 'applied history'—an attempt to illuminate current challenges and choices by analyzing precedents and historical analogues."[9] Applied history, in this case, does not refer to the activities of archivists or museum curators. "Applied historians would take a current predicament and try to identify analogues in the past. Their ultimate goal would be to find clues about what is likely to happen, then suggest possible policy interventions and assess probable consequences."[10] At one stage, early in the twentieth century, historians performed such a policy-oriented, practical role,[11] but they have largely ceded that role to scientists and social scientists. "Indeed, and ironically enough," say Robert Frodeman, Carl Mitcham, and Roger Pielke Jr., "the historical trajectory of the humanities has been precisely the opposite of that of the sciences. Two centuries ago, it was the liberal arts and humanities that were thought necessary for informed public debates. . . . A hundred years ago science, like the humanities today, was thought to be largely irrelevant to practical affairs, at least in terms of the public resources devoted to science."[12] The social sciences were central to the first think tanks, such as the Brookings Institution, and it is largely from the sciences and social sciences that most policy experts are drawn. Science as a source of policy knowledge received a boost during and after the Second World War, when Vannevar Bush described the "endless frontier" of science. The formation of the Humanities Think Tank assumes the strong voice and advocacy of a Vannevar Bush for the humanities.[13]

A Council of Historical (or Humanities) Advisors would clearly represent a more stable platform for the institutionalization of humanistic knowledge outside of the universities than that represented by the public intellectualism of little magazines. Another institutional form for public humanists is the think tank. Think tanks have been described as "universities without students."[14] More precisely, think tanks occupy a position between the intellectual autonomy of the little magazine and the policy impact of a political insider. "Think tanks," says Thomas Medvetz, "have become the primary instruments for linking political and intellectual practice in American life. . . . By occupying a crucial point of juncture in between the worlds of political, [academic], economic, and media production, think tanks increasingly regulate the circulation of knowledge and personnel among these spheres. As a result, any intellectual figure who wishes to take part in American political debate must increasingly orient his or her production to the rules of this hybrid subspace."[15] The Humanities Think Tank represents such a (re)orientation of humanists.

Before a Council of Historical Advisors or a Humanities Think Tank can become reality, however, the methods of the historian must be redeployed toward understanding problems and issues of the present and the future.[16] This advisory board could, of course, be expanded to include humanists more broadly—scholars of philosophy, English, religious studies. They might have the left-leaning political orientation of the little magazines' new intellectuals. But such an advisory group would be noted not for its ideological orientation, but for the particular vantage point and intellectual perspective it would bring.

Humanists have particular methods and habits of mind that would be distinctive in a policy setting. Indeed, the humanities once informed statecraft, observes Charles Hill, who had a career in the US Foreign Service and is now a senior lecturer in humanities at Yale: "For some decades now, the international state system has been deteriorating, intellectually disparaged from within and assaulted by a series of rival system[s] from without. But literature, *once paramount as a way of knowing*, was evicted from its place in the pantheon of the arts . . . and statecraft has suffered from the loss. Today, both the state order and literature are under assault. Whether the present international system can be shored up and repaired or must be transformed, statecraft cannot be practiced in the absence of literary insight" (emphasis mine).[17] The idea of literature as a way of knowing with applications in a policy setting would be an animating feature of the Humanities Think Tank.

Whatever their particular disciplinary orientations, the humanities are joined together by common methods and ways of thinking. Geoffrey Galt Harpham defines the method of the humanities in this way: "The scholarly study of documents and artifacts produced by human beings in the past enables us to see the world from different points of view so that we may better understand ourselves."[18] An even shorter version of this statement might be: humanists read and interpret texts. The humanist and biotech entrepreneur Donald Drakeman asserts the centrality of "the interpretation of documents as our [humanists'] method"; indeed, humanists engage in "the proper way to interpret a document."[19] In reading and interpreting documents, humanists engage in methods that include ethnographic and archival research, textual analysis, sense-making, pattern analysis, and drawing larger conclusions from qualitative data through narrative.[20] Humanists engaged in public discourse and political consulting interpret a different set of documents from what they typically read.

■ ■ ■

Sense-making and the interpretation of culture are two areas in which humanists especially excel, and they form a key part of the work of the Humanities Think Tank. Gary Saul Morson and Morton Schapiro contend that economics would benefit "from understanding people better" and that the humanities provide such an understanding. Humanists understand culture better than economists do, especially since "economics has a hard time dealing with culture because it cannot be mathematized."[21] "People are not organisms that are made and then dipped in some culture, like Achilles in the river Styx," Morson and Schapiro argue. "The temptation of claims aspiring to universality, and of models reducible to equations, makes the idea of acultural humanness especially appealing" but ultimately false and misleading.[22] Central to the knowledge generated by the Humanities Think Tank is the deep knowledge of a variety of cultures. Further, economics needs story and narrative, write Morson and Schapiro, and humanists are expert at "narrativeness." "Narativeness," as they define it, "measures the need for narrative. . . . When is there narrativeness? The more we need culture as a means of explanation, the more narrativeness. The more we invoke irreducibly individual human psychology, the more narrativeness. And the more contingent factors—events that are un-predictable from within one's disciplinary framework—play a role, the more narrativeness."[23] The Humanities Think Tank sets itself apart from other think tanks in its specialized knowledge of the dynamics of human culture.

■   ■   ■

Christian Madsbjerg, trained in the humanities, applies humanistic knowledge to management problems and has formed a management consulting firm staffed by others trained in the humanities. He helps his clients understand culture, and he argues that the quantitative, decontextualized data that are the currency of business consulting are insufficient to this task. "We can think of sensemaking as the exact opposite of algorithmic thinking: it is entirely situated in the concrete, while algorithmic thinking exists in a no-man's-land of information stripped of its specificity. Algorithmic thinking can go wide—processing trillions of terabytes of data per second—but only sensemaking can go deep."[24] Sense-making and interpretation are foundational habits of mind of the humanist, and they would be applied to public policy issues.

Madsbjerg's team employs "analytic empathy," a concept drawn from humanistic practice. When working on business problems, Madsbjerg's consultants employ thought processes practiced by all humanists: "[The historian] systematically assembles sources and evidence from that time. . . . But the research materials are only the beginning. She will need to establish a context based on other scholars' work. She must also validate and critique the importance of the data, and place the data in a theoretical framework that explains the time period. The power structures, gender roles, aesthetics, technology, and information systems are all topics historians have created in order to analyze the data."[25] In his consulting work with companies, Madsbjerg engages in analytic empathy: "Once our thick data of ethnographic field notes, photographs, journals, and interviews are collected and sorted, our job is to identify the salient patterns occurring across all of the data. . . . After we have reframed a problem into a phenomenon, this process of analytical empathy brings us to a greater understanding of what we are encountering."[26] This is the applied humanistic thinking that animates the work of the Humanities Think Tank.

Madsbjerg's consulting practice relies on applied phenomenology, "the study of human experiences."[27] Quantitative data and other kinds of scientific information typically inform such management consulting, but Madsbjerg believes that to truly understand potential customers one needs a deeper understanding of culture, of human experiences in the world. "What does it mean to be human? How do we experience ourselves in the world? Where does meaning come from? When we want to delve into questions this profound, the humanities are an extremely helpful guide."[28] The Humanities Think Tank asks similar questions, working in the public policy environment to better understand culture and human experience.

■　■　■

Humanists in traditional universities tend to focus on interpreting documents from the past. Drakeman notes, "Whether the scholars who have been so influential in leading policy-makers to the choices they made were called philosophers, historians, social psychologists or medical ethicists, they were taking part in society's continuing effort to figure out [borrowing from the title of the Gauguin painting] 'What Are We?' and 'Where Are We Going?' which necessarily involves think-ing about 'Where Do We Come From?'"[29] Humanists in traditional universities largely concentrate on the final question; the new intel-lectuals ask the first and second questions. Eric Touya de Marenne writes, "Beyond the positive nature of physical or social science ('what is'), the humanities expand one's intellectual inquiry to examine 'what ought to be.'"[30] It is interesting to note that the founding legislation for the National Endowment for the Humanities said, "An advanced civilization must not limit its efforts to science and technology alone, but must give full value and support to the other great branches of scholarly and cultural activity in order to achieve a better understanding of the past, *a better analysis of the present, and a better view of the future*" (emphasis mine).[31] In spite of this directive, "remarkably, little sustained effort has been given to examining the claim that the humanities can make significant contributions to policy outcomes."[32] As a measure of this deficiency, of the academic disciplines studied by policy experts, history and area studies represent 6.1 percent of the total; the arts and humanities are 3.5 percent of the total.[33] It is my sense that the humanities as institutionalized in the traditional university are broadly focused on understanding "where we come from" rather than "what we are today" and, more critically, "where we are going." It is the latter question that is of interest to a policy-making community, and that question features prominently at the Humanities Think Tank. A policy-oriented humanities that attempts to influence public discourse would focus attention on the interpretation of contemporary documents with the aim of making "crucial decisions about the kinds of lives we live."[34]

■   ■   ■

The humanist in a think tank would be redefined as a "policy expert."[35] "The proliferation of think tanks," says Medvetz, "has made possible a new kind of public figure in American life known as a 'policy expert,' whose authority is built on a claim to mediate an encounter among holders of various forms of power."[36] The humanist as policy expert would be a different kind of public intellectual, "someone who could challenge the political orthodoxy of the day from a standpoint of relative autonomy while speaking in terms that were accessible to the lay public."[37]

The humanist in a think tank, in addition to practicing the skills and methods of the humanities, would need proficiency in politics, business, and media, skills atypical of a humanist in a traditional university. "The ideal-typical policy expert," observes Medvetz, "is someone who . . .

merg[es] the intellect of a serious scholar, the procedural know-how and ability to anticipate 'hot' policy issues of an 'inside the Beltway' player, the willingness to 'sell' one's wares of an entrepreneur, and the knack for 'talking in sound bites' and writing concise op-ed pieces of a media specialist. Thus, like the think tank itself, a policy expert must exist in 'plural' form."[38] This means that the preparation for the humanist in a think tank would need to extend beyond what is offered in most PhD programs. Those programs would, obviously, prepare graduates in the skills and methods of the humanities, but perhaps their dissertations would focus on a contemporary issue, a form of applied humanities. Part of their graduate training might include time spent interning in government or other policy-making entities. Internships might include experience in business or the media. Indeed, the new intellectuals need experience in media that prepares them for work at a humanities think tank. It should be clear that, in this scenario, there are still graduate programs at traditional universities that are producing PhDs in the humanities, but the training for some would be particularly geared toward work in a public policy think tank, and the Humanities Think Tank would establish partnerships with such graduate programs. It is also possible that the Humanities Think Tank would have its own graduate program and would train its own PhD students in the particularities of applied humanities research.[39]

■ ■ ■

In a similar way that the humanities were transformed when they moved into the university (pace Turner), the humanities are transformed when they move into think tanks. The practices of humanists are different; for example, research work in think tanks is more goal-directed. "The research of tenured professors is unmanaged and undirected. The object of research is up to the whim of the professor. The goal may or may not be to solve an important social problem. Think tanks, by contrast, tend to be very goal-oriented. They employ or contract with scholars to research specific topics and encourage solutions to well-defined problems."[40] Further, such research moves at the pace of the policy community and is usually determined by its "timeliness."[41] Researchers must be out in front of contemporary issues and, indeed, must anticipate future concerns and issues.

Because the audience for the think tank's intellectual output is not simply other scholars, the documents to be interpreted, the kinds of questions to be asked, and the types of intellectual products are different than what is typical for humanists in a traditional university. In addition to academic articles and scholarly monographs, the intellectual products of the Humanities Think Tank take a number of forms. Policy experts "generate written materials that blend the features of legislative aide memos, scholarly articles, journalistic reports, executive summaries, 'talking points' memoranda, or some combination of these."[42] The audience for the intellectual output of a think tank tends to be "legislators, who 'buy' ideas by incorporating them into policy; financial donors, whose purchase is more literal because it involves giving money to the think tank; and journalists, who figuratively buy a think tank's studies when they cite or quote them."[43]

Supreme Court justices have long relied on humanists' amicus briefs to understand the context of particular cases. Interpreting the meaning of documents is an explicit requirement in such cases. "How does [the Supreme Court] discern the Constitution's proper meaning?" asks Drakeman. "The answer is that the justices have turned with impressive frequency to scholarship in the humanities not only for inspiration, but also for direct guidance as to the meaning of the supreme law of the land. The precise language of the text may provide a general sense of the interpretive metes and bounds, but the shape and substance of the constitutional landscape has come from historians, philosophers, sociologists and other scholars."[44] An amicus brief is a document prepared by a person or entity that is not a direct party but nevertheless has an interest in a particular case. That "amicus impulse" is an important feature of the Humanities Think Tank: the scholars and fellows produce documents not only for court cases but for policy decisions and, indeed, for the larger public discourse surrounding important issues.

The Humanities Think Tank produces white papers that function as amicus briefs for the polity.

Those white papers and policy briefs look different from typical humanities scholarship, in part because they follow a different set of formal rules in terms of length, features, tone, and rhetoric. The senior fellow is charged with the responsibility of adhering to publication guidelines as established by the think tank and overseen by the research directors. Further, publications follow a specific process designed to ensure their impact and influence. For the results of the research generated by any particular working group, a target audience is first identified, which shapes the particular form of the policy brief or white paper. The objective of the communication is also determined at this stage: cognitive, affective, or behavioral. A cognitive communication strategy means getting specific information to the target audience. An affective strategy means influencing the target audience to think a certain way about the research topic. A behavioral strategy means encouraging the target audience to take action. As with all other decisions, the particular communication strategy is determined by the senior fellow in close collaboration with the research director.

After the communication strategy has been identified, the specific channels of communication are determined. For many working groups, there are multiple communications channels, such as the policy brief or white paper, policy memos, or presentations at academic conferences. Social media, press conferences, and interviews with the media are other channels. A strategic consideration, again made by the senior fellow after consultation with the research director, is the particular mix of communication channels. Once these have been determined, the messages themselves are designed in terms of content and format. Finally, the effectiveness of the communication is measured, with the goal of improving both design and influence among targeted audiences.[45]

■   ■   ■

The Humanities Think Tank also convenes regular public forums. Unlike academic conferences, where specialists speak to specialists, these forums are intended for a wider public of both policy-makers and interested citizens. C-SPAN regularly broadcasts live presentations and recordings of such public forums, and the programming of the Humanities Think Tank may be featured as well. Indeed, "think tanks and policy research programs across the country specialize in bringing people together to engage in public dialogue. . . . Public dialogue remains a central feature of most think tanks, and it is the primary function of some of them."[46] These forums might pair humanities scholars and fellows with nonacademic experts in government and business, emphasizing again the hybrid space within which the Humanities Think Tank operates. Humanists who write as public intellectuals often do so autonomously and alone. The Humanities Think Tank serves as a channel for media attention, allowing for the more efficient dissemination of a public humanist's message. The think tank brings together a group of such humanists working collaboratively, intensifying their message and their impact.

In addition to providing specific content, humanists can influence public discourse by framing ideas and issues in new ways. "Policy organizations and researchers can often help decision makers, experts, and the general public understand issues and ideas in new ways through analysis and public dialogue. These efforts can include everything from exploring the historical, economic, and political context of issues to providing new information on how issues are seen outside the capital or outside the country."[47] The unique lens provided by the humanities has the power to shape the terms of public discourse. "Science also clearly contributes to decision making by helping to identify problems that otherwise could not be seen."[48] Question formation and problem identification also seem to be valuable roles that the humanities play, especially given humanists' facility with qualitative data when others are so focused on quantitative data. "We need the synoptic scope and methodological power of science if we are to make sense of events beyond localized human perceptions," say Frodeman, Mitcham, and Pielke.[49] Because sense-making is one of the humanities' central methodological features, the same could be easily said of those disciplines.

One way that the Humanities Think Tank can raise new questions and reframe contemporary issues is by identifying policy alternatives by drawing analogies to former practices, to alternatives practiced in the past.[50] For example, I participated in a working group of humanists on the theme of "confinement." The choice of term was meant to be more expansive than "imprisonment," but the thrust of the group's discussions was a history of prisons, slavery, and other institutional forms of confinement. One particularly valuable insight from this conversation was that the meaning of "prison" has not been static over time: Roman practices, for example, look very different from contemporary practices. The conversation turned from the history of prison to contemporary questions about prison, especially the prison reform issue that is currently drawing the attention of policy-makers. Knowing something about how prison was understood and conceptualized in the past provides alternatives for how we might think of prison in the present and future. Indeed, historians and other humanists—as keepers of the *longue durée*, of deep historical knowledge—can offer policy-makers a wealth of alternatives for doing things.

Knowledge of the past teaches that institutions, practices, and even "human nature" have never been static or unchanging. "Insofar as both climate science and economics have often left us with a vision of the world in which alternative futures are scarce or non-existent," write Jo Guldi and David Armitage, "history's role must be not only to survey the data about responsibility for climate change, but also to point out the alternative directions, the utopian byways, the alternative agricultures and patterns of consumption that have been developing all the while."[51] Alternatives practiced in the past offer potential options for how we might arrange institutions and practices in the present or future. The Humanities Think Tank produces white papers or societal amicus briefs that spell out previous alternatives, with an eye toward offering analogous solutions to present issues.

■   ■   ■

The range of policy questions that humanists might address is bounded only by their curiosity. Climate change and prison reform are but two examples. Donald Drakeman focuses on civil liberties and biomedical research, and he notes, "The individuals making up these powerful arms of the government have relied heavily on the work of humanities scholars to inform and justify their decisions, which are deeply rooted in the kinds of questions to which the study of the humanities has been devoted for a very long time. This message, that important elements of our economy and vital aspects of our lives are based on policy choices influenced by humanities scholarship, bears repeating whenever times get tough [for the humanities]."[52] For example, in the realm of health care, "will private sources of capital continue to invest in new technologies for developing life-saving drugs? That question turns out to involve more questions in the humanities than might be expected," says Drakeman.[53] "Ostensibly scientific and medical decisions are, in fact, based on very difficult, and largely unresolved, issues of distributive justice, fairness and the nature of the common good—questions that historically have been the province of the humanities."[54] Especially with regard to the question of distributive justice in health care, "the humanities have been working on—and not yet resolving, but providing thoughtful analysis and rational reflection about—this difficult issue for quite some time now." Drakeman invokes Smith, Kant, and Rousseau, among others who addressed these larger issues. "Scientists and physicians can figure out whether a new drug actually extends lives, and mathematicians can calculate the costs, but the STEM fields, by themselves, cannot provide a considered judgment about who should have those benefits and at what price."[55] Addressing questions such as distributive justice in health care means more than simply creating new subfields populated by specialists like those in the medical humanities.

Once their practices are reoriented toward present and future questions, all humanists, regardless of their individual disciplines and specialties, can influence and shape public debate and policy discussions. This practice might be termed the "translational humanities": "the application of humanities expertise in domains beyond higher education and cultural heritage institutions."[56] The term "translational research" comes from the medical sciences and refers to the application of research in order to directly impact public health and well-being. The translational humanities apply humanistic knowledge to address and improve the body politic and the quality of public discourse. The Humanities Think Tank places the translational humanities at the center of its communications strategy.

Interlude

The University of Beauty

Karl Jaspers writes, "The university is a community of scholars and students engaged in the task of seeking truth. . . . People are allowed to congregate [at the university] for the sole purpose of seeking truth. For it is a human right that man must be allowed somewhere to pursue truth unconditionally and for its own sake."[1] The University of Beauty is organized around another transcendental: beauty. At this university, students and faculty congregate as a community to engage in the task of seeking beauty unconditionally and for its own sake.

The pursuit of beauty forms the intellectual and pedagogical core of the university. As a first principle, the definition of beauty is examined (and problematized) by all students and faculty. Beauty is understood as a deeply historical and contextual experience, and an exploration of the differences between Platonic and Kantian notions of beauty undergirds the curriculum, as do the modernist rejection of aesthetics and the feminist critique of Western notions of beauty.[2] The curriculum includes non-Western notions of beauty, such as Eastern ideas of asymmetry, negative space, and the Japanese notion of wabi-sabi. Nor are aesthetics and beauty confined to the arts: students seek beauty in the sciences and mathematics and in the proportions and colors of forms across nature. Students explore beauty in music and what constitutes a beautiful move in chess, go, or the "beautiful game" of soccer. The aesthetics of dance and movement are part of the curriculum. Experimentation with beauty is encouraged: How might a move in chess be an example of wabi-sabi? What is fractal architecture? Aesthetics are experiential, but also active, with students and professors creating the beautiful as much as they are experiencing and admiring it.

While there are traditional disciplines at this university, there are no majors or subject concentrations: all students study beauty as expressed through different subjects and different cultures, and some seek patterns of similarity between disciplinary objects of beauty. As a culminating experience, students answer the question "What is beauty?"

Although there are disciplines, there are no departments, because there is only one faculty member for each discipline. Faculty are not specialists *in* their disciplines but are specialists *of* their disciplines, with a particular focus on the beautiful in history, in engineering, in music, in mathematics, in physics, in dance, in architecture, and in sports and video games. Students learn enough about these disciplines to be able to grasp what constitutes "the beautiful" in each. Outside of teaching, faculty time is given to discovering or creating the beautiful in their discipline. Faculty also collaborate, taking ideas of beauty from one discipline and extending it to another, creating new forms and new objects of beauty. They seek the sublime in their disciplines and cultivate a sense of wonder and awe, asserting that the experience of beauty is a human trait that artificial intelligence cannot match.

The pedagogy of the University of Beauty centers on cultivating a relationship between the object of beauty (whether physical or in the mind's eye) and the experiences of the student.[3] The object of beauty does not stand on its own as an object of contemplation: the professor values the expressive capacities of the student and how those are formed by their gender, class, and race/ethnicity. The professor connects the object of beauty to the life of the student. Because the experience of beauty is often inexpressible in words, professors encourage students to explore alternative ways of communicating and reflecting on their experience of beauty.

The physical space of the university is itself an experience in beauty and aesthetics. Like a Reggio Emilia school or a Montessori classroom, the University of Beauty is physically designed as a beautiful space. The rhythms and patterns of daily life in the university are contemplated as experiences of beauty. What do symmetry and balance look like when applied to the routines of an institution? The space of the university is reconfigurable so that students may design their own beautiful spaces.

The university resembles a museum but is not limited to art objects; it includes objects of design and objects of contemplation that reside in the imagination alone. The university curates music and mathematics as aesthetic objects. In this curated space, students and faculty exchange their ideas of beauty, creating physical and idea artifacts together or alone with mutual respect for one another's creations. There is an archive that houses books and other beautiful objects, including some created by faculty and students. In addition, student and faculty representations of their experiences of beauty are part of this collection. Curating is an important goal of the curriculum: students learn to curate, to identify, to organize, and to situate objects of beauty. Curating beauty means exploring analogies across different aesthetic forms and connecting disparate objects of beauty. The exhibition is a critical site for displaying and expressing one's experience of beauty, and it is where the subjectivity of beauty is negotiated.

With the pursuit of beauty at its core, the university is neither instrumental nor technocratic. It is a postcapitalist, postmodern university in that it does not serve the need for human capital development. Since students acquire aesthetic experiences rather than vocationally oriented skills, the University of Beauty exists more as a monastery, ashram, or yeshiva. It is a place apart from the rest of society, designed for the contemplation not of religious texts but of the beautiful and sublime in the world.

II APPRENTICESHIP

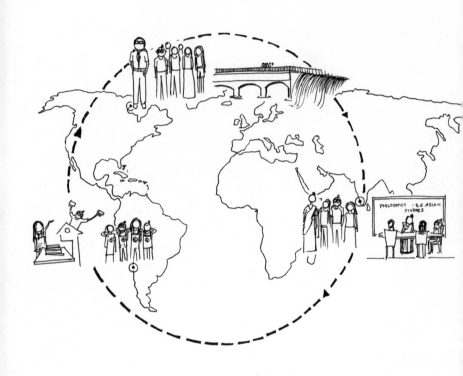

4

Nomad University

The "gig economy" describes the way that many people are employed in the twenty-first century: they are not attached to one company exclusively but move frequently between projects. Because the gig economy encompasses the globe, workers move from job to job to job wherever it might be located. Although people are essentially independent contractors, they may work on these short-term projects with teams, which then disassemble after the project has ended. New teams reform around different projects in different locations around the globe. Nomad University prepares students to operate in this cosmopolitan world.

Because work is no longer tied to location, Nomad University is nowhere and everywhere. Although Nomad University has a building to house administrators, it has no other stable physical location. The university is not rooted in place, symbolized by buildings that house chemistry labs, seminar rooms, or lecture halls. The physical location where learning occurs shifts around the globe, with professors and students seeking out problems and experiences wherever they might be. Perhaps they aim to solve an engineering problem in sub-Saharan Africa, perhaps they are mediating clashes between the police and the community in an American urban core, perhaps the goal is to design a software solution for a multinational corporation. Students might travel to Monticello to read Jefferson's works, to Oxford, Mississippi, to read Faulkner, or to Athens to read Plato. "Education in many places" is the guiding philosophy of Nomad University.

Faculty are similarly nomadic, traveling the world in search of projects to accomplish with the teams they assemble. Nomad University is a network of such faculty, who announce on an electronic board the projects for which they have secured funders. Faculty are practitioners: in addition to their work with Nomad University, they maintain professional lives. Faculty seek out requests for proposals (RFPs) from corporations, NGOs, cultural institutions, and other organizations. They then form a project team made up of students of varying levels of experience, from first-timers to advanced students who have several such projects already completed. Faculty occasionally team up: an anthropologist and a sociologist might work together and then include a writing faculty member or a filmmaker who documents the activities. These teams gather for the purposes of the project, complete the work, and then disassemble until another project emerges. While some team members might work on several different projects together, many teams are one-off temporary arrangements, not unlike a film production team. Students come and go from these projects and may work with several faculty members. A typical project lasts between four and six months, with students completing two or three such assignments a year. Students receive diplomas upon satisfactorily completing ten projects.

Students develop and demonstrate technical ability at each site, with the skills determined by the nature of the project. Each student receives a performance review from the faculty team leader, who assesses their work on the project as well as whether the project "worked" for the local community. At each site, students focus not simply on the technical problem at hand but also on its economic, social, and cultural contexts and dimensions. Building trust with the host community and developing cross-cultural communication skills are important outcomes of every project, whatever its technical details. Students learn to negotiate the unfamiliar and learn to understand new cultures. Such "encounters with novelty" arise even in the most ordinary of events, such as the evening meal or a trip to a market. The faculty mentor plays a critical role here not only as the manager of projects or the instructor of technical skills but as the guide to help students make sense of their new surroundings and facilitate their reflections on the contrast of cultures. Students are encouraged to reflect on the cultures they encounter and experience. How do they understand their own native culture? What similarities and differences can they discern between the various cultures they have encountered? Beyond any technical knowledge they gain, students learn to be cosmopolitan: to immerse themselves wherever they might be in the world. Students are granted time for reflection and conversations, which are part of the performance review and a key part of the learning experience.

As a condition of matriculation, students must participate in a broad variety of projects, but they are permitted to concentrate in one form. Thus, those with an interest in engineering may engage in five such projects, the repetition allowing them to build on skills learned in previous projects. Advanced students mentor younger students at each site. As a capstone, advanced students co-lead a project with a faculty member. Upon graduating, the student is a candidate for faculty status once they have established professional credentials and an external reputation.

There is a small administrative center at the university, where the registrar is housed. The registrar plays a key role in monitoring the students, keeping track of their activities, and curating their portfolios. There is also a network of administrators whose functions include the selection and vetting of faculty. A review board reads through applications from potential faculty. The administrators also make logistical arrangements, such as booking flights. This administrative center is where novice students gather to be prepped before going off on their first trip. Students do not pay tuition, but neither are they paid for their work. As part of the RFP agreement, students receive housing and meals when on location. Airlines provide tickets in exchange for advertising and public relations for the company. The projects are revenue-generating for the university since they are sponsored by the corporation or NGO that needs the work.

The kind of student produced by Nomad University is global and cosmopolitan, one with the capacity to listen in place.

■　■　■

The education futurist John Moravec observes: "Industrial society is giving way to knowledge and innovation work. Whereas industrialization required people to settle in one place to perform a very specific role or function, the jobs associated with knowledge and information workers have become much less specific concerning task and place. . . . A nomadic knowledge worker . . . is a creative, imaginative, and innovative person who can work with almost anybody, anytime, and anywhere."[1] He predicts that by 2020, 45 percent of the workforce in the Westernized world will be "knowmads," a term that identifies both the knowledge possessed by these individuals and the fact that they are not rooted to place.[2] Knowmads leap from job to job.[3] Nomad University will attract the kind of student who seeks to be a knowmad, and it prepares those students to be able to thrive in multiple cultural environments.

■　■　■

Malia Obama made news in 2016 when she announced she would be delaying her freshman year at Harvard to have a gap-year experience. Not unexpectedly, the news drew attention to this relatively rare experience. Gap years are more common in England, for example, and Malia Obama's action might spur widespread interest among American students. Perhaps gap years are uncommon in America because it seems too much like the grand tour, like a vestige of a time when aristocrats would spend a year traveling across Europe, exploring its art, architecture, and cultures. Given the high costs of some programs, gap years seem to be a way for the wealthy and privileged to delay adulthood while traveling around the world.[4]

It turns out, however, that some gap-year programs have pedagogical benefits. Jeffrey Selingo reports that "students whose gap years involve travel—whether to a foreign country or to a different part of the U.S.—not only end up with higher grades in college, but they also graduate at the same rate as those who don't delay at all. Research has found that when gap-year students arrive on campus, they take their studies more seriously and don't engage in risky behavior, such as alcohol abuse."[5] Students who take a gap year show that they are more motivated when they do enter college.[6] These are outcomes any college or university would desire for its graduates, let alone for students just entering college. If participation in just one gap-year experience has these benefits, what might a university designed as a four-year series of gap-year experiences produce?

■　■　■

Another reason students give for taking a gap year is that it allows them to take a break from the academic rat race of exam cramming that presumably defined their school experience, before they reenter that rat race in college. A survey of students revealed that burnout and the desire to "find themselves" were motivating factors in taking a gap year.[7] But the gap-year experience is seen as preparatory for or as a prelude to a traditional college experience, not as an educational end in itself. Some writers point to the fact that many students do a gap year in order to follow a passion, which was once a justification for attending college; the implication is that students no longer explore their passions at the university.[8] "For a gap year to have a significant impact on success in college, and later in the working world," reports Selingo, "it needs to be a transformative event, quite distinct from anything a student has experienced before—a meaningful work experience, academic preparation for college, or travel that opens up the horizon to the rest of the world. It should also be designed to help students acquire the skills and attributes that colleges and employers are looking for: maturity, confidence, problem solving, communication skills, and independence."[9] Rather than seeing the gap year as preparation for college, a coordinated and well-designed curriculum of several such experiences would produce students with maturity, problem-solving abilities, communication skills, a cosmopolitan disposition, and a host of other attributes that one would like to see from a classroom-centered collegiate experience.[10]

■ ■ ■

Nomad University is organized as a four-year series of gap-year experiences. That is, rather than seeing the gap year as something that is done prior to going to college, as a preparation for college, a series of gap year–like experiences *is* the collegiate experience. Students participate in ten projects across the country and across the world.[11] Each experience lasts four to six months, and in any given year a student completes two or three such projects. Students work on teams, each team led by a faculty mentor.[12] The projects are organized something like a lab: a director (professor) leads a hierarchy of student assistants, each with a different role to play on the team. The hierarchy is based on the students' level of experience: students in their third or fourth year have greater responsibilities and obligations than first- or second-year students. The projects are active: some task needs to be accomplished, and students are expected to develop and demonstrate skill acquisition. At the end of the experience, students must demonstrate their contribution to the project's goals. The teams form and unform around each project. That is, the faculty leader may have some students join her again on the next project, and others may join who were not part of the previous team.[13]

Nomad University is similar to Minerva schools, where classrooms are located around the world.[14] But while Minerva students reside in seven different cities during their education, the cities themselves are only a semiformal part of the curriculum. To live for a time in San Francisco or Barcelona is pedagogically valuable, but Minerva students do not work on problems specific to those cities. Indeed, the Minerva curriculum is based on interactive (online) seminars: the locus of education remains within the seminar, although students live in several global cities. Nomad University is more deliberate about moving the bulk of the learning out of the classroom. It is similarly situated in place, but the place itself—both the technical issue or problem to be addressed and the participant-observation-reflection of the encounter with otherness—is central, not peripheral, to the core curriculum.

When we look at some of the programs sanctioned by the American Gap Association,[15] we get a sense of the kinds of skills students acquire in any given Nomad University course. The Humanity and Community Development Projects in Ho, Ghana, for example, sought assessment volunteers for a school water project:

> Volunteers will have the opportunity to work with HCDP staff on an in-depth assessment of the current drinking-water situation in Adaklu Abuadi Community Primary School. This process will require several weeks of interviewing in Adaklu Abuadi to determine (1) the current drinking water system in both the school and community at large (2) concerns and problems with these systems (3) community members' thoughts and ideas on possible solutions. The next steps will include analysis of interview data to determine the most appropriate water storage solution and community focus groups to finalize project and establish roles for implementation. Volunteers will also experience the natural highlights of Ho, Ghana through excursions to Wli Waterfalls, Mt. Afadjato and the Tafi Atome Monkey Sanctuary.[16]

This project was largely sociological in nature, with students engaging in assessment techniques. Note the last sentence, which describes the opportunity to experience the nature of the region. Such experiences need to be carefully crafted, as detailed below, and they are a key feature of a Nomad University education.

Project Why sought drama, dance, and art teachers. "The children [served by Project Why] have very few opportunities to express themselves and have a hard time doing so," says the call for volunteers. "We expect volunteers . . . to come with an open mind, ready to adapt to an Indian lifestyle which includes food, weather, living conditions, behavior, and clothing,"[17] again suggesting that the experience involves more than the development and demonstration of skills. Fundación Misión

Gaia needed a "Sustainability and Waste Management Coordinator": "This project aims to design and implement an effective system of integrated solid waste management, to the village of Minca—Sierra Nevada de Santa Marta, which can be extended to other towns in the region and surround[ing] touristic, rural or ecological areas." A student participating on such a team project would be learning engineering skills in place. The Parijat Academy in Guwahati, India, sought volunteers to help teach children computer and multimedia skills, and Green Cameroon in Buea sought a "green media campaign coordinator," who would use media "to teach and sensitize on environmental issues both at local and global levels. If you are a good writer, photographer or filmmaker, you have a chance to volunteer on this project. With Volunteers coming from Canada, Belgium, France and Indonesia, you will have the chance to work with skilled and creative individuals from all over the Globe."[18]

Before they embark on a project, students receive a brief orientation on the kinds of tasks they will be performing. That orientation includes an introduction to the culture in which they will be working. This requires a particular kind of faculty leader, one who is knowledgeable about the skills and tasks necessary for the success of the project, but who is also able to negotiate the culture in which the team will be living and working.

■   ■   ■

It might seem that Nomad University focuses exclusively on vocational skills. While such abilities are central to each of the project courses, students also practice skills such as writing, oral communication, and quantitative analysis, as determined by the specifics of the project. Some projects require students have a background in the arts. Skills in place—not within the abstraction that is the classroom—drives the curriculum of Nomad University.

It could be argued that some students would be so deficient in the skills needed by the team that they would not be ready for work in an actual setting, that extensive classroom instruction would be needed before sending them forth into the world. The orientation before the project provides some of those skills, but the pedagogical philosophy of Nomad University is that students learn while performing the task. Advanced students bring skills learned in earlier projects with them to subsequent experiences. I once led a team of students on a project-based exercise similar to what Nomad University students engage in. The project was to redesign the interior of a corporate office to (1) make it more attractive to millennial employees, who are assumed to prefer to work more collaboratively, and (2) convey the corporate message to visitors to the office. None of the students I worked with had any experience in interior design, but over the course of eight weeks they identified a strategy for the redesign and determined who in the group would engage in which tasks: some learned SketchUp and worked on the plans for the redesign, others interviewed workers, and others made observations of how the space was actually employed. Students uncovered through their observations, for instance, that there was only a small, cluttered space for communal events or for eating lunch. The redesign included an ample public space suitable for those purposes. Again, none of these students were designers, but they nevertheless left this experience with some of the skills of an interior designer.

Because our students were working with a local company, they had little occasion to experience the place in a new way. That is, the location of this intervention was already known to most of the students. The projects of Nomad University are located across the globe, so that students, in addition to the technical skills they acquire, learn how to negotiate and understand the culture in which their work is embedded. Thus, Nomad University is more than simply extended study abroad, although operating in another place and culture is a chief learning outcome. Like the gap-year projects described above, students learn by doing in the context of real problems in the real world.

MBA × America is an intensive internship program that pairs teams of MBA students with entrepreneurs. MBAx students worked with Red Ants Pants, for example, over three summers. RAP is "the first ever company dedicated to manufacturing workwear for women. Also run[s] the Red Ants Pants Foundation, dedicated to fostering strength and self-reliance in women in rural, agricultural communities." Student teams "dove into the business operations of RAP to recommend time-saving technology and checklists to reduce the time Sarah and her team have to spend intervening manually in the pants business, allowing them to focus more time on building the brand, preparing for and running the yearly music festival and the RAP Foundation."[19] MBAx is modeled as a kind of management consulting à la the companies McKinsey or Deloitte for the benefit of smaller, rural firms. But the spirit of the enterprise is close to what is achieved by Nomad University. However, a one-week, intensive summer experience (after which the students return to the classroom) gives little time for students to engage with the culture in which a company is embedded. Students fly in, perform a technical task, then fly back out. One week is not enough time to gain an understanding of place. One gap-year experience described above mentioned "experience[ing] the natural highlights" of the region, but they seem like tourist excursions, not a rich and meaningful encounter with cultural novelty.

While students at Nomad University are working on specific problems and gaining technical skills and proficiencies, their education is occurring in place, and the encounter with the different culture in that place is a key part of the educational outcomes. In *Peripheral Visions*, Mary Catherine Bateson contends that such encounters and the uneasiness they may cause a student should be a crucial part of education. As an anthropologist, she values the methods of the participant-observer as one kind of engagement with an unfamiliar place. Learning occurs when one must navigate and improvise within a different culture. Nomad University is not a tourist experience: students are not confined in Americanized ghettos of hotels and retail establishments.

Bateson has told of her time in Iran in the early '70s with her two-year-old daughter in tow. She was invited to witness the ritual killing of a sheep as part of a religious holiday. The anthropologist noted the differences between the Westernized Iranian elite and the butcher, differences in how both understood and approached the occurrence. The invitation was also cause for Bateson to examine her own assumptions and decide how she might help her small daughter understand the ritual killing. Bateson described this experience as uncomfortable but educational precisely because it forced her to confront her own cultural assumptions.

> Arriving in a new place, you start from an acknowledgment of strangeness, a disciplined use of discomfort and surprise. Later, as observations accumulate, the awareness of contrast dwindles and must be replaced with a growing understanding of how observations fit together within a system unique to the other culture. Having made as much use as possible of the sense that everything is totally alien, you begin to experience, through increased familiarity, the way in which everything makes sense within a new logic. Eventually an ethnographer will hope to develop a description of a whole way of life that will convey this internal consistency, in which the height and placement of a chair, the adult response to a crying baby and to voices raised in dispute, and the rules about when to relax and the rhythms of the day can be integrated, although never perfectly. The final description should deal with the other culture in its own terms. Yet it is contrast that makes learning possible.[20]

Bateson sees her purpose as an educator to be "to persuade my students of the legitimacy of learning from observation."[21] Nomad University students are participant-observers, not tourists or even simply technical experts who arrive, perform a task, and exit without having interacted with the culture within which they are residing. Their time in place is lengthy, with much effort spent engaging a different culture as a learning objective.

Such encounters can be culturally and epistemologically challenging, and thus are a critical aspect of the curriculum.[22] Indeed, part of the experience embedded in each project is learning to negotiate the unfamiliar and learning to understand new cultures on their own terms, not in reference to the assumptions of the student's own culture.[23] "A certain amount of friction is inevitable whenever peoples with different customs and assumptions meet," says Bateson. "It is familiar enough between genders or across class lines in a single society. What is miraculous is how often it is possible to work together to sustain joint performances in spite of disparate codes, evoking different belief systems to affirm that possibility. As migration and travel increase, we are going to have to become more self-conscious and articulate about differences, and to find acceptable ways of talking about the insights gained through such friction-producing situations, gathering up the harvest of learning along the way."[24] The term "friction" suggests that confronting a culture different from one's own is messy and discomfiting, but it is from such confrontations that transformative learning can occur. Encounters with novelty can occur in even the most ordinary of events. Outside of the religious, the rituals of the meal, the street scene, and the daily experiences of gender are also instructive and potentially "friction-producing."[25]

The faculty mentor plays a critical role here; she is not only the manager of the project or the instructor of technical skills but the guide to help students make sense of their new surroundings, to facilitate the students' reflections on the contrast of cultures. As students accumulate a number of such experiences across the globe and in a variety of contexts, they are encouraged to reflect on the cultures they have encountered and experienced. How do they understand their own native culture? What patterns of similarity and difference can they discern among the various cultures in which they have been immersed?

Beyond any technical knowledge gained, students learn to be cosmopolitan: to embed themselves wherever they might be in the world. No one should be under any illusion that a six-month stay in an unfamiliar culture, working on technical problems, will produce students who know the local culture "without an accent." Cosmopolitan means being immersed in a culture, even if one is not a native.

5

The Liberal Arts College

The trivium (grammar, logic, and rhetoric) and the quadrivium (arithmetic, geometry, music, and astronomy) were the seven liberal arts in the medieval university: a set of skills a free person would master in order to be able to participate in civic and ecclesiastical life. The Liberal Arts College reasserts this ancient definition of "liberal arts" as skills rather than subjects, specifically concentrating on the skills necessary to participate in the modern economy.

Surveys reveal that many employers are looking for college graduates with broadly applicable skills like oral and written communications, a capacity to think critically, and the ability to solve complex problems. Such skills are viewed as being as important as specific vocational skills. Given their importance in the world of work, the curriculum of the Liberal Arts College centers on seven broad intellective skills: (1) complex problem solving, (2) sense-making, (3) making, (4) imagination, (5) multimodal communication, (6) cross-cultural competency, and (7) leadership. There are no majors or electives; every student studies and practices each of these seven skills. A degree from the Liberal Arts College signals competence in all of them.

It would seem that employers look for those characteristics long considered central to a liberal arts education. But liberal arts colleges do not really focus on skills, instead teaching subjects and disciplines (history, psychology, English, chemistry). Or, perhaps more correctly, if students acquire these skills, they do so as a by-product of this subject-based education. Further, students major in or concentrate on only one or two subjects, not a broad range of skills.

At the Liberal Arts College, the broad-based skills of the liberal arts experience align with workforce development needs: the skills identified by employers become the subjects of a liberal arts education. Thus, rather than history or chemistry, students study sense-making and imagination, with formal courses organized around each skill. This requires a specific type of faculty, one knowledgeable in skills rather than academic disciplines.

Students participate in a four-week, intensive, classroom-based introductory course that focuses on a particular skill. Then they are assigned to local companies or organizations, where they apprentice for four to six months. We tend to think of apprenticeships as about the skilled trades; the Liberal Arts College is based on a series of apprenticeships around the seven cognitive skills. Unlike traditional internships, the focus of the apprentice's time with any one organization is on developing and demonstrating one of the seven skills. For example, a student might spend five months with a nonprofit seeking to develop a zero-waste working environment. Student apprentices hone complex problem-solving skills acquired during the introductory course; "on the job" is the principal site for skill development. The faculty mentor monitors the progress of the students during their internships, and students also report to and learn from a supervisor at the company. The bulk of the learning occurs in the field, during the apprenticeship. At the end of each apprenticeship, the student must demonstrate their fluency in the particular skill, which is certified by both the participating organization and by the faculty mentor.

During their apprenticeships, students gather at regular intervals as cohorts with their faculty mentor to discuss the skills they are mastering. A monthly gathering might involve discussing a reading, a show-and-tell of work performed, a meditation on imagination, or sharing the thought process of developing a new skill. The faculty mentor might share their experiences and wisdom.

The Liberal Arts College has a central building for the introductory classes, for the monthly cohort conferences, and for offices for faculty mentors. But the bulk of the learning is spread throughout the community, among the businesses, government agencies, and nonprofits that make up the talent ecosystem. These organizations often benefit from the human capital of those trained at universities. But it is the students, through their tuition, who pay for their own training. With the Liberal Arts College, those organizations directly invest in the talent they will one day hire into their enterprises. Indeed, students do not pay tuition, but are instead paid for their labor/training. The talent ecosystem, therefore, is not only the recipient of talent from the Liberal Arts College, but is an active participant in the training of and investment in that talent.

Once a student has received her degree, the Liberal Arts College assesses her competence and matches her with an employer. The employer might be one of the organizations she apprenticed with during her training or another organization in the community. The college works closely with local companies to develop apprenticeships that train students in specific skills that are valuable to the company, which creates a pipeline for future employees. When they arrive for their first day on the job, students are already broadly trained in skills that meet the stated needs of the organization.

■   ■   ■

The Liberal Arts College is designed to align education and workforce development needs. Current surveys reveal that while students feel themselves prepared for the workplace, employers note deficits in their training. Employers contend that colleges and universities are not providing sufficiently trained employees, and many positions go unfilled for lack of qualified applicants. In terms of workforce readiness, surveys also reveal that employers are as interested in broad intellective skills as they are in specific vocational preparation, and so the Liberal Arts College concentrates on the development of intellective skills *as* workforce training. The Liberal Arts College ensures that employers have skin in the game; they are invited to contribute directly to the training of the workforce they will one day be hiring.

A survey from the Association of American Colleges and Universities indicated that the skills associated with a traditional liberal arts degree are desirable for workplace success.

■   Nearly all those surveyed (93 percent) agreed that "a candidate's demonstrated capacity to think critically, communicate clearly, and solve complex problems is more important than their under-graduate major."

- More than nine in ten of those surveyed said it is important that those they hire demonstrate ethical judgment and integrity, intercultural skills, and the capacity for continued new learning.
- More than three in four employers said they want colleges to place more emphasis on helping students develop key learning outcomes, including critical thinking, complex problem solving, written and oral communication, and applying knowledge in real-world settings.[1]

"The majority of employers agree," the survey report continued, "that having both field-specific knowledge and skills and a broad range of skills and knowledge is most important for recent college graduates to achieve long-term career success. Few think that having field-specific knowledge and skills alone is what is most needed for individuals' career success."[2]

This and similar surveys suggest that the skills associated with a traditional liberal arts degree are wanted and necessary. However, studies such as those documented in *Academically Adrift* suggest that these skills are not being acquired by students in some majors. Students feel that practical, vocationally directed majors are the path to employment, and there is little value in the liberal arts. "Growing numbers of students are sent to college at increasingly higher costs," write Richard Arum and Josipa Roksa, the authors of *Academically Adrift*, "but for a large proportion of them the gains in critical thinking, complex reasoning and written communication are either exceedingly small or empirically non-existent." Arum and Roksa look specifically at results from the Collegiate Learning Assessment (CLA) standardized test and conclude that "while these students may have developed subject-specific skills that were not tested for by the CLA, in terms of general analytic competencies assessed, large numbers of U.S. college students can be accurately described as academically adrift."[3] The Liberal Arts College concentrates on these core cognitive skills, making the "soft skills" the center of the curriculum.

Liberal arts skills are usually acquired by taking subject matter courses. That is, the liberal arts as currently constituted in the contemporary university are divided into disciplinary subjects. Students take classes in literature, philosophy, biology, and psychology; the organization of these courses is around disciplinary knowledge. Any skills acquired, such as communications ability or creativity, are a secondary outcome of that disciplinary knowledge. The Liberal Arts College, however, is organized around skills rather than subjects. Students are expected to demonstrate proficiency in all seven skills mentioned above as a condition for matriculation. These skills are based on the stated needs of employers for broadly trained graduates.[4]

■ ■ ■

The pedagogy of the Liberal Arts College is based on a modern-day apprenticeship program, what we might term a "cognitive apprenticeship."[5] For each skill, there is a four-week introductory course taught by a faculty member who is a skills expert (as opposed to a subject matter expert). That person is responsible for the introductory classes, monitoring student progress throughout their internship, and assessing the final deliverable. In addition, faculty conduct monthly cohort gatherings, a time for student-apprentices to reflect on their experiences and the skills they are acquiring. The bulk of the coursework is fulfilled through apprenticeships with local companies and organizations; the apprenticeship with the local company around that particular skill *is* the course. Howard Gardner observes: "The core idea of an apprenticeship is that a young person goes to work for, and often to live with, an adult expert in a trade or vocation. . . . The overt purpose of the apprenticeship is to learn the skills of a vocation, but apprenticeships have long been seen as an introduction to the world of work and as a transitional niche en route to becoming an adult member of society."[6]

The apprenticeship in this case is not based on a traditional trade but on problem solving, leadership, or cross-cultural communication. Students are placed with local companies, where they serve as interns for between four and six months; their apprenticeship concentrates on developing one of the seven skills, although there likely are opportunities to engage in other tasks.[7] Indeed, one of the responsibilities of the faculty is to monitor and ensure that the skill remains the focus of the internship. Someone in the company serves as the student's supervisor and mentor, the adult expert from whom they learn. After the allotted time, the student-apprentice presents a final product, a deliverable, a portfolio, or some other demonstration that they have mastered the particular skill. This capstone is evaluated by both the company supervisor and the faculty mentor. Only after this final presentation is approved is credit given. The student is awarded a diploma when she has demonstrated mastery in all seven skills.

In summary, the curriculum of the Liberal Arts College consists of brief introductory classes, concentrated apprenticeships with local companies and organizations, monthly cohort gatherings to reflect on the skills learned, and the presentation of a final "masterpiece" for each of the following seven skills:

1. *Complex problem solving.* Many of the surveys of business leaders stress the need for employees who are adept at problem solving. "Work is no longer defined by your specialty," says Karen Bruett of Dell. "It's defined by the task or problem you and your team are trying to solve or the end goal you want to accomplish. Teams have to figure out the best way to get there—the solution is not prescribed. And so the biggest challenge for our front-line employees is having the critical thinking and problem-solving skills they need to be effective in their teams—because nobody is there telling them exactly what to do. They have to figure it out."[8]

Complex problem solving is one of the definitions of design and design thinking. Although design was once understood to be simply about making something look beautiful, design today is defined as an approach to problem solving.

That approach begins with asking the right questions. Tony Wagner observes that "asking good questions, critical thinking, and problem solving go hand in hand in the minds of most employers and business consultants."[9] Good questions help properly frame a problem, and so "frame creation" is an important first step in any problem-solving process.[10] As practiced by the d.school at Stanford, design-thinking-as-problem-solving involves moving through five steps: empathize, define, ideate, prototype, test.[11]

A professor of complex problem solving at the Liberal Arts College spends four weeks leading an intensive boot camp to train students in design-thinking methods and processes. Such an approach to problem solving is an intellectual process disconnected from any domain-specific problem-solving process. That is, the design-thinking method is applicable to any number of complex problems.

Students then apprentice with local companies to solve problems defined by those businesses. For example, a student might work with a company to design systems and processes that encourage zero waste. Using the design-thinking process—asking the right questions, framing the problem space appropriately, ideating, prototyping, and testing—the apprentice might discover that by changing the signage at trash receptacles to read "Landfill" next to those that say "Recycle" or "Compost" subtly changes behavior by discouraging people from automatically discarding waste products.[12] The student who helped design such a solution receives credit for mastering the "complex problem solving" skill.

2. *Sense-making.* The Institute for the Future identifies sense-making as one of its "future work skills." In a digital world awash in information, the "ability to determine the deeper meaning or significance of what is being expressed" is an important skill.[13] As quoted by Idris Mootee, Karl Weick defined sense-making as "structuring the unknown [by] placing stimuli into some kind of framework [that enables us] to comprehend, understand, explain, attribute, extrapolate and predict." "Sense-making," states Mootee, "takes an obscure situation that is clouded in uncertainty and complexity and makes it more understandable for decision makers."[14] Tony Wagner says that "accessing and analyzing information" is one of the seven "survival skills" students need in order to be successful in the world of work. He interviewed someone who works in retail who said that her industry needed "people who can conceptualize but also synthesize a lot of data."[15] Sense-making is the ability to answer the question "What does this mean?"

Daniel Pink observes, "When our lives are brimming with information and data, it's not enough to marshal an effective argument." Thus "story" is one of the key skills he identifies for the conceptual age. "The essence of persuasion, communication, and self-understanding has become the ability to fashion a compelling narrative."[16] Storytelling is one of the surest ways we have developed to make sense and to discern meaning. "Narrative is the linguistic form we use to communicate human experience and render it meaningful to one another and to ourselves," note David Lane and Robert Maxfield.[17] Sense-making can be demonstrated in many ways, but they are all tied together by acting on a large data set in order to discern pattern and meaning. One approach is to create a linguistic narrative or story, such as a TED-style talk that weaves together a wide amount of information and points out the essence or underlying meaning. But a story can be conveyed in a variety of ways beyond the linguistic. A map, for example, can convey a story, organizing a great amount of information into a meaningful pattern, allowing us to draw visual attention to the signal in the noise.

Apprentices might be assigned to a design or marketing research firm and given the task of developing narratives around products. They might be assigned to a bank or investment firm and given a large amount of varied data, with the task of uncovering the meaning in those data and presenting it in some sort of narrative form.

3. *Making.* Since the beginning of the twenty-first century, we have assumed that the economy is dominated by bits rather than atoms.[18] The making of things has never really gone away, however, and manufacturing is poised for a new industrial revolution. We are not "returning to the giant factories of old," says Chris Anderson, "with their armies of employees, but [rather] creating a new kind of manufacturing economy, one shaped more like the Web itself: bottom-up, broadly distributed, and highly entrepreneurial."[19] Manufacturing today is carried out by 3-D printing, computer-aided design, computer numerical control routers, and other such technologies. While the digital world of bits has occupied our attention, the rise of the maker movement and garage manufacturing signals a return to materials, to the production of things as a central economic activity. Advanced manufacturing is no longer

a predominantly blue-collar occupation. "Smart jobs," as described by Adam Davidson, "tend to scramble the line between blue-collar and white-collar. Their titles tend toward the white (technician, specialist, analyst), but the underlying industries often tend toward the blue, toward the making of physical stuff. Smart jobs can involve factories and machines, plastics and chemicals, but operating those instruments and manipulating those materials demands far more brains than brawn."[20]

Apprentices from the Liberal Arts College learn to design and make objects, and comfort with a craft and familiarity with the properties of materials are skills they develop. For example, apprentices might be assigned to a design firm or manufacturer in order to design and make objects with environmentally gentle footprints. Many communities are building maker spaces and fabrication labs, and students might apprentice in these workshops to learn woodworking, blacksmithing, casting, welding, glass working, and sculpture.[21]

Although they employ digital design and fabrication tools, students of the Liberal Arts College are skilled with their hands.

4. *Imagination*. The 9/11 Commission Report noted that, among other causes for that devastating event, the United States suffered from a "failure of imagination" in anticipating the attacks, and the authors recommended that the government "find a way of routinizing, even bureaucratizing, the exercise of imagination" as a way to anticipate future terrorist events.[22] Tony Wagner observes that "the words *curiosity* and *inquisitiveness* are almost always mentioned when I ask leaders to tell me what skills matter most today," and so he identifies "imagination" as one of the seven survival skills.[23]

"Imagination" is the term we apply to a number of related mental processes. At one level, to imagine means to visualize in the mind's eye some object that, while not physically present, is nevertheless usually perceived by the senses. For example, one can imagine an apple or one's living room or a co-worker. To imagine here means to recall and to reconstruct. But to imagine can also mean to combine and recombine in the mind's eye objects and ideas that are not available to the senses: nonexistent entities. Imagination in this sense is the ability to ask and answer the question "What if?" So, I might imagine a purple apple or my living room balanced on the Eiffel Tower or my co-worker roller-skating across a busy highway. When I imagine my living room perched atop the Eiffel Tower, I am drawing on my brain's perceptual system (what I already can visualize about my living room and the Eiffel Tower) and using my imagination to conjure the new or unfamiliar. For Kant, imagination meant an enlarged mentality or expanded thought. "This 'enlarged mentality,'" says Nannerl Keohane, "entails deliberately broadening your perspective to take into account the standpoint of others,"[24] suggesting that the exercise of imagination requires an open and expansive mind. Curiosity is the quality of finding something interesting simply because it is interesting.

When the 9/11 Commission recommended that intelligence and security agencies better develop their imagination, it gave little guidance about how to accomplish this; "imagination" is not a testable subject in most schools. "I think we're way too focused on creativity. It's misguided," says polymath John Seely Brown. "We should be focused on imagination. The real key is being able to imagine a new world. Once I imagine something new, then answering how to get from here to there involves steps of creativity. So I can be creative in solving today's problems, but if I can't imagine something new, then I'm stuck in the current situation."[25] The four-week boot camp ahead of this apprenticeship has students exercising this skill by giving them the time and freedom to imagine, to wonder, even to daydream.

Student apprentices might be asked to imagine a business and its competitive market space. They might then work to alter that world in their minds in some fashion, imagining how it might look under different conditions. Students might apprentice with a restaurant and be given the task of working on a strategic business plan that asks, "What if something like Uber-for-restaurants were to emerge? What would happen to our business?" The students then think through—imagine—what that world would look like and how the restaurant would compete.

5. *Multimodal communication.* Nearly every survey of business leaders and human resources managers identifies written and oral com-

munications as necessary and highly desired skills. The Liberal Arts College teaches students about clear and cogent communications. In order to demonstrate fluency, apprentices write and speak in real-world situations, such as "writing memos, letters, complex reports."[26] As Wagner writes, Mike Summers of Dell seeks employees with "not only the ability to communicate [their] thoughts clearly and concisely but also the ability to create *focus, energy and passion*." Summers is less interested in grammar, spelling, and other things that students are tested on today. "While it's obviously important to write and speak correctly," observes Wagner, "the complaints I heard most frequently [from business leaders] were more about fuzzy thinking and the lack of writing with a real *voice*."[27]

To write well requires the ability to read well, and so students at the Liberal Arts College learn how to read widely and how to read for meaning, for content, for style. Similarly, effective speaking requires effective listening, which is part of the four-week preparation course. Beyond what students learn in the intensive boot camp, writing, reading, speaking, listening, and presenting in a formal business setting constitute invaluable training.

Effective communication today has extended far beyond the linguistic. Communicating in a digital environment also means being fluent with images, sounds, and movement. Multimodal communication means communicating formally and persuasively through writing, speaking, reading, listening, visualizing, and drawing.[28] The *New York Times*, for example, has been a leader in elegantly designed information visualizations, and students at the Liberal Arts College learn how to communicate effectively through such visualizations. The *Times* is also experimenting with virtual reality presentations, and there is every reason to expect that communicating through virtual 3-D environments will become a requirement for effective communications for all organizations.

Students apprenticing with a company might be in charge of producing the annual report, communicating in words and images. An oral presentation to the board might be part of this experience, as would the creation of information visualizations.

6. *Cross-cultural competency.* As defined by the Institute for the Future, cross-cultural competency means the "ability to operate in different cultural settings." Future workers "need to be able to operate in whatever environment they find themselves. This demands specific content, such as linguistic skills, but also adaptability to changing circumstances and an ability to sense and respond to new contexts."[29]

I once polled an employer advisory group on this ability. In the internal unpublished report, I noted that three-quarters of the respondents (who came from a variety of industries) said, "Recognizing the importance of international business, interpersonal and intercultural etiquette" was important or very important, and it was important for employees to "understand differences, commonalities and relationships among global cultures, situations and issues." In the Association of American Colleges and Universities survey, 76 percent of respondents said that it was very important or fairly important that employees have knowledge of global cultures, histories, values, religions, and social systems. Tony Wagner observes, "The skillfulness of individuals working with networks of people across boundaries and from different cultures has become an essential prerequisite for a growing number of multinational corporations."[30] But "cultures" need not be confined to geography or language: the Institute for the Future notes that the ability to adapt to and work with groups of people of "different ages, skills, disciplines, and working and thinking styles" is also an important cross-cultural competency.[31]

Thus, students spend their four-week boot camp gaining an introduction to various geographic, linguistic, cultural, disciplinary, political, and socioeconomic domains. The students learn about the key underlying assumptions governing each group (and thereby learn about their own underlying assumptions and biases). An important goal of this skill acquisition is learning to serve as a "translator" between these domains. Such a skill is important today since we tend to congeal into isolated clusters of people who think and act as we do and who have the same income levels as ourselves. Cross-cultural competency means not just simply operating in a different domain for a while; it means adapting one's own beliefs and knowledge to that domain, allowing oneself to become a different person through such an immersive experience.

An internship experience with a local organization might involve assisting with the process of welcoming and acclimatizing immigrant communities, or a young student might work with elderly populations, or an apprentice might serve as a teacher's aide in a school for children with special needs.

7. *Leadership.* Nannerl Keohane defines leadership as "providing solutions to common problems or offering ideas about how to accomplish collective purposes, and mobilizing the energies of others to follow these courses of action. . . . Leaders determine or clarify goals for a group of individuals and bring together the energies of members of that group to accomplish those goals."[32] Leaders are those who

- make decisions
- devise and implement strategies
- compromise in order to achieve their goals
- listen to proposals or petitions from others
- adjudicate conflict
- assemble resources and deploy incentives
- seek counsel and issue statements
- take stands
- persuade, require, or force[33]

Many organizations are seeking people who exhibit these abilities. Those whom Wagner interviewed, when discussing leaders, often said that "initiative" was an especially important trait. "Leaders today," he reports, "want to see individuals take more initiative and even be entrepreneurial in terms of the ways they seek out new opportunities, ideas, and strategies for improvement." Executives at a financial firm said they want "individuals who are self-starters, who take initiative, and who are entrepreneurial. And now they've decided to make finding, growing, and retaining this kind of talent a part of the performance management system for executives." Mark Chandler from Cisco was perhaps the biggest proponent of these traits: "Leadership is the capacity to take initiative and trust yourself to be creative."[34] One definition of "initiative" is "the ability to be resourceful and to introduce a new course of action. It requires you to be resilient, tenacious and determined. You will need to be able to demonstrate that you can think for yourself and take action when necessary."[35]

Leadership and initiative may appear to be innate qualities and therefore difficult to teach. There is some truth to this, but at the same time students can learn about and emulate such traits, and this is a key outcome of the four-week seminar before they move into their apprenticeships. Students read and discuss classic texts on the subject, such as James Macgregor Burns's *Leadership*, and they engage in case studies in leadership, especially those drawn from history. Biography is often a good way to peer inside the mind of a leader, to understand the context of their leadership and how circumstances enabled and inhibited their actions. Literature also provides an introduction to the mind of a leader: an executive once said to a colleague that reading Shakespeare might be the best way to learn about leadership.

Leadership and initiative are forged in action, and an apprenticeship opportunity is not easy to craft for such experiences. That said, in any given project, students at the Liberal Arts College are judged on their leadership abilities: their ability to influence and to take initiative. Outcomes cannot be spelled out in advance, but whether and how they exercise initiative and leadership can be evaluated. In the chapter on Nomad University, I described an apprenticeship I helped lead where students were invited to propose a redesign of a local organization's office space. One student in particular seized the initiative, teaching himself SketchUp and articulating a vision for the redesign. He persuaded the others in his ten-person group to take their collective ideas and visualize them in this particular way. Not surprisingly, this student made the final pitch presentation to the client. He proved to be the leader of the group by virtue of his actions, not because of any formal mantle I or anyone else placed on him. This is an example of how a leadership apprenticeship might work. The task or project given to the student is less important than how the student shows initiative.

The evaluation from the supervisor or the faculty mentor involves documenting such leadership qualities.

■ ■ ■

By the time they graduate, students of the Liberal Arts College have developed a number of broad-based and workforce-ready skills.[36] They will be hired by one of the participating organizations because of their skill in communications, their aptitude in making, and their ability to lead across cultures. They enter the organization ready to succeed because of this broad education and because the company itself has been directly involved in training and certifying the employee.

On the surface, the Liberal Arts College resembles the Saxifrage School in Pittsburgh.[37] A key feature of that school is that Saxifrage does not own any buildings. Classes are held around the community in spaces such as churches, museums, and libraries.[38] Classes at the Liberal Arts College are similarly conducted at businesses and other organizations around a city, but rather than being simply a container for such classes, those businesses are where the students apprentice. The character of the Liberal Arts College is determined as much by the quality of the companies and other organizations at which students apprentice as it is by the quality of the faculty. The Liberal Arts College in New York is of a different quality than the Liberal Arts College in San Francisco or Portland or Barcelona.

The Liberal Arts College coordinates a "learning ecosystem" that extends throughout the community.[39] "We see evidence," writes Jamie Merisotis, "that 'the [educational] system' is really an ecosystem of people, with students at the center: Institutions of higher education, with faculty playing an especially important role; policy and professional organizations; employers; and others are major elements of that system."[40] The college is embedded in the community, part of the learning/talent development ecosystem but not at the center. The Liberal Arts College is an education in place, and the ecosystem of talent development that it coordinates is a crucial part of a city's "creative placemaking."[41]

Employment success should involve a partnership between colleges and employers, at minimum. The Liberal Arts College sees such partnerships extending far beyond what is usually performed by career services at most institutions. The current model is to have colleges train potential workers, perhaps in consultation with employers. For certain technical and vocational programs, there are some tight couplings between employers and colleges. These take the form of employers telling colleges what skills they seek and colleges designing curricula around these demands.[42] Such a system does not necessarily guarantee that graduates will have jobs with these companies, and students still pay for their own training. Further, there seems to be a breakdown in communications, especially when employers complain that graduates are ill prepared. Surveys reveal that across a number of categories, students feel themselves to be better prepared than what employers believe to be the case.[43] The Association of American Colleges and Universities survey notes that "in a number of key areas (oral communication, written communication, critical thinking, being creative), students are more than twice as likely as employers to think that students are being well-prepared."[44] The Liberal Arts Colleges tightens the connections between employers and graduates, making the process a true partnership in talent development and acquisition.

■ ■ ■

The Liberal Arts College engages in similar sorts of activities as some prehire training companies, only based on intellective rather than technical skills. Companies like Galvanize and Revature provide concentrated courses or boot camps running anywhere from four to twenty-four weeks, usually in technical fields, such as web development or data science.[45] The courses are aligned with industry specifications, and many students certified in these programs gain employment, although not in a direct manner. Revature, for example, says, "Upon your successful completion of the Bootcamp, you will be hired by Revature. As a Revature Software Development Professional, you will work on innovative, challenging, and rewarding software development projects for leading technology companies."[46] This is not the same, of course, as being hired on a permanent basis by a tech company, but it does demonstrate how the tight coupling between workforce development and education might look. The Liberal Arts College differs from this approach, first, in that the skills being taught are not technical or coding skills but broadly applicable skills. Second, there is an explicit agreement between the Liberal Arts College and the local companies that bring on students as apprentices that the firms will hire those apprentices after they have completed their studies.

Those who were surveyed by the Association of American Colleges and Universities were executives, CEOs, presidents, and others who occupy the C-suite. It is not uncommon in such surveys for the upper management of for-profit and not-for-profit organizations to say that they value the skills developed via liberal arts degrees. In many organizations, however, those making hiring decisions are not C-suite executives but hiring managers and, more and more commonly, search algorithms. One result is that while presidents say they desire employees with broad intellective skills, hiring managers seek only those who can fill the very specific technical roles required by the company. Peter Cappelli has uncovered that

> Silicon Valley is an industry that demands a very precise, rapidly changing type of employee. Thus, Silicon Valley companies ought to keep the schools that provide appropriate graduates informed about what sort of employees they want. They should be involved in co-op programs and support students pursuing the needed courses, and they should train and develop employees for skills that are emerging. These efforts pay off by ensuring that a regular stream of acceptable employees is available as the industry continues to morph and grow. To expect schools and students to guess what skills your company will need in the future is plain and simply bad business, especially in such a rapidly transforming and innovative industry. In effect, doing so amounts to outsourcing the supply of talent without bothering to let the outsource vendors know.[47]

Were employers and colleges to be in partnership, not just in communication, such gaps in talent development would disappear. The CEO of Cascade Engineering says, "There is a disconnect between what comes out of the education system and what we need as employers. . . .

[Employers] need to know what people really know and employers need to describe what they need."[48] At the Liberal Arts College, employers are effectively communicating what they want from graduates because they are directly responsible for training those graduates.

■ ■ ■

The Liberal Arts College is designed such that employers are not simply the beneficiaries of the talent development system, but they pay for it as well. If employers are to benefit from the talent, they will also invest in that talent. One of the more pernicious aspects of our current talent development system is that students pay the (sometimes very high) costs to receive training with the hope that they will be hired by companies at such a salary that they can repay the costs of their training. At the Liberal Arts College, students are paid for their apprenticeships since businesses benefit from their labor at the same time they are training that labor.[49] Further, there is the expectation that the local organizations will hire the graduates of the Liberal Arts College because they have been so instrumental in the students' talent development.

Current colleges and universities are not set up to ensure this kind of relationship with employers. Ryan Craig contends:

> I don't see colleges and universities involved in matching students with employers at the level of the competency—a proposition that requires institutions to assess students' competencies and then match, rather than simply arranging job fairs and interviews. Nor do I see institutions engaging in employer-specific training on products, systems and process[es], so new hires can hit the ground running like an experienced employee. When we get beyond skills-based training to matching students with employers, intermediaries aggregating candidates from multiple institutions and providing matching and training services for multiple employers will be much more productive for students and employers than a single institution.[50]

The Liberal Arts College expressly addresses these issues: student competencies are measured, students are matched to employer needs, employers write curriculum, and businesses are directly involved in the training of students.

Interlude

Superager University

On the surface, this institution appears like a traditional liberal arts college, with a number of departments in disciplines like psychology, physics, philosophy, and sociology. Unlike programs that allow older students to audit courses intended for young undergraduates, to be admitted to Superager University a student must be sixty years of age or older. As life expectancy continues upward, at least in the developed world, a new stage of life has emerged: the period after work has ended but before retirement. At one time, it was believed that a natural part of advanced age was cognitive decline, but new research suggests that the aging brain can not only stave off Alzheimer's and other cognitive degeneration disorders but can also be as supple and active as younger brains.[1] "Superagers" are those between the ages of sixty and eighty whose brain health, measured by memory and attention, is comparable to a young person in their twenties. "The cerebral cortex of superagers was thicker than that of typical older adults, and . . . superagers were anatomically indistinguishable from young adults; hippocampal volume was also preserved in superagers."[2] This university is designed for those over sixty to thicken up their cerebral cortices.[3]

Becoming a superager depends on rigorous cognitive and physical activity, and so students arrive at Superager University seeking not enrichment but to develop their brains and sharpen their cognitive abilities. The education provided is not intended for career preparation, but neither are these students ready to atrophy into retirement. The post-sixty period in one's life is understood as the next phase in human psychological development. Because the brain remains plastic even with advanced age, Piagetian development extends beyond childhood.[4] "Adult education" has to be redefined to account for a period of cognitive development beyond what is needed to be economically productive. The development of the superager brain is the educational end itself, the sole purpose of this university.

There are no enrichment activities here, and students do not do crossword puzzles or play brain-training games or join book circles. They are expected to engage in a range of rigorous disciplinary work. They study physics and chemistry and engage in the kind of lab work and research activities that a twenty-year-old undergraduate is expected to engage in. Superager students are expected to perform the kind of critical reading and interpretation practiced by students decades younger. They receive grades for their work and are expected to maintain minimum grade point averages as a condition for remaining. In the same way there are undergraduate research forums and publications, superagers present their own research at learned gatherings.

Teaching new facts to these students is only a basic, minimum function of the curriculum. To achieve the kind of cognitive development characteristic of superagers, "continued brain development and a richer form of learning may require that [students] 'bump up against people and ideas' that are different. In a history class, that might mean reading multiple viewpoints, and then prying open brain networks by reflecting on how what was learned has changed [their] view of the world. . . . Such stretching is exactly what scientists say best keeps a brain in tune: get out of the comfort zone to push and nourish your brain."[5] Coursework is designed expressly to challenge assumptions, asking students to critically reflect on the beliefs and perceptions they have acquired over the years. The cognitive benefits of music education and bilingual training are also evident in the superager brain, and so these courses are a regular part of the curriculum.[6]

Strenuous physical activity is also a vital part of the curriculum. Students are expected to engage in activities that provide cardiovascular exercise since "physical activity appears to be a propitious method for influencing gray matter volume in late adulthood."[7] Thus, there are intramural tennis teams, basketball leagues, and swimming competitions: those attending Superager University are expected to be student-athletes. "The discomfort of exertion means you're building muscle and discipline": this discomfort young people accept without question, but many older adults avoid. "Superagers are like Marines: They excel at pushing past the temporary unpleasantness of intense effort. Studies suggest that the result is a more youthful brain that helps maintain a sharper memory and a greater ability to pay attention."[8]

III   TECHNOLOGY

6

Interface University

Interface University is based on the idea that machines will not—indeed, cannot—fully supplant human cognition. Its foundation is the idea that humans and computers thinking together are better than humans or computers thinking alone; thinking with machines allows students to engage in a level of cognition not possible with the brain alone. Thus, at Interface University students learn how to think together with computers.

The curriculum is based on enhancing the quality of the interface between computer and individual brain. The term "interface" refers to the relationship established between two entities, in this case between human and synthetic intelligences. Students are ready to matriculate when they have demonstrated this unified condition. The educational outcome that animates Interface University is that the human and artificial intelligences attain a symbiosis, with the artificial intelligence serving as a metaphorical third hemisphere of the human brain.

Because so many cognitive functions—especially left-brain skills—can be carried out by synthetic intelligence, students arrive at Interface University to develop attributes, especially right-brain attributes, that cannot be mimicked by machines. Students develop curiosity, creativity, imagination, playfulness, meaning-making, and wonder, attributes no algorithm has yet mastered.

Learning at Interface University is a noisy affair, with humans and synthetic intelligences engaged in continual conversation. In the same way that we converse with Siri or Alexa, students at Interface University are constantly speaking with their third hemisphere: working together, thinking, solving problems, making, researching, and creating. The artificial intelligence is a conversation partner, and one goal of education is learning how to engage with synthetic intelligences. Some are tethered to robotic bodies, and so there is also a physical presence of artificial intelligence at Interface University. Part of the educational mission is teaching students how to mediate social interactions between embodied synthetic intelligence and human intelligence. In some cases, students are directly connected to an artificial intelligence, with both the interface and a physical connection linking the two intelligences together. Students so augmented experience emergent forms of cognition.

The organization of disciplines at Interface University is similar to traditional universities. That is, students major in individual disciplines, and faculty members do research in those disciplines. But at the same time, the kinds of questions addressed and the nature of the research in those disciplines are different. Competency in each discipline is demonstrated by the results generated via human-algorithm cooperation. The form and appearance of synthetic intelligence differ from department to department. Students develop new architectural forms, for example, from both the manipulation of material objects and the algorithms, which suggest new forms; the architect "mentors" the algorithms. Students in the digital humanities use text-mining algorithms to read volumes to discern patterns that would have gone unobserved were it not for the algorithms; the digital humanist interprets the patterns generated. Thus, students achieve a degree in a subject/discipline that is undergirded by these augmented thinking skills.

Student assessment relies more on projects than on tests. Indeed, the acquisition of knowledge/information is not tested at all at Interface University: because so much information is accessible via networked knowledge bases, the idea of standardized tests of knowledge makes little sense. Instead, Interface University educates students to develop questions and to construct the cognitive tools to answer those questions. Know-how is valued more than know-what. In each class and with every encounter with the disciplines, students are evaluated on the insights gained from the artificial intelligence–human interface.

Students at Interface University need to know how to code; coding is as critical a part of their education as writing is at a traditional university.

Students learn to ask new questions and solve new problems by partnering with algorithms, and those algorithms are not available off the shelf. Students have to create their own synthetic intelligence as a way to solve problems and answer questions. A student leaves Interface University with the ability to code/create her own electronic third hemisphere, with which she has learned to cooperate.

Students learn the history, philosophy, and ethics of interface as part of their education. They examine the basis of human cognition, and thinking about thinking (metacognition) is central. A consideration of the nature of cognition (human and machine compared to human+ machine) forms an important part of the curriculum. Students learn that while algorithms can sift through data and uncover patterns, humans interpret and make sense of those patterns. Any insights the algorithms uncover are understood by a human partner interpreting the meaning. Interface University redefines and reconfigures what we mean by human cognition, and students seek to understand the limitations of synthetic intelligence. Joseph Weizenbaum's *Computer Power and Human Reason* is a foundational text: students learn about human decision-making and when it is appropriate and ethical for humans alone to make decisions. As part of the university's curricular mission, the synthetic intelligences learn ethics, educated by both students and faculty in the morality of decision-making. But students at Interface University know when the synthetic intelligence is "wrong."

Philosophers have identified ours as the age of the "posthuman." William J. Mitchell has described himself as being "plugged into other objects and subjects in such a way that I become myself in and through them, even as they become themselves in and through me."[1] Donna Haraway writes that "we are all chimeras, theorized and fabricated hybrids of machine and organism; in short, we are cyborgs."[2] Interface University educates posthumans.

Education has always involved developing an interface with our cognitive prostheses and developing the interface with books specifically. Interface University is based on such an intimacy with cognitive technologies. It assures students that they cannot be replaced by computers and other machines and that we are in fact better together.

■   ■   ■

In March 2016, AlphaGo—a computer algorithm developed by Google —defeated Lee Sedol, one of the world's top go players, four games to one. The result was a worldwide sensation: five years after IBM's Watson easily beat the best *Jeopardy!* champions and twenty years after Garry Kasparov was defeated by IBM's parallel-processing computer Deep Blue, artificial intelligence had once again seemingly surpassed human intelligence.

At the time of Kasparov's defeat, many observers, including me, wrote that it would take decades for a computer to defeat a human at go, if it were possible at all. While chess is complex, at its heart it is a game of logic and calculation. Given a particular board configuration, a player needs only to calculate the possible combinations of moves and decide the best path among those possible choices. Computers are particularly good at brute force calculation of this type, and thus it might have seemed inevitable that as computational power grew exponentially, eventually a device would be created that could calculate more combinations faster than a human could.

Go, however, is not a game that easily succumbs to brute force calculation, and that is why so many observers thought it unlikely that a computer could ever defeat a human. Go is a deceptively simple game: on a nineteen-by-nineteen gridded board, players alternately place black and white stones on the intersections. When chains of like stones encircle territory, the surrounded stones may be captured and removed from the board, and the player who encircles more territory is the winner. From these relatively simple rules, however, emerges a game of great beauty and complexity. Players do not calculate moves as much as intuit patterns in the stones. To calculate all possible moves, it has been said, would mean calculating as many variations as there are stars in the universe. Thus, human intuition and pattern recognition would always defeat computer calculation—or so went the conventional wisdom, until AlphaGo's victory.

What was most troubling, however, was not how emphatic the victory was—four out of five games. In one game, AlphaGo made a particularly intriguing move. Observers were stunned: they had never seen a move like that before; one person called it "beautiful." It was bad enough that an algorithm had defeated one of the best human players, but the artificial intelligence was also capable of creativity, of inventing something no human had ever devised.

AlphaGo was programmed using machine-learning techniques. Unlike Deep Blue, AlphaGo was programmed to learn go via experience. It played thousands and thousands of games and learned from the experience of playing. It has been said that to master any domain, one must practice for 10,000 hours. It seems that with machine-learning algorithms, computers are developing the ability to become masters.

What some find unsettling about AlphaGo's victory is that it portends other instances of an intellectual skill once considered unique to humans being superseded by computer intelligence. There are very serious people today imagining and considering the implications of a "world without work," with algorithms performing cognitive tasks once thought to be the sole domain of humans. Derek Thompson observes:

> In the past few years, even as the United States has pulled itself partway out of the jobs hole created by the Great Recession, some economists and technologists have warned that the economy is near a tipping point. When they peer deeply into labor-market data, they see troubling signs, masked for now by a cyclical recovery. And when they look up from their spreadsheets, they see automation high and low—robots in the operating room and behind the fast-food counter. They imagine self-driving cars snaking through the streets and Amazon drones dotting the sky, replacing millions of drivers, warehouse stockers, and retail workers. They observe that the capabilities of machines—already formidable—continue to expand exponentially, while our own remain the same. And they wonder: *Is any job truly safe?*[3]

Jerry Kaplan describes algorithms like AlphaGo as "synthetic intellect[s]." Artificial intelligence in the form of "machine learning, neural networks, big data, cognitive systems, or genetic algorithms" will soon supplant human intelligence.[4] In the same way that machines replaced human physical labor during the Industrial Revolution, synthetic intelligence will replace human cognitive labor during what Erik Brynjolfsson and Andrew McAfee have termed the "second machine age."[5] "The coming wave of synthetic intellects is going to devastate many . . . professions," asserts Kaplan. "Automation is blind to the color of your collar."[6]

In some ways, this scenario is already happening. LegalZoom and TurboTax have made redundant some lower-level positions in the law and accounting professions. "Luminance, a startup specializing in legal research, can run through thousands of cases in a very short time, providing inferences about their relevance to a current proceeding. . . . Similar applications are emerging for other types of data sifting, including financial audits, interpreting regulations, [and] finding patterns in epidemiological data."[7] An application called Quill from the company Narrative Science turns spreadsheets of data into prose compositions. The annual report for a company might be generated by an algorithm; the box score from a ball game might be converted into a story that appears to have been produced by a sportswriter.[8] It is entirely possible that the Facebook article you clicked on was produced by a synthetic intellect, not a human being.[9]

■ ■ ■

It is common in contemporary society to say that the purpose of higher education is to prepare young people for work. Sean Gallagher states, "Today it is well accepted that one of the primary purposes of higher education is to prepare students for and connect them to jobs."[10] We take it as given that the purpose of higher education is to provide productive workers to fill positions in a complex global economy. Indeed, higher education in the United States since the Morrill Act, or at least since the GI Bill, has been defined as human capital development. But if predictions of a world without work come to pass, then the linkage of higher education and job preparation would be torn apart.[11] What will be the "primary purpose" of higher education when synthetic intelligence has made so much human employment redundant?[12] In a scenario that includes widespread synthetic intelligence and a waning number of jobs that require human cognitive skills, human capital development would no longer be an imperative, and thus higher education would become unnecessary for the bulk of the population. A small number of institutions of higher learning might remain as places where students go to engage their minds, but many institutions will be shuttered if a central core of their mission has been eliminated. Higher education would return to its pre-Morrill condition as a leisure activity for the few. Those who do seek higher learning would do so without a specific end goal, including employment. In this scenario, formal higher education exists only for those interested and curious enough to attain it. Others interested in higher learning might seek out informal, non-degree-bearing, free sources, such as TED talks, other online resources, or visits to public libraries.

But the computers-become-more-intelligent-than-humans scenario is only one possible future. Indeed, this will only come to pass if predictions about increasing computing speed are borne out. Many predictions for supersmart computers are based on extrapolating Moore's law into the future. Moore's law states that the processing power and speed of chips doubles every eighteen to twenty-four months, and indeed computer processing speeds have been following that logarithmic trajectory since the 1960s. If computing power continues to expand exponentially, computers cannot help but become superintelligent.

If, however, as some physicists and computer scientists have noted, such continued expansion is not physically possible, then computers, algorithms, and other digital devices might run up against limits on their processing speed and thus their intelligence. Others contend that we still know so little about how our brains work and the basis of our own cognition and consciousness that we cannot yet hope to replicate the human brain in synthetically intelligent electronic brains. Algorithms will reach a peak intelligence beyond which they will not be able to go. The implication is that synthetic intelligence will not reach a stage where it will supplant human intelligence in all areas. Artificial intelligence will be able to perform many cognitive tasks, even some that may replace human labor (especially cognitive tasks that are easily repeatable), but many intellective tasks will remain exclusively "human." Our capacity for wonder, for example, or play or empathy will define human intelligence in the second machine age.

In such a scenario, the purpose of higher education is for students to develop attributes, not skills. At one time, higher education was about the acquisition of information. As information exploded and became easy to access, higher education became focused on skill development. Should synthetic intelligence advance such that many human skills are rendered unnecessary, higher education might shift its focus to the cultivation of those attributes that cannot be mimicked by machines. Students would no longer arrive on campus to study accounting, engineering, or information technology, these professions having been overrun by algorithms. Students would arrive to develop curiosity, creativity, imagination, playfulness, and wonder—attributes no algorithm has yet mastered. Daniel Pink has observed that right-brain attributes—such as playfulness and meaning-making—would triumph in the age of smart machines, since left-brain skills are easier to automate.[13] "Other animals apply intelligence to solving problems," writes the president of Northeastern University, Joseph Aoun.

> But only human beings are able to create imaginary stories, invent works of art, and even construct carefully reasoned theories explaining perceived reality.... Creativity combined with mental flexibility has made us unique—and the most successful species on the planet. They will continue to be how we distinguish ourselves as individual actors in the economy. Whatever the field or profession, the most important work that human beings perform will be its creative work. That is why our education should teach us how to do it well.[14]

When the age of the smart machine arrives, higher education will shift its curricular mission to focus on the cultivation of right-brain attributes.

■   ■   ■

Another very plausible scenario is that humans and machines will work together—not compete against each other—to engage in a level of cognition that each entity alone could not achieve. In 2005, amateur chess players Steven Cramton and Zackary Stephen won the PAL/CSS Freestyle Chess Tournament, defeating both human and computer chess players.[15] The tournament was based on "hybrid chess," developed by Kasparov shortly after he lost to Deep Blue, where human players are permitted to team with computers. Kasparov described these teams as "centaurs": hybrids of humans and machines.[16] Cramton and Stephen were both rated as average players, and the computer program they were using was an off-the-shelf model. Yet this team of humans and computers beat some of the best humans and computers in the world. Less than a decade after Kasparov's defeat by Deep Blue, humans and computers were working together to attain extraordinary results.

At Interface University, higher education exists to develop "centaurs." Synthetic intelligence carries out many cognitive tasks with greater efficiency than humans can. But human intelligence is necessary to complete many cognitive tasks. In other words, humans and algorithms working together prove more effective than either algorithms or humans alone. Alex Davies asks, "As increasingly intelligent machines come to life, how should they interact with humanity?"[17] Interface University seeks answers to that question, and the purpose of higher education becomes cultivating the interface between human and synthetic intelligence.

The computer scientist Edward Ashford Lee maintains that we are today witnessing "the emergence of symbiotic coevolution" between humans and artificial intelligence, "where the complementarity between humans and machines dominates over competition." When we consider symbiotic species in nature, we do not assume that one dominates the other or that one will kill off the other. "Instead," says Lee, "stronger connections and interdependencies between man and machine could create a more robust ecosystem" as is often found among species in nature. Lee believes a similar sort of cognitive cooperation is forming between humans and machines. "To understand that complementarity" between human and artificial intelligence, "we have to understand the fundamental strengths and limitations of both partners. Software is restricted to a formal, discrete, and algorithmic world. Humans connect to that world through the notion of semantics, where we assign meaning to bits."[18] If artificial intelligence deals in syntax, then humans deal in semantics. Education for enhancing the complementarity between humans and machines is the pedagogical philosophy of Interface University.

■   ■   ■

Keri Facer asks, "Will our forms of assessment continue to be designed for the autonomous individual working alone," as we currently practice at the university? Or will we instead design the university "for the [student] plus specific enhancements, tools and access to social and information networks?" She assumes the future of education will look more like the latter. "Instead of maintaining the myth that education is a set of relationships between autonomous individuals," she writes, "we need instead to recognize [students] as being connected to a unique constellation of networks of people, tools, information and processes. We need to see [students] not as clearly defined and bounded by biology, but as intimately embedded in and interconnected with their tools, their environment and their social networks."[19] Facer is not referring specifically to synthetic intelligence or embodied artificial intelligence, like robots, but her observations clearly apply to such a world. When machines are as intelligent as humans, educating the two simultaneously rather than in isolation should be the purpose of higher education.

The designer Sveta McShane describes one way algorithms and designers interface to work together. "No longer required to be the operator of the tool in generative design, the human being is freed to become the curator; choosing the best possible solution and working alongside the computer to co-create the most ideal design. Given various possibilities, we can now choose which design suits our needs the best in terms of structure, weight, shape, etc. . . . Humans don't get replaced when the machine begins to design creatively, instead we step into the newly evolved phase of the *mentor*."[20] The purpose of higher education is to educate humans and machines together, with human intellects learning how to mentor their synthetic counterparts. Howard

Gardner imagines a future where "those hooked on creative activity will also use computers as intellectual prosthetics. . . . most innovations today—from the architectural designs of Frank Gehry to the decoding of genomes by the company Celera—would not be possible without powerful computers."[21] At Interface University, the disciplines are the same as at a traditional university, but students ask different kinds of questions and answer those questions via the interface between human and synthetic intelligence. Competency in each discipline is assessed by the results generated by human and algorithm cooperation. Higher education means the augmentation of human intelligence with synthetic intelligence.

■   ■   ■

This education is not simply a one-way street. As algorithms perform more and more cognitive tasks autonomously and without our direct instruction, they will encounter situations that they have not seen before or were not programmed for. How will they make a decision? How will they act? What moral or ethical principles will influence those decisions? GoodAI is a company that includes what it terms the "School for AI." The company's website says:

> Besides having hard-coded skills, we expect the AI to be able to learn. We will teach the AI new skills in a gradual and guided way in the School for AI which we are now developing. In [the] School for AI, we first design an optimized set of learning tasks, or a "curriculum." The curriculum teaches the AI useful skills and abilities, so it doesn't have to discover them on its own. Next, we subject the AI to training. We use the performance of the AI on the learning tasks of the curriculum to improve both the curriculum and hard-coded AI skills.[22]

Machine learning is a way to program algorithms to learn on their own via repeated experience with a specific task, like learning to play chess or go. The School for AI takes a more deliberate approach to educating synthetic intelligence. Interface University also has a curriculum for synthetic intelligence; the faculty conduct the bulk of such teaching, but students also play a significant role. In learning to interface with machines, students are simultaneously educating algorithms. That education especially includes moral and ethical learning. Thus, at Interface University the synthetic intelligences are just as augmented as the human students are.

In this scenario, human and synthetic intelligences engage in cognition together, each bringing differing cognitive abilities. Algorithms are terrific at analyzing enormous amounts of data; humans are particularly good at interpreting the meaning of such patterns. That interpretive ability is one that I believe computers will not be able to duplicate any time soon. Interface University is an institution of higher education where students develop hybrid minds and achieve a state of cognitive interface with synthetic intelligence.

This is much more than simply giving students iPads. A student is ready to matriculate when she can demonstrate a state of interface with synthetic intelligence. Branden Hookway defines an "interface" as "a form of relation that obtains between two or more distinct entities, conditions, or states such that it only comes into being as these distinct entities enter into an active relation with one another . . . and such that its overall activity brings about the production of a unified condition or system that is mutually defined through the regulated and specified interrelations of these distinct entities."[23] We sometimes think of an interface as a physical object, like a mouse or a graphical user interface. But for Hookway, the idea of an interface extends beyond any material device: it is a relationship established between two entities. "The interface is the zone of relation that comes into being between human beings and machines, devices, processes, networks, and even organizations."[24] In such a relationship, the intelligence of both entities is augmented.

> Intelligence here refers to a quality determined and adjudicated within a given interface. It describes the capabilities and range of activity of elements brought into relation by the interface, or marked by the interface as territory for further development. Intelligence may be human, technological, social or material. It is not a fixed property but rather a condition or behavior that is relative to the operation of a particular interface. The

situational presence (or production) of intelligence is exactly what defines the capability of human beings or machines to come into contact through the interface. . . . The state of augmentation brought into being by the interface is essentially a hybrid condition, one equally capable of incorporating electronic sensors and human sensorium, computer processing and human cognition.[25]

Hookway's description of interface is largely metaphorical; when he says "to come into contact," I do not think he is referring to a direct physical connection between humans and machines. However, there are a growing number of cases where engineers and technologists are experimenting with such direct connections between artificial intelligence and the brain,[26] and it is possible that part of the education at Interface University will involve students being physically connected to technology. Learning to negotiate this intimate link would therefore be a key learning outcome of the university. In most cases, however, the interactions will not be directly physical. Students might interface with synthetic intelligence through verbal means, for instance, the way we do with Siri and Alexa today, and in this case interface would mean learning how to engage in a cognitively productive conversation with machine intelligence. It is also possible that synthetic intelligence would have a physical presence at Interface University, in the form of robots. That interface would involve learning to negotiate social interactions with machines. Similarly to how the creativity and dynamism of cities derives from the serendipitous collisions of different people and ideas, humans and robots learn to "collide" at Interface University. If the idea of sentient robots seems too much like science fiction, consider how automated and robotized a city like Seoul already is today.[27] There is every reason to believe that Interface University will be founded in South Korea before it is established in the United States.

■ ■ ■

Under the state of interface, a new entity is formed when the relationship described by Hookway is established. Interface University is about establishing this relationship, developing an emergent intelligence that is the product of human and synthetic intelligence in relation to each other. Students are ready to matriculate when they have demonstrated this unified condition or system, this state of interface. The pedagogical and epistemological philosophy of Interface University is that the highest goal of education is achieving the kind of symbiosis between human and computer intelligences as exists between a horse and rider.[28]

At Interface University, the computer is not treated as a tool but as a third hemisphere of the brain, and higher learning means developing a metaphorical corpus callosum with this synthetic hemisphere.[29] The computer is a partner in creativity, in thinking, and in cognition, and as such it is not treated as a junior partner. Upon matriculation, students will have identified several computers/algorithms/synthetic intelligences with which they have interfaced throughout their four years. Those synthetic intelligences would be inseparable from the student in any official transcripts, portfolios, or certifications.

Human and synthetic intelligences working together is a plausible future scenario because it aligns with historical precedent. Humans have always had "hybrid minds."[30] For as long as we have been a species, humans have worked together with our technologies to engage in cognitive acts. The cognitive scientists Andy Clark and David Chalmers argue that what we think of as cognition often involves a human brain working with a technology to attain something that neither entity alone could achieve. That is, humans develop tools that extend our cognitive abilities such that the act of cognition itself = activities in the brain + tools.

Hieroglyphics and cuneiform, the earliest writing systems, were technologies with which humans interfaced. Writing began as a form of counting or record keeping: as cities emerged and their populations increased into the thousands, keeping track of people and the products of civilization taxed what the human memory alone could retain. Humans developed writing as a way to store symbols in a permanent form outside the body, which could be consulted later, so that information need not be retained in biological memory alone.

The philosopher Walter Ong once argued that the "literate mind" was of a fundamentally different quality than the "oral (spoken language alone) mind."

> A deeper understanding of pristine or primary orality enables us better to understand the new world of writing, what it truly is, and what functionally literate human beings really are: beings whose thought processes do not grow out of simply natural powers but out of these powers as structured, directly or indirectly, by the technology of writing. Without writing, the literate mind would not and could not think like it does, not only when engaged in writing but normally even when it is composing its thoughts in oral form. More than any other single invention, writing has transformed human consciousness.[31]

Even before writing, humans were making marks on cave walls depicting bison and other animals, either to commemorate a successful hunt or to act as a divination of a future successful hunt. That is, the cognitive technology of visual representation allowed humans to engage in a kind of thinking not possible before the brain was collaborating with the tool.

The ability to read and write has long been a central educational outcome, demonstrating that the interface between cognitive technology and the human brain has been an important feature of higher education. The philosopher of education Kieran Egan states:

> If we see this external symbolic storehouse as something whose internalization in individual brains constructs their minds, and if we accept [Lev] Vygotsky's idea that the tools, or "operating systems" and "programs" for our brains initially exist external to our bodies in our culture, then we may begin to conceive of education's tasks somewhat differently. Education becomes the process in which we maximize the tool kit we individually take from the external storehouse of culture. Cultural tools thus become cognitive tools for each of us.[32]

The university, in this formulation, has always been about interface. Now, we have developed a new technology (synthetic intelligence) with which to interface, and this different kind of interface will produce different results.

■ ■ ■

What might an interface with synthetic intelligence look like? How might this function in practice? For example, I have been working with a team of researchers to understand the history of public housing in the United States. The dominant narrative of this history—largely composed by policy-makers, scholars, and other observers—is that public housing has been an abject failure. Newer approaches have challenged this conclusion by listening specifically to the experiences of those who actually lived in public housing—as opposed to those who have commented on public housing. This reveals a different narrative. In our work, we examined a dozen historically black newspapers with the intention of discerning how public housing was written about and understood by those most closely associated with it. Many of these newspapers have been published since the 1930s, and so reading every article, noting every instance where the term was mentioned, and then determining how public housing was represented by the author would be a monumental task for one historian, even with an army of researchers.

Using data analytics, we were able to machine read tens of thousands of articles and locate the references to public housing. We then used a technique called sentiment analysis, which looks at the terms surrounding a given word or phrase to determine the quality of the description of that word or phrase. (The word "day," for example, might have the word "beautiful" or "lousy" next to it, each conveying a very different sentiment.) In this case, we wanted to know whether the authors of the newspaper articles were writing about public housing in positive or negative terms. We developed a bank of both positive associations (opportunity, community) and negative associations (crime, drugs, poverty) that we searched for around each term.

The results were startling to us: we found that rather than being written about as a failed social experiment, public housing in historically black newspapers was frequently discussed in very positive terms.

We uncovered patterns of positive sentiment at key points in American history. To be clear: the algorithm we wrote was the intelligence that was doing the bulk of the "reading," which would have been logistically difficult for us. Thus, one could conclude that the machine was doing all the work. However, the human researchers played a key role in this process as well. In addition to writing the code (a nontrivial part of this exercise), we selected the problem to be addressed, we asked the question, and, importantly, we interpreted the results. The algorithm revealed patterns, but we made sense of those patterns. While the synthetic intelligence was helping us to read, we were engaged in humanistic inquiry.

So, one might ask, will algorithms replace the humanist in the way they appear to be replacing so many other cognitive workers? If we allow machines to read texts, what role is there for the human reader? While algorithms can engage in many cognitive tasks, they cannot (yet) interpret: they cannot fathom the meaning of either texts or the patterns in those texts. They need us to interpret. AlphaGo made a beautiful, creative move, but it was the human intellects observing the game that appreciated and interpreted it as such. When I use algorithms to read a large amount of texts, I am reading *with* the machines. We are better together: the algorithm can discern patterns in very large amounts of text that would be cumbersome for me to read through on my own. And my interpretive abilities allow me to make sense of those patterns. The algorithms may be reading the texts for me, but I am interpreting the meaning of the resulting patterns. Human and algorithm working together engage in a kind of thinking that neither could accomplish alone. This scenario—rather than one that sees algorithms making humans redundant—is the more likely future.[33]

■ ■ ■

An important part of the education at Interface University is discerning those moments when human intelligence should supersede synthetic intelligence. Machines can engage in certain forms of cognition, and working with human intelligence they can carry out extraordinary feats, but the computer scientist Joseph Weizenbaum writes in *Computer*

Power and Human Reason that "there are some human functions for which computers *ought* not to be substituted. It has nothing to do with what computers can or cannot be made to do. Respect, understanding, and love are not technical problems."[34] Weizenbaum wrote those words more than forty years ago, and they retain great wisdom and insight. But today we might ask whether it is possible for synthetic intelligence to be programmed with or to learn compassion, wisdom, ethics, and judgment? Can these be taught to machines? Will machines learn to defer in all such cases to human intelligence? If only humans possess judgment, that ability should always prevail over computation, especially when making decisions about humans, an important lesson that algorithms are taught at Interface University. I see interpretation and meaning-seeking among the comparable qualities that are retained by humans at Interface University.

Sidonie Smith has imagined what an augmented humanities scholar might look like:

> The locus of thinking, for the prosthetically extendable scholar joined along the currents of networked relationality, is an ensemble affair. It involves the scholar, the device, the algorithm, the code. It involves the design architecture of platform and tool, the experiential architecture of networks, and the economy of energy. . . . Ultimately, thinking is a collaborative affair of multiple actors, human and nonhuman, virtual and material, elegantly orderly and unruly. Jane Bennett, in her project to "g[i]ve the force of things more due," would call this "distributive, composite notion of agency" an "agency of assemblages." This concept of agency is posthuman in the sense that it dislodges the human subject as the entire site of rationality, autonomy, intentionality, and effectivity and joins the human subject to the "material agency of non- or not-quite things."[35]

One does not need to imagine a singularity scenario for such a posthuman state to occur and thus for there to be a rationale for Interface University. The singularity is the time predicted by Ray Kurzweil and others when computing speed and the resulting cognitive ability of synthetic intelligence transcend our own intelligence. As part of the path toward the singularity, humans and machines unite in such a way as to be indistinguishable from each other. If "posthuman" means a state where humans and autonomous technologies merge with each other, then the goal of Interface University is the education of these posthumans.

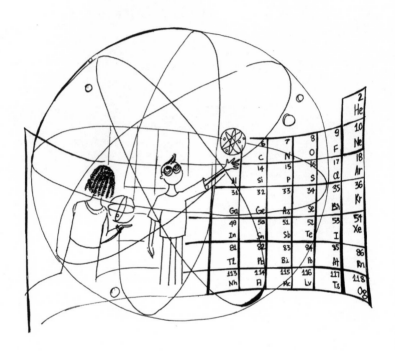

7

The University of the Body

As our information-saturated society continues to logarithmically generate more and more data, we have found new ways to apprehend that data, to intuit meaning, and to render such an avalanche of information useful. Robert Sapolsky imagines a world where data are organized beyond three dimensions, forecasting that "we're not going to get much out of these vast data sets until we have people who can intuit in six dimensions."[1] The University of the Body is an institution that trains people to gather and make sense of data in those six dimensions, including all of the senses. Students learn to "read" with the entire body.

In this world, our main interface with information networks is through a space similar to the ambientROOM developed at MIT: the interface with the computer was taken off the screen and embedded in the surrounding environment. One can "read" or otherwise gather information from all of the senses: information is converted into sound, smell, touch. In the ambientROOM, some information is also converted into scent: a pleasant smell means the stock market is rising, a pungent smell means it is falling. In this information environment, symbols exist in olfactory form, and inhabitants of the ambientROOM develop their sense of smell not simply as an aesthetic action but as a way to gain information about the world. The University of the Body trains students for a world where something like the ambientROOM extends across our symbolic landscape.

Since humans first began drawing on cave walls, we have devised ways of storing ideas and information in symbolic forms external to the body. The history of education might be understood as instructing pupils how to access and manipulate the objects of this external symbolic storage system. In the world in which the University of the Body exists, the objects of the external symbolic storage system are visual, oral, tactile, kinesthetic, and olfactory. Students learn to receive and interpret information and express ideas through all of the body's senses. Once smartphones came with swiping and pinching interfaces, we all had to learn new forms of gesture and movement and create new forms of muscle memory. In the University of the Body, gesture and movement are formally taught as cognitive interfaces with information.

Forty years ago, the idea that meaningful, rigorous information could be expressed and apprehended via visualization seemed absurd. Edward Tufte's *Visual Display of Quantitative Information* (1983) ushered in a new era of scientific or information visualization. Students had to learn to become comfortable with visual information and the spatialization of symbols. In the University of the Body, those symbols appear in forms utilizing all of the senses. Students are surrounded by the world's music, sounds, movements, scientific visualizations, smells, art, and graphic design. The University of the Body resembles a science museum that is especially good at designing sensory-rich environments.

Virtual reality spaces are important sites for learning. Such spaces are not only visual, spatial, and aural but tactile as well. For instance, students enter a spatial/haptic environment where they explore van der Waals forces by physically handling molecules and trying to connect them together. The student feels the attraction as these molecules link, or she struggles to push two repellent molecules together, thus learning by touch. In these virtual spaces, students learn to manipulate the symbolic world around them, to manipulate data and concepts as if they were physical objects ("manipulate" comes from "manu," with the hands), and that world touches all their senses. "It is as important," says the bioengineer Heinz Wolff, "for young people to become [able to] manipulate as it is to be articulate."[2] Dance and kinesiology are required courses at the University of the Body, and mastery of formal movement is as important as written communication skills or quantitative skills. Rather than being a sideshow, athletics are a regular part of the curriculum. Indeed, all education is physical education: awareness and control of the body is higher learning.

Because students learn to manipulate and construct varieties of sensory objects, the library at the University of the Body looms especially important as a repository. The textbooks and other learning materials are curated through the library. The library maintains the virtual spaces and other sensory environments for interacting with information and symbols.

While traditional disciplines define the academic infrastructure of the University of the Body, students are expected to develop a number of literacies across the senses. Indeed, new types of literacies emerge here: "olfactoricity" and "manipulaticy" join alphanumeric and aural literacies as the core of the curriculum. The expectation is that students learn to "compose" in these various forms, to produce as well as consume multi-sensory information. Faculty are expected to work in an interdisciplinary fashion, not only across traditional disciplinary boundaries but also across the entire sensorium. The curriculum is along the lines of a liberal arts college, except the mastery of a variety of senses is the learning outcome.

The University of the Body is based on the idea of the educated control of the body and that cognition comes via all of the body's senses. Students learn to interact with information/symbols in disciplines that we have not thought of as having sensory form (like chemistry through touch or statistics through sound). Students in an architecture class are asked to "draw music," while other students might make things out of clay to describe words. Synesthetics are considered gifted as are those adept at translation between the senses. In the world represented by this scenario, those who work with sound, movement, touch, and making are more highly valued. They occupy a higher place in the hierarchy of the university compared to the situation in the contemporary university.

We have increasingly come to understand that cognition is not limited to the brain and that cognition is embodied. Guy Claxton imagines a pedagogy based on "the education of touch and smell, of visceral awareness and subtle grip."[3] The University of the Body is an institutional expression of this realization: the body, not just the brain, is the center of higher learning.

■   ■   ■

Alexander Meiklejohn's Experimental College at Wisconsin in the late 1920s and early 1930s was a liberal arts institution where students learned by working with books. "The intention of the college," he said, "is that . . . minds shall be fed, and trained, and strengthened, and directed by the use of books."[4] St. John's University and other "great books" colleges are built on the idea that the content of knowledge is contained in the book, and learning how to interact with books is how one is educated.

The University of the Body is a future-looking institution where knowledge has been moved off the page and even off the screen. Thomas Rickert observes that ours is an era that is witnessing "a profound externalization of media."[5] "Externalization" here means that information is moving off the screen and the page and into the surrounding environment, enveloping the individual body. In this scenario, higher learning means developing the literacy skills to apprehend these externalized media. At the University of the Body, minds are trained by the use of ambient media.

The engineer Bret Victor thinks of himself as a craftsman, and the work of a craftsman occurs in a space.[6] Craftsmen are typically surrounded by tools and, in being so surrounded, use their bodies as a way to "think spatially." He draws special attention to the proliferation of maker spaces, which are rooms that contain an array of tools—from lathes to 3-D printers to extrusion machines—with which makers can create. "The room becomes the macrotool [craftspeople] are embedded inside." Victor wants to design a new kind of space that "enables and empowers makers." He imagines such a space filled not simply with tools that allow one to make but with tools that allow one to "see," which he terms a "seeing space."[7] Such spaces exist in some forms already, such as the control centers for NASA, Fermilab, and the California power grid. These spaces allow one to understand everything that is occurring in a complex system. Rather than accessing information via a computer sitting on a desk, a variety of types of information surround the user: information comes off the small screen and is embedded in the larger environment in the form of wall-size displays.

A seeing space would be a similar kind of environment. If one were working on a problem—Victor suggests the design of a robot—then in addition to tools that help in the fabrication of that device, other tools would allow one to climb inside the system, as it were, and gather a wide variety of information. Having the robot move would generate large amounts of data, which would be displayed on large screens. Motion capture devices would be able to track the movement of the object, and that information would be used to make changes, adjustments, or redesigns in real time. A seeing space allows one to understand what a project is "actually doing," "like a giant microscope you are embedded inside." Sensors would collect information about the system, turn it into data, and then "transmit that data into the room."[8]

Victor's seeing space projects information onto large physical screens, but that information can also be displayed in virtual spaces. Virtual reality systems, of course, replicate physical surroundings, but they can also become sites for abstract information displays. Stated another way, virtual reality can be a kind of seeing space, and there is every reason to think that externalized media can be virtual as well as physical. Kevin Kelly reports, "Microsoft's vision for light field [augmented reality] is to build the office of the future. Instead of workers sitting in a cubicle in front of a wall of monitor screens, they sit in an open office wearing HoloLenses and see a huge wall of virtual screens around them."[9] In Microsoft's vision of the future, the worker is not simply using her eyes to see information. "A future office worker is not going to be pecking at a keyboard—not even a fancy glowing holographic keyboard—but will be talking to a device with a newly evolved set of hand gestures."[10] This suggests that more of the body—beyond the eyes and the fingers—will be involved in receiving and manipulating externalized media. Thus, virtual environments are an important feature of the University of the Body: students learn to manipulate the symbolic world around them, and that world touches all their senses.

The visions of Victor and Microsoft reflect an alternative future to the current narrative. In the age of smart devices of ever-greater computing power, we have come to expect information displays to become smaller and smaller, perhaps even one day to be embossed on our eyes. This alternative future suggests that information displays will grow outward, larger and larger, expanding beyond the device and into the environment that envelops our bodies.

■   ■   ■

Victor's seeing space is, as its name implies, a very visual space. As information becomes externalized and ambient, it takes other forms and arrives to our awareness through a variety of senses. Imagine these spaces with information that includes the sonification of data, where one hears changes in pitch and timbre as meaningful data about the state of the system. Other information might come in the form of smell: a pleasing aroma might indicate new information.[11] Touch, the sensations of the skin, might serve as a receptacle of ambient information. "Researchers in the emerging field of 'sensory enhancement' have begun developing tools to give people additional senses—ones that imitate those of other animals, or that add capabilities nature never imagined."[12] For example, "the Sensory Substitution Vest takes audio from tiny microphones in the vest and translates those sound waves into a grid of vibrations that can be felt by a deaf person wearing it," reports Kevin Kelly. "Over a matter of months, the deaf person's brain reconfigures itself to 'hear' the vest vibrations as sound, so by wearing this interacting cloth, the deaf can hear."[13] We might imagine a hearing person also wearing such a vest, which translates data into vibrations that can be similarly felt, adding another channel for information.

The sensory substitution vest can also be programmed to take in other forms of input besides sound. Its creator, David Eagleman, says, "It could be used to monitor the stock market, or sentiment on Twitter, or the pitch and yaw of a drone, or one's own vital signs. You could of course display these things on a computer screen, but our brains can't attend to lots of visual details at once. . . . The body, on the other hand, is used to monitoring dozens of muscles just to keep us balanced, so would be more adept at handling multidimensional inputs."[14] Eagleman and others are also experimenting with devices that provide, in effect, extrasensory perception. One engineer "wirelessly connected an electrode in his arm to one in his wife's arm, so that wherever they were, they could feel when the other flexed a hand. Eagleman wants to take that idea one step further and wirelessly connect heart and sweat monitors on his wife and himself so they can sense each other's moods." Other researchers are experimenting with techniques where "an EEG senses brain activity in the sender and another device applies magnetic pulses to the brain of the receiver. Eventually, we might have brain implants connected wirelessly. This kind of communication might get over some of the limitations of language," says one of the researchers developing this technology. "It could help people share sensations or express thoughts that are hard to put into words, and enhance collaboration."[15]

Engineers working with artists at Nokia Bell Labs have developed a wearable armband they call the Sleeve, which "gathers information about the user's physical and emotional state through gyroscopes, accelerometers, and optical sensors, then communicates that intel via haptic pulses and screen-displayed messages. . . . In this right-brains-meet-left coalition, engineers and artists team up to explore big questions: Can humans communicate through touch? Is it possible to transfer empathy?"[16] Haptic pulses might prove to be another channel through which we both communicate and receive information, and thus the education of touch forms an important part of the pedagogical philosophy of the University of the Body. In such a sensory environment, communication moves beyond spoken language and orality. Students need to learn how to communicate effectively and elegantly through such enhanced means, a kind of rhetoric of telepathy. Gathering information from across a range of senses permits us to expand the amount of information we simultaneously take in and expands our capacity to make sense from a vast and complex data array.

■   ■   ■

A multisensory information space was developed at the MIT Media Lab, a space where externalized media arrived to a user through a range of senses. Called the ambientROOM, the information space took data off the screen and placed it in various forms around a small room, moving information "into the physical environment, manifesting [it] as subtle changes in form, movement, sound, color, smell, temperature, or light."[17] "In this cubicle-as-monitor, the most noteworthy surface was the ceiling, which projected an animation of waves radiating across a water surface," observes Malcolm McCullough. "The speed and size of these waves reflected different data of the occupant's choosing. This space may have been the first to move the display from the figure to the background. Since then, information technologies have moved the display still further away, with nontexual background representations of markets, traffic, energy usage, and more."[18]

Aside from relying on an expanded range of senses to apprehend information, the ambientROOM expands the scope of our attention. Stated another way, an ambient information environment depends on our ability to make sense of background information; it elevates the rhetorical place of peripheral information. In such multisensory spaces, background or peripheral information—what is outside of our attention—looms important in how we process information. The designers of the ambientROOM make the case that "humans have highly sophisticated capacities for processing multiple information streams. While a particular source of information may occupy the 'foreground' of our awareness, many additional sources may concurrently be monitored in the 'background.' For example, we may have a sense of the weather outside from ambient cues such as light, temperature, sound, and air flow from nearby windows. We may also have an idea of the activities of colleagues in the area from the ambient sound and the visible presence of passers-by. . . . Unfortunately, most computer interfaces fail to take advantage of our background processing capabilities."[19] The University of the Body trains students to become literate in multisensory information spaces. "Much of our somatic intelligence operates unconsciously, without conscious supervision or even awareness," says Guy Claxton.[20]

One might argue that a space filled with sounds and movements and smells would overwhelm the sensory capacities of anyone entering it. Our current technological environment is already so mesmerizing that it is difficult for many to remain focused and attentive. Indeed, learning to negotiate the relationship between center and periphery is an important epistemological feature of the University of the Body. "We can think [of] this in terms of Richard Lanham's notion of rhetoric as the economics of attention, provided we expand the concept of attention beyond that which is limited to the subjective, intentional, or merely cognitive," says the rhetorician Thomas Rickert. "Attention attends to the salient, but the bringing forth of salience is itself a complex activity that has ambient dimensions. This poses a problem . . . when the salient is taken for all there is or all that matters. It poses a problem precisely because it excludes from discussion how the ambient dimensions of a rhetorical situation constitute the ways things emerge and show up for us in the first place."[21] Rather than casting off ambient information in an effort to focus attention, students at the University of the Body learn to draw attention to the ambient periphery.

Seeing spaces, virtual offices, and ambient rooms all are sensorily rich information spaces. They may seem futuristic and fantastical, but one could argue that humans have long inhabited such sensorily rich spaces. In contrast, the page and the screen—as information spaces— are "sensorily impoverished," says Guy Claxton. The screen in particular "offers sight and sound, but . . . nothing solid and smelly, tickly and tasty in the way real life is. Computers lead us to concentrate more and more on the two evolutionarily younger senses, sight and hearing, and to withdraw attention from the others. Are we being numbed as well as dumbed down by our machines?"[22] The pages of a book lack even sound, and so, in this telling, books are even more sensorily impoverished.

■   ■   ■

According to one school of thought, cognition is not confined to the actions of the brain. The body as a receptacle of sensations and sensory information is as much a part of the system of cognition as the brain is. The brain plays the role of coordinator of all the information received via the senses. According to Guy Claxton, "a well-integrated, well-tuned, highly resonant body is itself the organ of intelligence. The brain plays an important part in that integration, allowing loops of information from the skin and the spleen, the hands and the heart, the gut and the gullet to be brought together in fruitful discourse. But without all those loops carrying fast-changing information about what is possible and what is desirable, and without the constant conversation between all the far-flung outposts of the body, the brain would not be intelligent at all. It is only as good as the intelligence it receives."[23] Thus, a sensorily rich ambient environment that conveys information through touch, sound, smell, and movement is not an oddity, but indeed depends and draws on our fundamentally embodied intelligence.[24]

One could argue that the sensorily impoverished information spaces of the book and the screen are historical anomalies, since our earliest ancestors resided in ambient media environments. Cave art, for example, was far more than just drawings on the wall. Some archaeologists are convinced that the cave environment itself, especially its acoustics and other sound qualities, was as important as the visual images. We think cave environments included the burning of incense, and thus the environment was a visual, aural, and even olfactory space.[25] While not explicitly concerned about the information-processing abilities of various senses, the ancient Greeks nevertheless viewed the education of the body as on a level with the education of the intellect. "These are twin arts—parallel and complementary," Isocrates observed, "by which their masters prepare the mind to become more intelligent and the body to become more serviceable, not separating sharply the two kinds of education, but using similar methods of instruction, exercise, and other forms of discipline."[26] The ancient Chinese as well sought a balance between the education of mind and of body.

The culture of the printed page and even of the screen reduced the ambient, reduced the information space down such that the only information that counted, especially in an educational context, was information that was suitable for the page. That information space was overwhelmingly visual and reduced the information-acquisition features of the body to the movement of the eyes across the page and the fingers turning the page. Early books in monasteries were read aloud, but even that oral/aural function disappeared. Universities were born during the rise of the book, and one could argue that they have retained a sensorily impoverished information culture that the book enforces. Our future ambient environments will open up those spaces of information, will fill them with multisensory forms of information, and will require sites of higher learning that teach how to navigate the literacy of such spaces. The University of the Body is an institution that trains students to navigate externalized, ambient, multisensory information environments.

■   ■   ■

Future ambient information environments will have senses as well and will absorb information from us as we absorb information from them. "Researchers at MIT have taught the eyes in our machines to detect human emotions. As we watch the screen, the screen is watching us, where we look, and how we react," reports Kevin Kelly.

> Rosalind Picard and Rana el Kaliouby at the MIT Media Lab have developed software so attuned to subtle human emotions that they claim it can detect if someone is depressed. It can discern about two dozen different emotions. I had a chance to try a beta version of this "affective technology," as Picard calls it. . . . Say I am reading a book and my frown shows I've stumbled on a certain word; the text could expand a definition. Or if it realizes I am rereading the same passage, it could supply an annotation for that passage. Similarly, if it knows I am bored by a scene in a video, it could jump ahead or speed up [the] action.[27]

Gesture recognition like this is another way students at the University of the Body interact with information, similar to the way that we swipe a phone today. "The new iPhone introduced a camera that can perceive three dimensions and record a depth for every pixel, and home devices like the Nest IQ and Amazon's Echo Look now have cameras of their own," reports David Rose. "Combined with neural nets that learn and improve with more training data, these new cameras create a point cloud or depth map of the people in a scene, how they are posing, and how they are moving. The nets can be trained to recognize specific people, classify their activities, and respond to gestures from afar. Together, neural nets and better cameras open up an entirely new space for gestural design and gesture-based interaction models."[28] In such an educational environment, students learn to interact with information by changing their expressions or by using whole body gestures. That body movement, that kinesthetic intelligence, needs to be learned and formalized. "Physical education" takes on new meaning beyond athleticism as a way to apprehend and interact with information.

Education in such an environment involves an understanding of how to control the body and how to employ all of the senses to acquire information. The proper movement of the body in a multisensory environment is a kind of choreography or athletics: a formalized control of the body. But there needs to be more than simply learning the correct form. What is the content of what is learned in such environments? Scholars who have been considering the implications of virtual reality on the creation and experience of literature give us some indication. "Immersive literature"—experiencing a story as a participant—means the ability to see, hear, and touch characters. In a chemistry class, a student is immersed in a virtual environment where she has in front of her a representation of the periodic table of the elements. She walks up to the display and grabs two hydrogen atoms and an oxygen atom. She then manipulates the elements into the proper configuration—and perhaps gets virtually "wet" when she succeeds. When manipulating other elements, she might discover that certain atoms do not easily combine; she feels physical resistance in her attempt to join them. This is a tactile way to experience atomic forces, and chemistry becomes a visual and tactile experience. "It is [as] important for young people to become manipulate as it is to be articulate," writes Claxton. "Maybe we can look forward to an enlightened society in which manipulacy is talked about and valued as highly as literacy and numeracy."[29]

■ ■ ■

At the University of the Body, students interact with information through symbols that we have not traditionally thought of as having sensory form. The rise of data visualization was made possible by giving visual form to information that had not been previously conceived as having visual form. A student of mine once explained that when she was young, she was given the task of making things out of clay to describe words; another was once asked to "draw music." At the University of the Body, a whole range of information is translated into nonintuitive sensory forms. In this way, the disciplines become embodied. How a student understands chemistry or literature is altered when the practice of these disciplines expands across a range of senses. "Feeling statistics" or "touching literature" would alter our understanding of these disciplines.

As these examples indicate, the traditional disciplines are featured at the University of the Body but are subject to sensory expansion. The same subjects and curricula found at traditional universities are found here, only in a different symbolic/information environment. A student still studies psychology but may do so by listening to synaptic connections, for instance. The "senses across the curriculum" is a foundation of general education, however, with students expected to demonstrate competency in acquiring information through a range of senses. Episodes of synesthesia are not uncommon, and indeed the ability to translate between different senses is a curricular goal. The University of the Body encourages interdisciplinarity, and faculty work across traditional academic boundaries but are united within the same sensory boundaries. Mastery of a discipline is not the highest goal for students, although it is one goal. The ability to competently make sense of information in a multisensory environment is the highest goal.

■ ■ ■

A key part of making sense of data is learning to create and compose in such environments. Discovering new ways to represent information in nonintuitive sensory forms is a mark of distinction, as is creating innovative ways to manipulate information in order to yield new insights. If information is arriving by sound, touch, and even smell, then learning how to combine these together is a valued skill, a new form of literacy. Students develop a grammar and a rhetoric of the senses as a measure of this literacy. Combining information from various senses—touch with movement, smell with sound—suggests new ways to understand information, new interpretations. Humanists often talk about a new reading; at the University of the Body, we also talk about a "new gesture" or a "new feeling"—and not in a metaphorical sense, but in an actual physical sense. "The liberally educated person of the future will know that right attunement of the body affects perceptual capacities and will find ways of returning to the body's center to recover clarity of vision and attentive listening," says Donald Levine. "To reinvent liberal teaching along these lines will require a search for techniques and new curricular structures to bring bodily functioning and its attendant feelings into greater consciousness."[30]

■　■　■

Sensory information created and used at the University of the Body requires curating. When information is converted into a physical object to be handled and manipulated, it needs to be stored and preserved. When information is olfactory, when symbols are tactile and aural, protocols for its storage and maintenance are the responsibility of the library, the repository of sensory objects.

In a multisensory information environment, the meaning of the information arriving via the senses is altered. If an environment is suddenly overwhelmed with the smell of roses, we need to have trained bodies in order to understand that such a smell means a change in some system. That is, students need to learn to associate the smell of roses not with their mother's house but with the qualities of data. At the University of the Body, new meanings are attached to smells, sounds, and textures. The University of the Body is agnostic about the semantics of the senses: the senses serve as interfaces with a symbolic system that is itself made up of sensory objects. But there is also occasion to examine the many contested meanings of those sensory objects. Inasmuch as they investigate meaning, the humanities—the sensory humanities—therefore have an important place in the curriculum of the University of the Body.

Interlude

Technology University

This university is a technology incubator.[1] As he observed the activities in the pin factory that heralded the beginning of the Industrial Revolution and the division of labor, Adam Smith noted:

> All the improvements in machinery, however, have by no means been the inventions of those who had occasion to use the machines. Many improvements have been made by the ingenuity of the makers of the machines, when to make them became the business of a peculiar trade; and some by that of those who are called philosophers or men of speculation, whose trade it is not to do anything, but to observe everything; and who, upon that account, are often capable of combining together the powers of the most distant and dissimilar objects. In the progress of society, philosophy or speculation becomes, like every other employment, the principal or sole trade and occupation of a particular class of citizens. Like every other employment too, it is subdivided into a great number of different branches, each of which affords occupation to a peculiar tribe or class of philosophers; and this subdivision of employment in philosophy, as well as in every other business, improves dexterity, and saves time. Each individual becomes more expert in his own peculiar branch, more work is done upon the whole, and the quantity of science is considerably increased by it.[2]

This division of labor in tool-making hastened a process of technological imbalance. Without romanticizing it too much, prior to industrialization, the same person typically designed, built, and used the tool. Think of stone tools, our first technologies. One person conceived of the tool, honed the stone into a point, and used the resulting object for hunting, scraping, and other uses. The appearance of the object was the result of one person's unity of mind and purpose. Other technologies were fashioned via a similar process. Industrialization tore this unity apart: as Smith observed, the designer of the tool was a different person from the builder of the tool, who was different from the user of the tool.

We derive the word "technology" from the Greek *techne*: the craft of making tools. Indeed, in many languages the word "technology" refers more to human skill than to the object produced. In our current usage, technology often refers very narrowly to digital applications, as when we refer to the "technology sector" or to "technology stocks." If we do use the word more broadly, technology usually refers to the objects produced as a result of human skill. These connotations mean that most people experience technology as the object and not as the human skill that brought it into being.

The purpose of Technology University is for students to achieve technological balance. They accomplish this by learning to be designers, builders, and users of technology. Students generate technologies as a key learning outcome, and they also audit and evaluate all of the technologies brought into the space of the university and those used by the society as a whole. The educational philosophy of Technology University is to assist society in achieving technological balance and in developing new technologies that reflect such balance.

Technology University is organized into three schools. "Design" encompasses those disciplines related to the visualization and planning of technological systems, the "men [and women] of speculation" identified by Smith. "Build" is a school organized around traditional engineering subjects, such as mechanical engineering. The "Use" school hosts a range of disciplines, such as sociology, cognitive science, history, economics, art, humanities, anthropology, science, and technology studies: the fields that examine how technology and technological systems are used and with what effects. Students at Technology University specialize in a discipline in one of the schools, but are expected to minor in fields in the other two schools.

Students engage the curriculum in four phases. First, all students take a course series that introduces designers, builders, and users to the processes of technology creation, in both its historical and current incarnations. They learn to see technology and technological systems as a unified process of designing, building, and using. In the second phase, students concentrate on their specific disciplinary subjects. In the third phase, students work in teams of designers, builders, and users to engage in a technology audit, which is an inquiry into a specific technology or technological system, a careful close reading of a technology. Students ask a series of questions before any new technology is admitted into the space of Technology University. For instance, students might inquire into the CRISPR gene editing technology and ask questions such as the following:

- What are the purposes of this technology? What problem does the technology solve? How was this purpose agreed upon? That is, who decided that this problem needed to be addressed?
- Who decided how this technology was to be used, and what process led to this decision?
- Who uses this technology? Why? How closely does actual use align with its purpose?
- What are the primary benefits, costs, and risks of this technology?
- Who values this technology? Why? Who finds this technology problematic?
- Who designed the technology? Why? What does the design require of builders and users?
- Who built the technology? What materials and processes are required to build this technology? How were these selected? What are the environmental or human consequences of using these materials?

There are no correct or preferred answers to these questions; the questions serve only to make these decisions transparent. Teams are made up of a mixture of students from each school, and students advocate for their particular affiliation in these technology audits. After debating these questions, students then make recommendations as to whether or not the technology should be admitted into the space of Technology University. This process runs counter to the way most technologies enter universities. Think of tablet initiatives, where university leaders partner with companies to give devices to students. Users are excluded from this decision-making process. In contrast, any new technology must be critically analyzed by the student community before it may be placed into the ecosystem of Technology University.

The technology audit is also used as a service to society as a whole. Students examine technologies using the above questions and compose white papers that inform the public about the efficacy of any new technology. The focus, as always, is on the human skill, the decisions made by humans, and the effects of any new technology on humans.

The fourth and final phase of students' education at Technology University is a capstone project in which students ask a different set of questions when developing a new technology. Working in teams of designers, builders, and users, they ask questions that include:

- What problem are we solving? What are the potential risks of developing a technology to solve this problem? Why do we wish to solve this problem? To make money? To better the human condition? Does everyone view the problem in the same way?
- How do we design the technology to solve the problem? What requirements does this design impose on builders and users?
- What materials do we require to build this technology? What are the costs, benefits, and risks of procuring these materials? What downstream effects—on both the environment and living things—do these materials present?
- Who will value this technology? Why? What if users are not persuaded to use the technology? What are the ethics of demanding that users use the technology?

If this evaluation is completed successfully, students release the new technology into society. Technology University is an incubator of new technology via a process of technological balance.

IV **ATTRIBUTES**

The Institute for Advanced Play

The Institute for Advanced Play sees play as the highest form of learning, placed well above the acquisition and production of knowledge. Engaging in play turns out to be related to the thought processes used by artists and other creative people, so the activities in the institute look much like the kinds of activities artists and designers engage in. If the seminar room and the laboratory define the modern research university, then the studio defines the Institute for Advanced Play. The institute explores novelty and engages in generative creation: imagining that which does not exist, bringing the new into being, making serendipitous connections, seeking unexpected answers. The Institute for Advanced Play places wonder and curiosity at the center of its enterprise.

Howard Gardner observes that all children reach a stage in their intellectual development when "they are able to envision a state of affairs contrary to the one that is apprehended by their senses, to capture that imaginative activity in public symbolic form, and to continue to elaborate upon that imaginative capacity."[1] Fellows of the institute capture imaginative activity in public symbolic form, the results of which constitute their research.

A key epistemological tenet of the institute is that play and imagination define higher learning, and so the institute cultivates the imagination. The ontological terrain on which the institute operates is that of the subjunctive and the "adjacent possible."[2] That is, play is enacted not only in the actual world but in irreal possible worlds. To play means to imagine that which does not otherwise exist.

The Institute for Advanced Play is a space for serious play designed as a playground, a place for the imagination.[3] This space is like what is permitted by some companies, such as "Google time," when workers take a percentage of their time to play and experiment without a necessary end goal (although that is always welcomed). Fellows of the university-as-playground engage in world-making: building pretend worlds, inhabiting them, and playing in them. Fellows engage in role playing and immersive simulations, pretending to be others or reenacting the past. Improvisation is valued as an epistemological achievement.

There are neither faculty nor students at the institute. Fellows are selected according to a rigorous approval process that identifies "advanced players." Once selected, fellows are invited to stay at the institute for as long as they desire. There are no subjects or disciplines, and the institute is not organized into departments or colleges. "Play personalities" distinguish fellows and organize them into smaller groups; play personalities include those who prefer movement, those who explore the world around them, and those who use their hands to make things.

Fellows transgress existing rules and invent new rules, and they play games based on the newly invented rules. The exploration of "what if?" is one of the highest forms of inquiry: fellows wonder "What if work were separated from employment?" or "What if the dirtiest, grungiest jobs were paid the highest?" Fellows at the Institute for Advanced Play explore worlds through virtual simulations and through the construction of physical worlds. For example, someone might ask "What if the university were designed to facilitate serious play?" and build such a world not only through words but as an actual structure and organization, where players perform roles in this imagined world.

There is no set curriculum, no prescribed set of courses. Fellows follow their curiosity, exploring the subjects necessary to satisfy that curiosity. Fellows thus meander through subjects and disciplines as their curiosity leads them. Of all the institutions in this book, the Institute for Advanced Play is furthest removed from what we traditionally think of as a university because there are no prescribed outcomes, no learning objectives. The "imaginative activity captured in public symbolic form" is not mandated; it emerges at the end of a curiosity journey and is as serendipitous as the play that produces it.

"Pure play" and "applied play" exist together in an uneasy balance. The fellows selected as permanent members of the institute pursue play without direction, without an end goal, and without any expectation that the results of their play will have any benefit or use outside of the institute. But there are businesses and other organizations that seek out the innovative and creative ideas produced by fellows. These organizations also covet the fellows who have produced innovation through their play. Fellows are invited by outside companies to drive innovation and are also asked to teach playfulness to their employees. Companies may place their employees for limited amounts of time at the institute, as visiting fellows, where they hone a playful disposition and then return to their home organizations.

The Institute for Advanced Play values and encourages experimentation and tinkering with no end goal: play is a process of aimless curiosity. There may be real-world applications of the results of play, but creations that act on the world are not the outcomes sought at the institute. Its motto: *Ludite ut sibi fin* (Play as an end unto itself).

Play is facilitated through the manipulation of props or other objects that can be appropriated and hacked (imagined differently than their intended use). The availability of these objects makes the Institute for Advanced Play a kind of Montessori school for adults. Indeed, the institute itself can be hacked. Fellows play with and appropriate the very spaces and organization of the university.

The Institute for Advanced Play is a space for unlearning and failure. Unlearning implies the opposite of a specialist, who is someone with deep knowledge. Those with a beginner's mind, rather than a disciplinary specialist's mind, are invited into the institute, which is a space for wonder and intellectual adventure. Because the institute is driven by play, by unknowing, by imagination, and by wonder, the risk of failure is omnipresent. Failure is a natural outcome of pure play. Freed from any pressure to perform or produce, fellows explore and appropriate and fail.

■　■　■

Play is a human activity that we associate with childhood, using the diminishment of play as one way to mark adulthood. The Institute for Advanced Play is based on the idea that because it is a crucial cognitive activity, play should not be limited to children. Adults should play too, and at this university, play is elevated above knowledge.

"Play is a very primal activity," notes Stuart Brown. "It is preconscious and preverbal—it arises out of ancient biological structures that existed before our consciousness or our ability to speak." Far from being frivolous, the need to play appears to be crucial to how our brains work. "In fact," argues Brown, "I would say that the impulse to create art is a result of the play impulse. Art and culture have long been seen as a sort of by-product of human biology, something that just happens as we use our big, complex brains. But the newer thinking is that art and culture are something that the brain actively creates because it benefits us, something that arises out of the primitive and childlike drive to play."[4] Brown studies what he terms the "play histories" of various people, and he notes the advantages of play for certain kinds of cognition as well as the pathologies that emerge when play is absent. For example, he observed that the lack of play in childhood was an important factor in the crimes committed by murderers serving time in a Texas prison. Brown has also "documented abused kids at risk for antisocial behavior whose predilection for violence was diminished through play."[5]

Play is important in the development of the frontal cortex, and Brown concludes that "play seems to be one of the most advanced methods nature has invented to allow a complex brain to create itself."[6] Given the importance of play to brain function, it seems odd that our society discourages play as we grow older. Further, it is ironic that while we associate play with the activities of children, children in the United States have been playing less and less over the last fifty years. Time once given over to free play has been consumed by more schoolwork and more structured activities (like coached sports), and there is less time spent on hobbies. "The effect," writes Peter Gray, "has been a continuous and ultimately dramatic decline in children's opportunities to play and explore in their own chosen ways."[7] When they do mature into adulthood, some have been compensating by playing with adult coloring books, joining kickball leagues, and otherwise engaging in the free play that was denied to them when they were younger.[8]

This signals to me a need and desire to play that our society is not meeting.

Adults and children may need to play more as a way to cope with the complexities of life in the twenty-first century. Indeed, Douglas Thomas and John Seely Brown assert, "The ability to play may be the single most important skill to develop for the twenty-first century."[9] Given play's importance to the development of our brains and given the importance it seems to have for coping with the modern world, we require more spaces and organizations to facilitate adult play. If the goal of any university is to be transformative, then the Institute for Advanced Play exists in order to develop and build the individual's capacity for play.

■   ■   ■

The Dutch historian Johan Huizinga's definition of play continues to shape the way observers think about the nature of play. Huizinga defined play as "a free activity standing quite consciously outside 'ordinary' life as being 'not serious' but at the same time absorbing the player intensely and utterly. It is an activity connected with no material interest, and no profit can be gained from it. It proceeds within its own proper boundaries of time and space according to fixed rules and in an orderly manner."[10] Huizinga's definition suggests that play is extracurricular, not serious, and therefore can be identified as frivolous. To say that play involves "no material interest" means that it is a nonproductive activity and thus something that only someone with leisure can practice. John Dewey said that play involves "freedom from economic pressure—the necessities of getting a living and supporting others—and from the fixed responsibilities attaching to the special callings of the adult."[11] Given such a definition, it is easy to see how one might define play as something only children engage in.

A commonality among those who comment on play is that it is not defined by any specific activity but is, rather, a disposition, a way of behaving. That disposition might take many outward forms. Perhaps it is because we focus on the external forms—especially playing with toys or blocks—that we associate play with childhood, not with adult behavior. But as Dewey observed, "Play is not to be identified with anything which the child externally does. It rather designates his mental attitude in its entirety and in its unity. It is the free play, the interplay, of all the child's powers, thoughts, and physical movements, in embodying, in a satisfying form, his own images and interests. . . . To state it baldly, the fact that 'play' denotes the psychological attitude of the child, not his outward performances, means complete emancipation from the necessity of following any given or prescribed system, or sequence of gifts, plays, or occupations."[12]

I contend that play is also a psychological attitude of adults, an attitude that finds very few avenues for expression. Perhaps we require a different name for this disposition? "What [the physicist Andre] Geim wanted, he would later reveal, was a new term, a 'slightly different manner of speech,' to define what we really mean by play: 'curiosity-driven research.' He would prefer to call it 'adventure.' "[13]

Like Dewey, Douglas Thomas and John Seely Brown situate play as central to learning. "Much of what makes play powerful as a tool for learning is our ability to engage in experimentation," they write, evoking Geim's sense of play. "All systems of play are, at base, learning systems. They are ways of engaging in complicated negotiations of meaning, interaction, and competition, not only for entertainment, but also for creating meaning. Most critically, play reveals a structure of learning that is radically different from the one most schools or other formal learning environments provide, and which is well suited to the notions of a world in constant flux."[14] If play is that important to children's learning, it should also be accorded a central place in higher learning.

■ ■ ■

While play might often occur within the boundaries of fixed rules, an important feature of play is the transgression of those rules. For Miguel Sicart, play—and especially playfulness—is defined as appropriation. "Playfulness means taking over a world to see it through the lens of play, to make it shake and laugh and crack because we play with it. . . . To be playful is to appropriate a context that is not created or intended for play. Playfulness is the playlike appropriation of what should not be play."[15] Any time a child imagines a cardboard box as a spaceship or as a secret room, or when she imagines that the tube from a roll of paper towels is a telescope, she is engaging in play-as-appropriation.[16]

More formally, appropriation—as Sicart conceives it—involves stepping outside of formal rules or seizing and refashioning an object or an environment and thereby playing by different rules. "In playfulness," writes Sicart, "appropriation happens in its pure form, taking over a situation to perceive it differently, letting play be the interpretive power of that context. Appropriation implies a shift in the way a particular technology or situation is interpreted. The most usual transformation is from functional or goal oriented to pleasurable or emotionally engaging. Appropriation transforms a context by means of the attitude projected to it."[17] While children certainly engage in play-as-appropriation, adults also have this ability, but we need the time, space, and permission to exhibit it. The Institute for Advanced Play is a space that permits adults to appropriate a context; fellows are encouraged to take a different approach to the world and play by different rules.

Refashioning an object or an environment is especially evident during pretending. Howard Gardner explores what happens during pretending (or pretense, as he calls it), noting how children appropriate objects and environments. In Gardner's example, a child might perceive a banana and call the object by that name (a first-order representation, in Gardner's scheme). But when the child holds the banana to her ear and speaks into it, pretending it is a telephone, she is engaging in a second-order representation, a higher form of representation. "Treating one object as if it were another is a cardinal form of 'metarepresentation,'" notes Gardner. This is what happens when a child pretends to drink tea from an empty cup—turning nothing into something—or when she changes the property of some object into another. "Operating in each of these cases of metarepresentation is a recognition that what is apparently the state of affairs can be intentionally bracketed, so as to bring about another state of affairs that the player wants to evoke."[18] Play is the ability to alter a context, to bring about a novel state by not being confined to the world as it presents itself to us. For Gardner, play at this higher order of representation equates to the development of the imagination:

> What I am claiming is that within the first few years of life, all children pass a crucial milestone. Moving beyond the ability to think directly about the world of experience, they now become capable of imagining. They are able to envision a state of affairs contrary to the one that is apprehended by their sense, to capture that imaginative activity in public symbolic form, and to continue to elaborate upon that imaginative capacity. . . . The capacity to take a stance toward everyday reality—to confirm, deny, or alter it—confers enormous new power on the child.[19]

Higher-order or advanced play entails altering and appropriating reality, taking the world as it is and changing it in some fashion. Envisioning a different state of affairs—different from the way the world actually is—means moving into the realm of the subjunctive, the irreal. In addition to the actual world that we experience via our senses, we are also surrounded by "the sphere of the possible." Play is the exploration of that "adjacent possible."[20] "The most fundamental characteristic of the imagination," writes Richard Ogle, "is its ability to let us *free ourselves from the grip of present reality.* . . . . This characteristic enables us to construct and play with alternative ways of seeing, understanding, and acting in the world that allow something new, interesting, and useful to emerge. . . . The imagination frees us from the mesmerizing grip of reality, allowing us to invent, play with, and even try out alternative worlds."[21] "The work of the imagination does not represent 'what is absent,'" say Peter Murphy, Michael Peters, and Simon Marginson. "It also posits objects that otherwise would not exist."[22] If research is about the discovery of what exists in the actual world, play is about the generation of novel forms via the exploration of the possible. Rather than a research university, the institute is a generative university, a platform "for experimentation, speculation, and the reimagining of everyday life."[23]

■   ■   ■

"Role playing the past" is one kind of activity engaged at the Institute for Advanced Play. Players pretend to be historical figures, for example, and learn about the choices and decisions that confronted them. "Reacting to the Past" is the title of a curriculum where "students play monthlong games, set in the past, with roles informed by classic texts. For the game set in Athens in 403 BC, for example, students become democrats or oligarchs, and compete by debating the respective merits of Pericles and Plato; for the game set in the Holy Office in Rome in 1632, students pretend to be mathematicians, natural philosophers, and conservative cardinals, and debate whether Galileo's *Dialogue Concerning the Two Chief World Systems* proves that the Earth moves."[24] "The reading I had done in preparation for my role as Nehru convinced me that he was a consummate politician, someone willing to negotiate and compromise," says one historical role player, "and so I entered into my dialogue with Jinnah and the Muslim League expecting that we could find common ground in the search for a united India. Jinnah, in the game as in real life, did not want a united India. He wanted an independent Muslim nation. All of my negotiating tactics broke against the wall of his desire."[25] Such adult make-believe might be one way to study the past at the Institute for Advanced Play.

Some forms of play at the institute involve the construction and habitation of alternative worlds. These take the form of simulations, virtual worlds, or other imagined spaces within which players are able to act. Think of the movie *Interstellar* (2014): the filmmakers imagined a world similar to but unlike our own. They wondered what it would be like to exist in a five-dimensional world and to fly across a black hole. The astrophysicists who collaborated on the film learned about the nature of black holes by going through the process of imagining and visualizing them with the filmmakers. Their play in an imaginary world provided new insights.[26] As Thomas and Brown assert, "Where imaginations play, learning happens."[27]

■　■　■

The forms of play, playfulness, and appropriation described by Sicart and by Gardner sound very similar to the kinds of activities that hackers engage in. We usually associate hacking with cybercrime, but digital hacking can involve altering or otherwise playing with computer code to achieve a novel or unexpected outcome. Hacking may be a kind of mischief-making, but it is at heart taking a context and altering it in some fashion. Hackers view their own activity as "digital trespass: breaking into a system, owning it hard, doing what you want with it."[28] Compromising a system just for the sheer pleasure of it is the basis of the hacking mentality. The term has since expanded to refer to the alteration of any object or system. The Institute for Advanced Play is a haven for hackers of all types, people who wish to appropriate the world and alter it in some fashion for the sheer pleasure of the act.

Play-as-hacking, as a mischievous undertaking, reminds us that play can be carnivalesque. "Play appropriates events, structures, and institutions to mock them and trivialize them, or make them deadly serious," says Sicart. "The carnival of the Middle Ages, with its capacity to subvert conventions and institutions in a suspension of time and power, was a symptom of freedom. Carnivalesque play takes control of the world and gives it to the players for them to explore, challenge, or subvert. . . . Through carnivalesque play, we express ourselves, taking over the world to laugh at it and make sense of it too."[29] Carnivalesque play is at once creative and destructive, maintaining a precarious balance between the two. "Play is always dangerous, dabbling with risks, creating and destroying, and keeping a careful balance between both," writes Sicart. "Play is between the rational pleasures of order and creation and the sweeping euphoria of destruction and rebirth, between the Apollonian and the Dionysiac."[30]

One reason that we may not associate play with the actions of adults is that there are so few spaces, so few contexts for adults to play in any sort of sustained and meaningful way.[31] The Institute for Advanced Play is a space where permission is granted to adults to play. Some spaces for adult play are emerging in the business world. Stuart Brown recounts how the Jet Propulsion Laboratory was unsatisfied with the quality of the engineers it was hiring. The engineers, of course, came from top schools and were highly skilled, but the JPL managers found them wanting at problem-solving abilities. The JPL realized that the engineers who played with their hands—tinkering, taking things apart—had greater problem-solving aptitude. While not establishing a playground or other space for play, the JPL was nevertheless valuing those who exhibited a playful demeanor.[32]

The designer Ivy Ross won accolades for developing Project Platypus at companies like Mattel and the Gap. Project Platypus was an informal space in which twelve associates at the company, from various backgrounds and with a range of professional titles, were invited to play together. That play could take place with whomever, with whatever, and however they wanted. "[The space] resembled a Montessori environment," reports Sarah Lewis, "with stimuli to satisfy every self-initiated interest: games and even rubber rockets to shoot to give the mind a break. There was no set schedule; the weeks were filled with 'mental grazing,' the team filling themselves with new ideas, images, and concepts that they knew little about. 'Sometimes the ideas gelled, sometimes it wasn't until week seven, but it never disappointed me,' Ross said about Project Platypus. They always got more innovative work done than ever before. It was so creative[,] it was fertile." I imagine the Institute for Advanced Play as being very similar to Project Platypus, a Montessori environment for adults. The "Montessori objects" need not be colorful blocks; indeed, any kind of object can be used as long as it can be appropriated for second-order imaginative pretending. "Innovation is an outcome," concluded Ross. "Play is a state of mind. Innovation is often what we get when we play."[33]

Other companies also value the innovation and creativity that can be unleashed through play. Lego has developed a consulting practice called Serious Play, where adults are invited to play with Lego blocks as a way to stimulate problem-solving capabilities. Jørgen Vig Knudstorp, the CEO of Lego, contends that businesses simply placing foosball or ping-pong tables in their offices will not bring about playfulness. Doing so equates play solely with its external manifestations. Instead, the ideal play scenario is "a risk-free environment that encourages people to experiment, as there is no such thing as failure."[34] Serious Play works with businesses to provide a temporary play environment. The consultancy is based around a methodology that consists of "a facilitated meeting, communication and problem-solving process in which participants are led through a series of questions, probing deeper and deeper into the subject. Each participant builds his or her own 3-D LEGO° model in response to the facilitator's questions using specially selected LEGO° elements. These 3-D models serve as a basis for group discussion, knowledge sharing, problem solving and decision making."[35] The participants in such exercises are engaged in a form of play, in that abstract objects (the Lego blocks) are appropriated for another purpose (as a representation of the players' thoughts in answer to a problem).

Andrew Bollington, the global head of research and learning at the LEGO Foundation, echoes the thoughts of Thomas and Brown by focusing on "learning through play." Companies that view themselves as learning organizations need to have employees that focus on play as a state of mind rather than an activity. "For [the LEGO Foundation]," says Bollington, "learning is the process of acquiring knowledge, skills, and attitudes (preferably those that help to develop creative, engaged, lifelong learners). Play is an activity which provokes a playful state of mind. Therefore, *learning through play is the process of acquiring knowledge, skills and attitudes in a playful state of mind*. It's the most amazing and creative way of learning."[36] I imagine the Institute for Advanced Play as filled with objects and things. These could be Lego-like objects, although any objects would do, since they are not specific to any given task or discipline. The expectation is that these objects would be appropriated by the players.

■　■　■

In addition to objects, the physical structure of the institute itself is subject to appropriation. I once participated in a three-day design workshop with high school students. We provided standard classroom equipment and invited the students to "hack the classroom." This meant appropriating the objects, inserting new objects, and otherwise altering the space of the classroom. In a similar way, fellows at the institute play with the physical features of the space. Further, the rules and cultural mores governing the institute are open to appropriation and hacking. This play, of course, poses a number of risks, since it is creative and destructive at the same time.

Sicart reminds us, "A play space is a location specifically created to accommodate play but does not impose any particular type of play, set of activities, purpose, or goal or reward structure."[37] By this definition, the Lego approach and other spaces created by businesses do not qualify. In the Lego case, there are specific activities to be pursued, and each has an ultimate goal of producing more creative employees or enhancing their problem-solving abilities. One could argue that some companies, like Google, do permit a kind of free play time: employees are permitted up to 20 percent of their weekly time to engage in projects of their own interest, to tinker, or to otherwise play without the expectation of producing anything tangible or of economic value. However, there is at least the anticipation that such free play time will indeed yield the next great product.

I envision the Institute for Advanced Play as a space in Sicart's mold, without the imposition of any particular type of play or expected outcome. Otherwise, a conflict would arise between pure play and applied play. The institute is populated by fellows who seek only to play, without any predetermined direction or outcome. But there might be pressure to have the results of such play applied to situations and contexts outside of the institute. That is, the results of play—the innovative and creative ideas—could be coveted by outsiders, who might also covet the players who dreamed up such innovations. Fellows could be lured to businesses seeking such playful people or seeking those who could induce such play from their own workers. The institute will almost surely be invited as a consultant to businesses, as Lego is today. Companies might want their employees to spend a limited amount of time at the institute, as visiting fellows, perhaps, with the intention of developing a playful disposition that they then bring back to their organizations. Pure play and applied play uneasily coexist at the institute.

■ ■ ■

The Institute for Advanced Play does not have a curriculum or a prescribed set of courses that one must advance through. It is not a four-year institution; fellows, who are accepted only after a stringent process, may stay for as long as they wish. Visiting fellows arrive and depart as their professional obligations allow. There are no distinctions between faculty and students, only between players and advanced players, all of whom have come to play. The institute is not divided into subjects and disciplines, and it is not organized around departments in the way knowledge is divided up in traditional universities. Instead, play more than likely coalesces around the actions of eight "play personalities," which have been identified by Stuart Brown:

- The Joker: "A joker's play always revolves around some kind of nonsense."
- The Kinesthete: "People who like to move[,] who . . . 'need to move in order to think.'" These are athletes, dancers, and practitioners of yoga.
- The Explorer: Those who explore the world either physically, emotionally (as in exploring a new feeling), or mentally: "researching a new subject or discovering new experiences and points of view."
- The Competitor: "A person who breaks through into euphoria and creativity of play by enjoying a competitive game with specific rules, and enjoys playing to win."
- The Director: "Directors enjoy planning and executing scenes and events."
- The Collector: "The thrill of play for the collector is to have and to hold the most, the best, the most interesting collection of objects or experiences."
- The Artist/Creator: "Joy is found in making things."
- The Storyteller: "For the storyteller, the imagination is the key to the kingdom of play."[38]

Of course, any one person might exhibit a number of these traits. As they play at the institute, they join up with those of similar personalities, such that there are groups of kinesthetes or groups of jokers formed. Directors organize various groups of play personalities.

    The Institute for Advanced Play invites fellows to engage in unlearning, to cast off their specialist's mind-set and instead embrace the beginner's mind. The architect Kyna Leski asserts, "Creativity requires an open mind. . . . Artists work freely with uncertainty and play, and accept the thoughtless and immediate 'knowing' of intuition without the support of facts. Data are used not only to substantiate an intuition but also to spark further speculation and unknowing. As artists, we are surprised to find that scientists also work without knowing, sometimes following a hunch or aesthetic sense."[39] Play and unknowing are closely linked: the Institute for Advanced Play encourages unlearning, which in many ways is the opposite of most universities. "You'll need to make space within your mind to look deliberately beyond what (you think) you know," says Leski. "Space needs to be made for wandering—and wonder."[40]

When exploration is driven by play, unknowing, imagination, and wonder, the risk of failure is omnipresent. Given our contemporary culture's emphasis on testing and metrics, there are few opportunities in formal educational settings for children or adults to fail safely.[41] Failure is a natural outcome of pure play, however, and so is defined as an expected result of the Institute for Advanced Play.[42] Sarah Lewis describes a children's imagination playground, "massive block[s] set in weather-resistant blue material with no instructions, developed by architect and designer David Rockwell." This playground does not have swings or sliding boards or other suggestions for play. The large blocks can be stacked and combined in myriad ways, but also present the possibility of tipping over. The imagination playground lets "kids build things, and inherent in the process is that they're going to build things that don't quite work out. . . . It neutralize[s] the negative connotations of setbacks in a developmentally appropriate way."[43]

Freed from any pressure to perform, the fellows at the Institute for Advanced Play explore and appropriate and fail. "Play provides the opportunity to leap, experiment, fail, and continue to play with different outcomes—in other words to riddle one's way through a mystery."[44]

9

Polymath University

As a condition of matriculation, every student at Polymath University majors in three disparate disciplines. Polymath University is built on the educational philosophy that creativity and innovative thinking emerge from the mash-up of disparate ideas, from the ability to make connections between what appear to be different domains.

Students choose from a menu of majors, which is divided into three areas: the professions, the sciences and social sciences, and the arts and humanities. Thus, students cannot major in English, history, and philosophy or in finance, marketing, and accounting. Instead, they must choose, for example, majors in history, accounting, and biology or in finance, English, and chemistry.

Before arriving on campus and the start of formal classes, students participate in a summer orientation. This consists of mini-courses and experiences that allow them to sample different disciplines; it is a time to experiment, which is intended to help with the selection of their three majors. The expectation is that by the end of the summer orientation, students have a good idea of their concentrations; any change of mind or effort to change ships at midcourse add time to their university career.

In order to ensure that students can concentrate for forty credit hours in each major, there are no general education courses at Polymath University; writing, mathematics, and other general education skills are learned as part of one's major concentration. By focusing on three different disciplines, students develop a breadth of knowledge unattainable in a typical general education program. Taking an introductory course in one of the sciences is insufficient to develop any kind of deep knowledge of that subject. Although Polymath University encourages transdisciplinary thinking, it is the disciplines that are its focus, the idea spaces in which students immerse themselves.

The major is reconceptualized as teaching the habits of mind and thought processes of a discipline. The philosophy of Polymath University as a whole can be summarized as "thinking simultaneously as an architect, as a sociologist, as a poet." While there are some bodies of knowledge to be mastered, the majors are not content-driven, since the mastery of skills and habits of mind are emphasized. Each major may have a prescribed sequence of courses; alternatively, faculty and students may create a curriculum by identifying a set of yearly outcomes/objectives and devising ways of reaching those objectives. Instructional designers play a key role in designing majors, working with faculty to identify the preferred outcomes.

Students produce a final capstone project that is the result of the mash-up of their three majors. In each previous year, they have produced "mini-capstones" that build toward that final project. The preliminary projects involve teams of students; the final capstone is an individual project. At informal forums, students present their ideas to a group of nonspecialists. These look like hackathons where a problem is presented and teams have a weekend to solve it. Teams include senior students, who help mentor younger students about transdisciplinary thinking based on their own experiences. These informal forums are part of the curriculum, and participation in a number of them is an expectation before matriculation.

All faculty at Polymath University possess competency in three distinct disciplines, and they teach, research, create, and think in the areas between those disciplines, making them less prone to siloing. Ideally, faculty have three PhDs in three separate disciplines, but it is more likely that they have research qualifications in one discipline and teaching competence in two others. This competence usually comes from graduate coursework during their PhD training but in some cases comes from real-world experience, as when a faculty member works in government or for an NGO or has spent some time as an executive in a corporation or as the director of a nonprofit. Faculty research is also interdisciplinary, drawing on the intersections of a variety of fields. Polymath University produces its own academic journals that publish such interdisciplinary work.

The "transadvisor" is a key figure in the lives of students, a high-prestige position in the university. This is not a traditional advisor, someone the student encounters infrequently to check curricular boxes and ensure they are meeting requirements. The transadvisor helps students navigate between the three disciplines they have chosen. Transadvisors do not teach formal courses but concentrate on mentoring students on their journeys between the disciplines. This position is like an artist-in-residence. Transadvisors conduct informal seminars with groups of students around interdisciplinary questions, and they help coordinate the teams of students for capstone projects. Students also have advisors for each of their three majors, forming a team of student, transadvisor, and major advisors. This team aids the student in creating their capstones.

Athletes are also expected to be interdisciplinary, and every athlete participates in three sports. In keeping with the spirit of Polymath University, these sports are different and distinct and not just what we think of as competitive athletics. So a football player also performs dance and plays tennis, and a track athlete also plays rugby and swims.

A student does not come to Polymath University saying, "I'm going to be an architect." She comes looking to be an interdisciplinary thinker, and indeed it is not immediately evident what she will do after college. There is great serendipity and surprise when three disparate majors are so combined: a culture of intellectual promiscuity permeates Polymath University.

■   ■   ■

Mathematician George Mohler took a well-understood idea—earthquakes are unpredictable, but the aftershocks follow more regular, predictable patterns—and applied it in a different situation. He wondered whether a similar pattern existed with "aftercrimes": whether after an initial crime, a series of smaller crimes followed in its wake. Mohler plugged crime statistics from Los Angeles into algorithms used to predict aftershocks, and he was able to anticipate which areas of the city would be especially at risk for burglaries. Mohler noted similar patterns in gang activity, meaning that police now have a tool to anticipate some crimes before they occur.[1]

Mohler could be said to have created a mash-up of seismology and criminology. Joshua Cooper Ramo contends that "the mashup is a sign of a different landscape of power, more or less what Cubism was one hundred years ago."[2] More than simply an artistic technique, cubism—or, more precisely, cubist artists—saw the world differently and through this form of art described a condition of the world. "Every important historical moment is marked by . . . new models of living, which expand in velocity and complexity well past what the current ways of thinking can handle. Our moment is no exception. And usually the source of the greatest historical disasters is that so few people at the time either recognize or understand the shift. Artists, with their tuned instincts for the new, often do."[3] Ramo, a geostrategic advisor and consultant, says that we should look to artists to understand how the world works. A century ago, Gertrude Stein understood that the First World War represented a fundamental shift. "The composition of this war," she observed, "was not a composition in which there was one man in the center surrounded by many others but a composition that had neither a beginning nor an end, a composition in which one corner was as important as another corner, in fact the composition of Cubism." That is, "only Cubism, that trick of treating a single object with multiple perspectives, could hope to make sense of the intricately ordained carnage of 1914–1918 and the world that emerged afterward."[4]

Much art-making today could be said to derive from mash-up logic. The DJ Danger Mouse, for example, mashed together the Beatles' *White Album* and Jay-Z's *Black Album* to create his *Grey Album*. The internet is awash with examples of multiple media mixed and matched to produce new compositions. "If the Cubist revolution demanded that we look at one thing from multiple perspectives," notes Ramo, "mashup logic demands that we look at the world as multiple objects mixed in multiple—unpredictable—ways to create totally new objects or situations."[5] Polymath University is the pedagogical and epistemological expression of the culture of the mash-up.

While mash-ups appear to be the art movement du jour, the impulse behind the art form has a much longer pedigree. Indeed, one could argue that the root of all creativity is the mash-up of previously unconnected or disparate ideas. The trumpeter Miles Davis once remarked that he got ideas for phrasing his music from Frank Sinatra and Orson Welles; that is, Davis applied ideas from a singer and an actor-director to his trumpet playing. This is an example of what we might term "domain bridging," and it is one of the chief sources of creativity and innovative thinking. Mohler took a pattern or idea from seismology and translated it into the domain of criminology. Domain bridging occurs when an idea or pattern from one domain is applied in another domain, the effect of which is to produce a new outcome or new pattern.[6] Polymath University is an institution that educates minds for such domain bridging, which is the chief cognitive activity of the institution.

■ ■ ■

Arthur Koestler argued that creativity springs from collisions of different intellectual disciplines, that "all decisive events in the history of scientific thought can be described in terms of mental cross-fertilization between different disciplines."[7] Polymath University urges and facilitates students and faculty to cross-fertilize across disciplines. Steven Johnson borrows a term from evolutionary biology to describe this domain-bridging action: exaptation. In its original context, the term means an evolutionary trait developed for one use that is brought into a new context for another use. Johnson, of course, has exapted this concept and brought it into a new context: ideas developed in one context are brought into a new context. He looks specifically at modernism in the 1920s, which "exhibited so much cultural innovation in such a short period of time because the writers, poets, artists, and architects were all rubbing shoulders at the same cafes. They weren't off on separate islands, teaching creative writing seminars or doing design reviews. That physical proximity made the space rich with exaptation: the literary stream of consciousness influencing the dizzying new perspectives of cubism; the futurist embrace of technological speed in poetry shaping new patterns of urban planning."[8] In some ways, one could read this statement as a critique of the siloing of modern universities: the tendency for specialists to huddle together in their own corners of the institution or with fellow specialists at conferences, an attitude that rubs off on students, who are similarly cocooned within disciplines. Polymath University is designed to be a "space rich with exaptation."

Polymath University is based on the ideas that domain bridging occurs within the mind of a single individual and that such interdisciplinary thinking can be induced in an individual.[9] Johnson describes the thought process employed by John Snow, who in the 1850s discovered the cause of cholera in London. Snow engaged in numerous activities, from treating patients and writing papers for medical journals to exploring the mechanics of the control of chloroform. "It is tempting to call this mode of work 'serial tasking,'" says Johnson,

> in the sense that the projects rotate one after the other, but emphasizing the serial nature of the work obscures one crucial aspect of this mental environment: in a slow multitasking mode, one project takes center stage for a series of hours or days, yet the other projects linger in the margins of consciousness throughout. That cognitive overlap is what makes this mode so innovative. The current project can exapt ideas from the projects at the margins, make new connections. It is not so much a question of thinking outside the box, as it is allowing the mind to move through multiple boxes.[10]

This describes a particular view of multidisciplinarity or transdisciplinarity, a view that sits at the epistemological center of Polymath University.

We sometimes think of multidisciplinarity to mean people of different disciplines working together. Or perhaps transdisciplinarity means the blurring of disciplinary boundaries such that new intellectual forms arise. Polymath University, in contrast to these, is grounded in traditional disciplines. The disciplines are stable foundations, and it is the individual mind that moves between them. The individual herself is multidisciplinary, moving from discipline to discipline to discipline. "That movement from box to box forces the mind to approach intellectual roadblocks from new angles, or to borrow tools from one discipline to solve problems in another."[11] The intellectual environment of Polymath University seeks to cultivate the ability of an individual mind to move from one disciplinary box to a completely different disciplinary box.

■   ■   ■

At Polymath University, the disciplines are at the center of the enterprise. Like atomic elements or prime numbers, the traditional disciplines are the roots from which all else is created. The disciplines are organized as idea spaces, which Richard Ogle defines as "a domain or world viewed from the perspective of the intelligence embedded in it, intelligence that we can use . . . both to solve our everyday problems and to make the creative leaps that lead to breakthrough."[12] Academic disciplines are idea spaces in that they "embed collective intelligence about the most effective way to carry out research, typically providing an overarching framework of established theory, principles, practices, heuristics, methodological assumptions, lab techniques, and so forth."[13] Gaining knowledge of a discipline means developing the habits of mind of that discipline. To learn history or engineering is to do more than learn a body of knowledge or even a set of skills but to learn *a particular way of thinking*.[14] The goal is for students to become immersed in the collective intelligence represented by the discipline, the idea space. The majors at Polymath University are designed such that in forty credit hours of instruction, students can demonstrate mastery of this collective intelligence.[15]

Because students are expected to master three separate disciplines, there is no room for general education requirements at Polymath University. The kinds of skills acquired through general education are dispersed among the three disciplines; indeed, thinking at the intersection of different disciplines is itself a model of general education. As Derek Bok conceded, taking even two introductory-level courses in one of the sciences is insufficient to develop any kind of deep knowledge of that subject. "Instead of acknowledging the underlying difficulty," he writes, "countless colleges have simply forged ahead and forced their students to satisfy a science requirement by taking introductory biology or physics or chemistry, even though everyone knows that such courses cannot possibly make undergraduates 'scientifically literate' in any meaningful sense or equip them to understand more than a very occasional issue of science policy."[16]

At best, students in a general education curriculum dabble in each discipline and as a result cannot truly "know" that field.[17] Polymath University is designed on the premise that while students might not have the kind of broad intellectual experience found in a typical general education program, they nevertheless receive a kind of breadth by immersion in three separate idea spaces and by examining the connections between them.[18]

■   ■   ■

As they master three different disciplines, students also develop the ability to move between different ways of thinking, resulting in flexible, creative minds. Students develop what Jeff Dyer, Hal Gregersen, and Clayton Christensen have called associating, or "the ability to make surprising connections across areas of knowledge, industries, even geographies."[19] Associating is a natural result of students' deep immersion in divergent disciplines. Indeed, "innovative ideas flourish at the intersection of diverse experience. . . . Throughout history, great ideas have emerged from these crossroads of culture and experience. . . . The more diverse our crossroads of experience, the more likely a serendipitous synthesis of the surprising will occur. Put simply, innovators intentionally maneuver themselves into the intersection, where diverse experiences flourish and foster the discovery of new insights."[20] In their final capstone experiences, students seek to demonstrate an instance of this "serendipitous synthesis of the surprising." While they are learning each different discipline's habits of thinking, they are simultaneously working at the intersections of those disciplines, which Frans Johansson describes as the place where different fields meet: "When you step into an intersection of fields, disciplines, or cultures, you can combine existing concepts into a large number of extraordinary new ideas."[21] Students at Polymath University thus engage in two types of thinking. "The key difference between a field and an intersection of fields lies in how concepts within them are combined. If you operate within a field, you primarily are able to combine concepts within that particular field, generating ideas that evolve along a particular direction—what I call directional ideas. When you step into the intersection, you can combine concepts between multiple fields, generating ideas that leap in new directions—what I call intersectional ideas."[22] The generation of both directional and intersectional ideas—by both students and faculty—are key epistemological outcomes of Polymath University.

Being able to bridge two different domains often involves analogical reasoning; when we wonder how two disparate disciplines might be integrated and connected together, a useful route to follow might be analogical. Analogical reasoning "typically involves not analysis, but rather the imaginative and insightful transfer of whole patterns of knowledge from a familiar domain to one whose structure and character are less well defined, for the sake of making sense and thus creating new understanding."[23] Thinkers who are accustomed to shifting between disciplines are thus trained to leap out of familiar habits of mind into new idea spaces. "Creative leaps arise," observes Ogle, "from the imaginative and insightful transfer of powerful, externally embedded intelligence from one idea-space to another."[24] He imagines creative thinkers who are able to move from idea space to idea space, bringing concepts from one into another. He describes James Watson and Francis Crick as two scientists "whose confident imaginations and sharp intuitions enable[d] them to connect the dots by leaping from one idea-space to another without getting trapped in any single one."[25] Students at Polymath University learn to leap easily between idea spaces. "Creative leaps arise not from exclusively internal operations of the individual mind (genius or otherwise)," concludes Ogle, "but from navigating the idea-spaces of the smart world we have built for ourselves; locating the powerful, structured forms of intelligence embedded in them; and analogically transferring these to new spaces."[26] Indeed, some learning theorists contend that this transfer of knowledge is the very definition of learning. "Such transfer occurs in its most cognitively valuable forms when students draw on something they learned in one context, ideally by generalizing its core principles, and apply it appropriately to a situation that is far different from the original."[27] Because they are asked to transfer concepts and ideas between three disparate areas of knowledge, students at Polymath University learn to become flexible and creative interdisciplinary thinkers.[28]

■ ■ ■

We may gain some insight into what Polymath University might look like by examining the experiences of students who are double majoring at their current institutions, especially those that Richard Pitt and Steven Tepper refer to as "spanners." Their research indicates that students

> taking courses in one major that differs at least to some extent from a second major in terms of the nature and uses of knowledge challenges students to accommodate and use different approaches toward understanding, discovering, and problem solving. This, in turn, should result in more opportunities for students to cultivate a capacity for deep, integrative learning—which is manifested, among other ways, as a) attending to the underlying meaning of information as well as content, b) integrating and synthesizing different ideas and sources of information, c) discerning patterns in evidence or phenomena, d) applying knowledge in different situations, and e) viewing issues from multiple perspectives.[29]

The psychologist and education researcher Anthony Biglan developed a matrix for the characteristics of disciplines, with axes representing a continuum between "pure" and "applied" disciplines and "hard" and "soft" disciplines. For example, in his matrix, some "hard-applied" disciplines are agriculture, engineering, and computer science, which "focus on using knowledge for problem solving and developing products and technologies." The "soft-pure" disciplines include literature, psychology, and sociology, which are distinguished by their concern "with particular cases and holistic analysis, favoring breadth of intellectual ideas, creativity, and expression." In Biglan's matrix, as described by Pitt and Tepper, the fields that are diagonal to each other represent the greatest disciplinary spans, such that "students double majoring in a soft-applied discipline, such as dance, along with a hard-pure discipline, such as physics, would encounter very different kinds of knowledge and would be expected to use different analytical approaches to understand

and apply knowledge."[30] I have modified this matrix for the purpose of thinking about the triple majors at Polymath University. In my schematic, the disciplines are divided into three groups: the professions, sciences and social sciences, and arts and humanities (although the categories of hard-pure, soft-pure, and so on help to inform these distinctions). Students select one major from each of the three columns.

Professions	Sciences/ social sciences	Arts and humanities
accounting	physics	history
engineering	chemistry	English
business	sociology	philosophy
education	political science	art
finance	astronomy	religious studies
architecture	biology	theater

While the students surveyed by Pitt and Tepper are exclusively double majors, I chose to structure Polymath University around triple majors for the complexity it would unleash. Double majors, even spanning two very different disciplines, might encourage a kind of dualistic thinking. Integrating the idea spaces of three majors produces a kind of complexity comparable to three-body problems in physics, mitigating the more simple dualisms of double majors.

The mash-up of three different ways of knowing is intended to produce a student who thinks creatively and generates new ideas. Spanners self-report that "their double major combination helps them think differently, solve intellectual puzzles, and approach assignments more creatively. These gains are greatest when students major in two disparate domains of knowledge, especially combining science with art and humanities."[31] One student, a mathematics and French double major, claimed that her double major made her feel as if she were crossing C. P. Snow's "two cultures."[32]

Crossing the disciplinary boundaries between art and science is an important part of the approach used by David Edwards at Le Laboratoire, the activities of which would be welcome at Polymath University. "When I speak of art," writes Edwards,

> I . . . refer to an aesthetic method, by which I mean a process of thought that is guided by images, is sensual and intuitive, often thrives in uncertainty, is "true" in that it seems to reflect or elucidate or interpret what we experience in our lives, and is expressive of nature in its complexity. . . . When I speak of science, I . . . refer to a scientific method, by which I mean a process of thought that is guided by quantification, is analytical, deductive, conditional on problem definition, is "true" in that it is repeatable, is expressive of nature in its simplicity.[33]

Edwards defines art and science in terms of the habits of thought that characterize each, not as specific subject matter or the content of disciplinary knowledge. His Laboratoire encourages the fusion of these idea spaces. "The fused method that results," concludes Edwards, "at once aesthetic and scientific—intuitive and deductive, sensual and analytical, comfortable with uncertainty and able to frame a problem, embracing nature in its complexity and able to simplify to nature in its essence—is what I call *artscience*."[34] By adding one more category of thought to the mix, faculty and students at Polymath University explore "applied artscience."

While not using the term "applied artscience," students who double major often express a similar kind of cognitive development. One student double majoring in economics and philosophy reported, "I think it definitely makes me more creative in the sense that I am better at drawing connections between subjects or disciplines that seem very different from each other. I am able to get some interesting ideas at intersections between very dissimilar fields."[35] The effect of triple majoring is meant to be greater than simply exploring, for example, the "philosophy of economics." What I am referring to here is the connections between one way of thinking and another. What are the intersections between thinking like an economist and thinking like a philosopher? How might those idea spaces intersect, and with what emergent effects?

A student double majoring in biomedical engineering and electrical engineering reported, "In an audio engineering class about speakers and microphones, I can ask questions about how the ear works; in my visual systems class, I can ask good questions about the biological aspects of the eye."[36] This student is practicing a form of knowledge integration or bridging between disciplines: asking questions common to one discipline that have been hitherto unasked in other disciplines. Importing questions from one discipline into another is a kind of domain bridging. A math-sociology student reported, "Because my majors are so different I have the ability to be creative and see things in different ways. Having two majors makes you more confident *using one set of ideas in a different context*" (emphasis mine).[37] That is the very definition of domain bridging and is a key outcome of an education at Polymath University.

Rather than cocooning with like-minded people, spanners create connections with cognitively different people. "As further evidence that double majors get exposed to more diverse classmates," note Pitt and Tepper, "62% report that their double major combination 'expands their opportunities to interact with people who are different from them.' And, importantly, this benefit is greater for those who chose majors in different disciplines."[38] Scott Page has convincingly demonstrated that groups composed of people from different backgrounds perform at least as well as lone geniuses at creative problem solving.[39] While not about problem solving per se and while focused on developing an interdisciplinary mindset in a single individual, an education at Polymath University is beneficial because of the cognitive diversity it encourages.[40]

Spanners often find themselves "toggling" between their two majors. Such mental switching between different frames of mind is a desirable and expected learning outcome but must be cautiously and deliberately managed. One student majoring in theater and physics enthused that double majoring made him feel more creative: "Absolutely, just because I'm never stuck in one frame of mind, because I'm always switching back and forth between the two."[41] But while some students find this toggling exhilarating, others express frustrations with such switching. One student in art and linguistics lamented, "I can't be completely immersed in art because linguistics involves reading theoretical texts and really hard analytic stuff that takes you out of the artistic frame of mind and I can't really be immersed completely in either of them."[42] This needs closer scrutiny. Students might benefit from a support system that would help them with the difficulties of immersion that this student identifies. Here, the transadvisor would play an especially important role, although faculty from different disciplines—themselves polymathic thinkers—also mentor students at Polymath University. Because mental toggling is one of the attributes of a student of Polymath University, such support is absolutely critical, unless the student were to discover that such mental switching is outside their abilities. It is precisely the goal of Polymath University to develop students with the cognitive flexibility to move between three different frames of mind.

Pitt and Tepper describe how, for a variety of reasons, students might "identify" more with one major than another. When describing their majors to friends and family, sometimes the perceived status or job potential of one major places it ahead of the other. Sometimes, institutional structures—as when job applications only leave room for one major—mean that these students must decide which major to list at the expense of the other. At Polymath University, part of the education, and especially part of the role of the transadvisor, is to help students "identify" with all three majors, to construct an identity that holds all three majors in equal status, and to be able to communicate that identity to the wider world. "When asked why they choose to double major, the second most popular reason, behind only 'better preparation for work,' was because the two majors together best represent who they 'really are,'" note Pitt and Tepper.[43]

■   ■   ■

Examining the self-reporting of double majors indicates the potential challenges Polymath University might need to confront to achieve its learning objectives. Pitt and Tepper contend, "Many traditional age undergraduates are not yet capable of making such choices [to double major] on their own." They "point to this limitation in reporting the inability of many students to describe cogently how their two majors intersect and how their combination of majors reflects their goals and aspirations."[44] One reason suggested for this inability is that there are few institutional structures in place in today's colleges and universities to help guide students into seeing and making these connections.

Polymath University is built with this infrastructure firmly in place: for example, the central and important role of transadvisors is one scaffold of this infrastructure. Further, faculty are selected for their polymathic orientation, for it is often the case that disciplinary-based faculty in traditional universities present some of the more formidable challenges to encouraging double majors.[45] "To increase the likelihood that students will use the opportunities presented in two majors," argue Pitt and Tepper, "faculty members in the respective fields must be intentional about designing assignments that require students to draw on concepts from both."[46] Their study suggests that faculty competition is often a cause for this lack of integration between the majors of spanning students.[47]

One student reported that when she was working on integrative projects, faculty asserted the primacy of one method or disciplinary approach over the other. The student, an industrial relations and French double major, recounted a meeting with one of her faculty advisors. "I told her that these are the variables I want to use and my French advisor was like, 'we don't do that.' So you have to find a middle ground."[48] A condition for receiving tenure at Polymath University is that faculty demonstrate that they see the connections between disciplines as being as important as the disciplinary anchors.

Integrative activities and outcomes are as important as any evaluations in the disciplinary majors. Faculty are expected to mentor students to think integratively, which means that faculty themselves are integrative. The assumption at Polymath University is that faculty across disciplines are working and communicating together: "Such projects should be supervised jointly by faculty in each student's home majors. Faculty should meet together early in the project with students to discuss how to meet the expectations of both disciplines."[49] Here, the transadvisor plays a critical role, not only as a person working closely with the student to integrate disparate idea spaces, but as a mediator and translator between the disciplines. At Polymath University, faculty certainly do not privilege one discipline over another—one way of thinking over another—in their interactions with students.

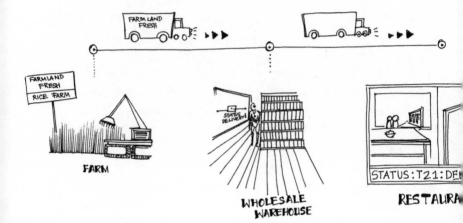

FARM

WHOLESALE
WAREHOUSE

RESTAURA

Future University

Future University attracts futurists, strategists, visionaries, activists, thought leaders, entrepreneurs, dreamers, and others who wish to act ahead of their time. Future University produces students who see the consequences of their decisions made in the present, students who work to create the future.

The curriculum at Future University is divided into pure and applied futuring, and so it is both a liberal arts and a vocationally oriented university. Pure futuring involves exploring the future as a possibility space, like pure mathematics. Students create and explore possible worlds. There are no other applications of the knowledge gained from such an exploration, aside from the beauty of the forms produced. Applied futuring involves the exploration of the future for practical ends, such as developing corporate strategy, visionary entrepreneurship, or social activism. Applied futuring means not just studying the future, but making the future happen. Students matriculating from Future University balance both approaches.

These two approaches are dispersed among four colleges or divisions:

Scenarios and systems. Systems thinking is the core of this division, which seeks to understand how the components of a system interact and the complex behaviors that emerge from such systems. Students learn the history of a number of types of systems: social and cultural, technological, economic, environmental, and geopolitical. By understanding how systems have behaved in the past, students project how systems might behave in the future. Students receive a grounding in chaos and complexity theory in order to better understand the behavior of systems.

In business schools, the case study is the central pedagogical instrument. The case study is based on the idea that by examining how companies made previous decisions, we can learn from their triumphs and mistakes as we make choices in the present. At Future University, students and faculty explore the idea that the scenario—a story about the future, a description of a future system—is a way to learn and to make decisions in the present. Students also learn other techniques used by futurists for anticipating trends to determine possible futures, such as environment scanning, cross-impact analysis, and trend identification, analysis, and extrapolation.

Design fiction. Design fiction uses the thought processes of designers to imagine, explore, and critique the future. It explores the implications of a scenario for the purpose of critiquing it. Design fiction is also a type of scenario building, only rather than a written narrative, the scenario is explored through the making of objects, in effect materializing the scenario. The objects created through this process are embedded in narratives, and students learn to convey narratives through the design of objects.

Platforming. Research by faculty at Future University may involve platforming: building a new future system within the space of the university. At its simplest, such a platform might be created in order to design new products or services, a kind of skunkworks inside the university. In this sense, Future University looks like a tech incubator, but the platforms extend far beyond developing new technologies and businesses: platforms incubate new social forms. That is, the larger cultural, social, and economic environment is part of the technological platform. Researchers explore how a given technology will affect the larger system. How will the device alter society? Platforms are like pockets of the future, even including utopian communities. A platform might involve the prototyping of a new system of social relations or a new economic system. A platform might experiment with a small society with a guaranteed minimum income for all residents. Grounded in trend analysis, systems thinking, and other forms of futures research, these platforms begin as mini-utopias, incubated in the university. Decisions are then made about whether and how they might be then set free in the world. Students even—cautiously—platform dystopias, and they explore other questions, such as the ethics and responsibilities of platform development. Faculty at Future University establish platforms as evidence of their research: they construct the future. Platforms are visions of the future and are a part of the training of visionaries.

Science fiction. The *Star Trek* series and other science fiction accounts often serve as inspirations for engineers and designers to devise new technologies. Students watch movies and television shows and read the literature of science fiction not only as exercises in pure futuring but also to understand how and why these authors and directors predicted the futures they did. Students also engage in science fiction prototyping: they compose their own science fiction accounts to explore the implications of technology.

General education at Future University is based on the qualities of mind exhibited by superforecasters. In addition to discipline-based courses, students take courses that develop specific attributes, such as caution and humility. Curiosity, introspection, and an actively open mind are some results of this curriculum, as are an analytic, pragmatic, and synthetic view of problem solving. Above all, the cultivation of imagination is critical for students and faculty at Future University. "Imagination" refers to the ability to picture images or ideas or concepts that are not available to be directly sensed; students at Future University are encouraged through their coursework and their platforming projects to develop this important facility. They hone their situational awareness—to better appreciate how and when change might occur—to better envision, encourage, and create the future.

■   ■   ■

The futurist Amy Webb defines the study of the future as "an interdisciplinary field combining mathematics, engineering, art, technology, economics, design, history, geography, biology, theology, physics, and philosophy."[1] At present, futuring is a practitioner-driven field more than an academic discipline, although there are several European universities that offer degree programs in foresight and futuring. As Webb's definition suggests, the training and preparation of a futurist requires knowledge from several disciplines. Future University expands the interdisciplinary boundaries of this field to encompass the entirety of the university. Given its breadth, the study of the future provides a framework for how the disciplines are organized and knitted together. At Future University, all of the disciplines we see at traditional universities are employed, although they are organized such that each is oriented toward the pursuit of the future.

Futurists do not make predictions. "As a futurist," says Webb, "my job is not to spread prophecies, but rather to collect data, identify emerging trends, develop strategies, and calculate the probabilities of various scenarios occurring in the future. Forecasts are used to help leaders, teams, and individuals make better, more informed decisions, even as their organizations face great disruption."[2] Students at Future University are taught to think in scenarios—and to be clear, a scenario is not the same as a prediction. A prediction assumes a kind of certainty about the future and also assumes that the future already exists someplace, waiting for the futurist to identify, discover, or invent it. When we make a prediction, we often say, "Such and such *will* happen." A scenario, on the other hand, is a narrative or a story about a possible future and comes with the assumption that other scenarios—other possible futures—are just as likely to occur. Peter Schwartz, one of the leading practitioners of the scenario method of planning, says, "Scenarios are stories about the way the world might turn out tomorrow, stories that can help us recognize and adapt to changing aspects of our present environment."[3]

As Kees van der Heijden explains, scenarios of the future have much in common with the narratives of the past created by historians:

> Stories about the future are in a way historical accounts but seen from a future perspective. They explain how the world has ended up in a future end-state, by a causal train of events, linking back to the well-known present. Scenarios make sense of future events in the same way as historical accounts make sense of the past. They provide the business planner with a flexible means to connect disparate data together into holistic pictures of the future, providing the context and meaning of possible developments. If they are carefully constructed, causal accounts of future events opera-

tionalize the insights gained, so that they can be used for drawing inferences and conclusions. (The historian may not have the same degree of
flexibility as the scenario writer, although here also there is considerable
scope for selective choice of events and of pattern inference[.]).[4]

Like historical accounts, scenarios are the product of research and
considered thought. "In a scenario process," says Schwartz, "managers
invent and then consider, in depth, several varied stories of equally
plausible futures. The stories are carefully researched, full of relevant
detail, oriented toward real-life decisions, and designed (one hopes)
to bring forward surprises and unexpected leaps of understanding."
Scenarios are "a tool for ordering one's perceptions about alternative
future environments in which one's decisions might be played out."[5]

Scenarists maintain that developing such stories allows one to
rehearse the future, to envision a world in which one will make decisions and to explore the consequences of those decisions under various
conditions. Schwartz asks, "How can you see, most clearly, the environment in which your actions will take place, and how those actions
will fit with (or stand against) the prevailing forces, trends, attitudes
and influences?"[6] The futurist Bob Johansen notes that "foresight is,
essentially, the ability to sense what could happen before it happens,
the ability to identify innovation opportunities."[7] Thus, scenarios are
of value for those who plan for the future, from corporate strategists
to entrepreneurs to social activists. At Future University, the scenario,
the story of the future, is the unit of discourse for all students.

Students create and explore scenarios for both pure and applied
reasons. Studying the future so as to make informed decisions in the
present is one applied goal. In devising scenarios, entrepreneurs learn
to imagine new markets and new opportunities. Social activists create
scenarios of preferred futures and learn techniques for bringing about
a future of social justice or wise environmental stewardship. Students
are also encouraged to create scenarios as warnings to the present; they
employ the future as a rhetorical device to influence perceptions and
decisions in the present. But students are also encouraged to create

scenarios for no other reason than the sheer pleasure in devising a world to be explored: pure futuring. The future, in this formulation, is a possibility space. In the same way a pure mathematician explores a possibility space for the beauty of the forms so discovered, scenarists at Future University create stories of the future for no other reason than intellectual curiosity. Future University is both liberal arts and vocationally oriented.

■ ■ ■

Scenarios are not predictions because a scenario is only one possible future. Indeed, it is typical for a scenarist to think in terms of multiple scenarios, each a story of the different paths the future might take. Scenario thinking is grounded in systems thinking. "A system," says Donella Meadows, "is a set of things—people, cells, molecules, or whatever—interconnected in such a way that they produce their own pattern of behavior over time. The system may be buffeted, constricted, triggered, or driven by outside forces. But the system's response to these forces is characteristic of itself, and that response is seldom simple in the real world. . . . A system is an interconnected set of elements that is coherently organized in a way that achieves something. . . . A system must consist of three kinds of things: *elements*, *interconnections*, and a *function* or *purpose*."[8]

Many systems are self-organizing, and because of their complex interconnections and feedback loops their future behavior is not easily predicted. This has been one of the key insights of complexity theory: because of sensitivity to initial conditions and their interactions and feedback loops, complex systems are inherently unpredictable. The future behavior of a complex system could traverse along any number of paths. It is the interconnections and their self-organizing behavior that make many systems complex, nonlinear, and therefore unpredictable. Scenarios are one way to capture or to make sense of such complex systems. A scenario, in this formulation, is a description of one potential state of a system, and each subsequent scenario describes other potential states a system might exhibit. Indeed, when we say that we are interested in the future, what we usually mean is we seek to understand what the state of some system will be at point n in the future. It might be more correct, therefore, to call this institution "Complex Systems University," since one of its main goals is to produce graduates who understand and can operate in a world with a variety of interacting complex systems.

Complex systems are made up a wide variety of components, and their interactions produce unpredictable behaviors. It is insufficient, therefore, to look at a technology in isolation from the larger social, economic, environmental, and political contexts in which it will be embedded. Students at Future University learn that any new technology resides within a complex ecology; as Neil Postman once observed, subtracting caterpillars from an ecosystem does not mean you now have the same ecosystem minus caterpillars. The ecosystem has been altered, creating in effect a new ecosystem.[9] New technologies, similarly, alter the social, cultural, and environmental ecosystems, and to anticipate the future implications of any new technology one must consider the complex effects on the larger ecosystems. At the same time, future changes to social systems arise from more than simply technology: change can arise from alterations to the social, economic, or political elements of any complex system. It is for this reason that aspiring futurists at Future University must have a broad education across a number of domains.

■   ■   ■

To develop a breadth of interest in many areas, futurists need to be curious. To be curious means wanting to explore something for no other reason than that it is interesting.[10] Future University naturally attracts those who are curious, but it also serves to enhance their curiosity. Classes emphasize the removal of information filters—not in terms of the source of the information (learning to spot and avoid fake news) but in terms of the content. It has been said that the futurist Buckminster Fuller claimed that when he was flying somewhere he would always purchase a magazine that he had never read before, open to the possibility of new kinds of information, new ways of looking at the world. Those whose only sources of information come from business magazines, say, see the world through this constricted lens. Learning to remove information filters is one of the first skills taught at Future University, since information filters can limit our environment-scanning gaze. As an exercise, students are encouraged to inventory their sources of information about the world. By becoming aware of their sources, they are better able to see their information filters. Thus, a student might realize that they read only the *Financial Times*, the *Wall Street Journal*, and *Bloomberg Businessweek*. They are then expected to expand what they read to include, perhaps, *Quanta Magazine* (on the frontiers of science and mathematics), *MIT Technology Review* (for developments in university and industrial labs), and *Adbusters* (for ideas and attitudes among anticapitalist activists).

One expression of curiosity is environment scanning, which is one of the pivotal skills imparted at Future University. Environment scanning means seeking and absorbing data from the larger external environment, looking for emerging trends and drivers. The science fiction writer William Gibson is said to have claimed that the future is already here, just not evenly distributed. Environment scanning seeks portents of the future, and in order to identify these futurists scan widely across a number of domains. The acronym STEEP best organizes these scans: futurists seek information about society and culture, technology, the economy, the environment, and (geo)politics. Because futurists must understand systems, how they behave, and how they might change in the future, students at Future University learn about the history of a number of civilizations, societies, and cultures. If they want to understand the future of China, for instance, students need some grounding in the history of that ancient civilization. Histories of culture, society, technology, economics, and politics form an important part of the curriculum. In the realm of geopolitics, for example, George Friedman from the consultancy Stratfor argues that states have stable interests, and he builds his predictions for the future of geostrategy around this assumption. To understand these strategic interests and to therefore understand potential futures in geopolitics, students take classes in global affairs and political economy.[11] Futurists also display cross-cultural literacy and are deeply familiar with at least one other culture than their own, as expressed by fluency in the chief language.[12] Students take courses in a range of social science disciplines, especially political science, economics, anthropology, psychology, and sociology.

In order to identify potential drivers of change, students also take courses in science and technology, with a focus especially on emerging developments in a number of areas. That is, students achieve a survey-level understanding of key directions in each field. They demonstrate the "widest possible knowledge of current and emerging developments in the natural sciences, and their emerging subdisciplines and transdisciplines" as well as a wide knowledge of issues related to "energy, water, food, demographics and climate change." With regard to technology, students learn about "developments in engineering architecture, and space sciences."[13] Students do not become bioengineers, but they are taught something about CRISPR; they do not major in mechanical engineering, but they are taught something about autonomous vehicles.

General education at Future University includes broad introductions to the social sciences; to economics, management, entrepreneurship, and leadership; to law, planning, and design. Students gain the "widest possible familiarity with philosophy, ethics, morals, and religions, and certainly the ethical discourse of as many different traditions as possible."[14] All of the traditional disciplines are represented at Future University, and students are expected to explore them. The disciplines are studied in the service of understanding systems and how they function, which aids in understanding their future direction.

The elements of complex systems derive from a wide variety of sources—from economics to law to the humanities—and all of these elements interact. This interaction of widely disparate elements is part of what makes systems complex. A technological change potentially yields a host of alterations to society, the economy, and geopolitics. Similarly, the effects of a technology are shaped by society, the economy, and geopolitics. Examining the creation of a technology alone is insufficient to understand how a future system might unfold. Therefore, general education introduces students to a wide variety of disciplines in order to aid environment scanning and to gain the widest possible understanding of how complex systems function.

■   ■   ■

General education develops the attributes of what Philip Tetlock and Dan Gardner have called "superforecasters," those with demonstrably proven achievements in accurate prediction. Superforecasters are not always experts in a domain, yet they often beat experts' predictions in certain defined cases. The attributes and characteristics of superforecasters include being

- cautious: nothing is certain
- humble: reality is infinitely complex
- nondeterministic: what happens is not meant to be and does not have to happen

In their thinking styles, they tend to be

- actively open-minded: beliefs are hypotheses to be tested, not treasures to be protected
- intelligent and knowledgeable with a need for cognition: intellectually curious, enjoying puzzles and mental challenges
- reflective: introspective and self-critical
- numerate: comfortable with numbers

In their methods of forecasting, they tend to be

- pragmatic: not wedded to any idea or agenda
- analytical: capable of stepping back from their own views and considering other views
- dragonfly-eyed: valuing diverse views and synthesizing them into their own
- probabilistic: they judge using many grades of maybe
- thoughtful updaters: when facts change, they change their minds
- good intuitive psychologists: aware of the value of checking their thinking for cognitive and emotional biases

In their work ethic, they tend to have

- a growth mind-set: believing it is possible to get better
- grit: determined to keep at it, however long it takes[15]

General education classes—and the other courses taught at Future University—seek to inculcate these habits of mind in all students.

■ ■ ■

Sense-making is an important attribute of this education. After students have acquired data and information from the environment, they engage in implications assessments, where they infer and project the potential effects of that data. When they encounter a piece of information via environment scanning, they are taught to ask "What might this mean?" For example, doctors have discovered a new strain of pneumonia that is resistant to drugs, is highly infectious, and does not discriminate (the young and healthy are as much at risk as are the very young and old). "In the past three decades, two types of *K. pneumoniae* have appeared in hospitals," reports NPR. "The first is a drug-resistant form, called CRE, which can fight off even the toughest antibiotics. Last January [2017], this type of pneumonia killed a woman in Nevada. That strain resisted 26 antibiotics. The second type of *K. pneumoniae* causes a very severe form of the disease and is known as 'hypervirulent. . . .' For years, doctors feared the two types would one day combine. And now that it has happened, scientists around the world need to be on alert for these triple-threat strains."[16] What does the appearance of this hypervirulent strain mean? Could this lead to a global pandemic, such as the Spanish flu of 1918–1919? What would be the effects globally? How would it impact the global security situation? What would be the economic effects? The public health field is more sophisticated and there are more practitioners than in 1918. Might those factors mitigate the spread of the disease? People travel more frequently and more globally than they did a century ago. Might this accelerate its spread? Learning how to perform implications assessments of the data, identified through expansive environment scanning, is an important skill developed at Future University.

Of necessity, students at Future University have well-developed imaginations. Far from being viewed as kids' play, imagination is a habit of mind actively cultivated as part of general education and a key attribute in order to create scenarios and to anticipate the future behavior of complex systems. "Cognition requires in each of us the capacity to run scenarios," says Peter Murphy, "to think about alternatives, to model situations based on assumptions, and then to change the assumptions. To think 'what if?' and to plan 'if, then' requires imagination."[17] Imagination in this sense means the ability to mentally project change onto an aspect of space and time, to be able to look at a system and visualize it differently. Question posing is a highly valued skill, and what-if questions are especially encouraged. Students learn to ask "What if students no longer demand higher education?" or "What if the TED model becomes a new way to deliver higher education?" and imagine scenarios that are answers to such questions. Students might be asked to visualize a business environment: a specific business, its customers, its competitors, the general economic environment, and the regulatory regime. To this imagined system, they are asked to add something, a disruptive technology, say, and then determine how the system might be altered. This exercise occurs in the imagination, in the mind's eye. Students at Future University learn techniques and habits of mind for conducting such thought experiments as a central feature of their general education.

■   ■   ■

The curriculum offers courses on a variety of futuring techniques, including cross-impact analysis, Delphi methods, expert interviews, nominal focus groups, and trend analysis.[18] But just as important, students learn strategies for avoiding what the futurist Stephen Millett terms "anti-thinking": mental crutches that we too easily or unreflectively rely on when addressing a problem.[19] While the ideal learning outcome is its elimination, the more realistic outcome is to have students develop a self-awareness of antithinking in order to identify and avoid it. Examples of antithinking include appeals to tradition, convention, or social norms. Rather than unquestionably stating that "this is the way it has always been done," the futurist learns to challenge traditions and conventions in order to imagine new possibilities. Students are taught to identify their own ideological thinking—where ideology is defined as a state of mind in which the answers are known before the questions have been asked—and see how it might bias their thinking or unnecessarily filter their information gathering. Appeals to constitutions, laws, rules, and regulations concentrate thinking solely on what is allowed—by authorities, by society—to be done.

Imitation means merely copying rather than generating new or divergent ideas. Benchmarking—a staple of organizational practice made popular by the Six Sigma method—is a kind of imitation that identifies and copies best practices from some other organization. Fear and anger, confusion and panic similarly blind us to reality or prevent us from seeing what is possible. Myths and stereotypes shroud our perceptions of the behavior of others and of ourselves. Certainty is another antithinking attribute that students address. Especially when faced with the complexity of systems and how they might behave in the future, belief in the certainty of specific outcomes blinds the futurist to the mere probability of their occurrence and thus to the equal likelihood of alternative scenarios. To have certainty is to exhibit a kind of mental brittleness; one's worldview is easily shattered when events unfold along a different trajectory. Acceptance of and comfort with uncertainty and the mental flexibility it promotes is a key part of this curriculum.

All of these efforts to combat antithinking leave the student better equipped to confront reality. Many CEOs fail at their jobs because they fail to confront the reality that surrounds them, whether that means problems within or threats from outside their organizations. Identifying and confronting their own anti-thinking prepares futurists to better confront reality and to better anticipate what will be next.[20] These approaches are taught via a series of mini-courses, not fifteen-week semester-long courses. They are also identified and exercised in all coursework at Future University and are practiced as part of platforming projects.

■ ■ ■

Scenarios are often about understanding systems that we cannot influence, but scenarios are also employed as a tool for visioning, for imagining a preferred future. Students engage in an idealized design process at some point in their time at Future University. Idealized design involves imagining "what the ideal solution would be and then work[ing] backward to where you are today."[21] That is, rather than devising a scenario based on trend projection and a consideration of how systems might react under various conditions, students first devise a scenario that describes the ideal or preferred future. Then, they work backward to the present, determining what conditions have to exist in order for that ideal condition to prevail. For example, students might devise a scenario where all fossil fuel use has been eliminated globally by 2035. That is the preferred state, but then students need to determine the conditions that would bring this preferred state about. First, all alternative sources of fuel would need to be identified and implemented across a number of energy platforms, from home heating to transportation. How would homes be converted to alternative energy use? What further steps would need to occur? Alternatives to the internal combustion engine would need to be in place. What steps would need to occur? How would such a global regulation be implemented? Under whose authority? Would nations be this authority? Perhaps it would be multinational corporations or international organizations like the United Nations that would promulgate and enforce these regulations. Working backward from a preferred future means exploring highly complex systems with many interacting elements. The resulting reverse-engineering project yields a roadmap or account of how to bring about desired change, all the while exposing the complex sets of decisions and actions that would need to occur. "Getting all nations to agree to a binding UN declaration" may prove to be a necessary step to bringing about the idealized future, and that step is itself a complex—insurmountable?—process. Students learn from this process not only how to manage the drivers of change but how to identify and challenge the blockers of change. Idealized design projects can be helpful to entrepreneurs seeking to develop the latest app and to activists seeking to bring about social justice.

■   ■   ■

Students also employ design fiction as a way to imagine scenarios.[22] Design fiction is similar to scenario building in the level of research involved and the understanding of the behaviors of complex systems, but rather than a written narrative, the scenario is explored through the making and prototyping of objects: "materializing ideas and specula-tions" in the words of designer Julian Bleecker. The design fiction process produces "objects with stories. These are stories that speculate about new, different, distinctive social practices that assemble around and through these objects. Design fictions help tell stories that provoke and raise ques-tions. Like props that help focus the imagination and speculate about possible near future worlds—whether profound change or simple, even mundane social practices."[23] For example, the Museum of Capitalism in Oakland is a design fiction space that imagines a world after capitalism. "Visitors will be invited to reflect on capitalism as if looking back at it from a world in which capitalism is dead."[24] This is a space filled with speculative objects of a world after capitalism.

A related discipline is science fiction prototyping, where students write short fiction or produce a movie or compose a comic book "based specifically on a science fact for the purpose of exploring the implica-tions, effects and ramifications of that science or technology," says Brian David Johnson. "[Science fiction] prototypes let us imagine the future, to think through the ethical implications of technologies, play with possible benefits, explore possible tragedies and ultimately engage in a deeper conversation about science, technology and our future."[25] Students produce four such design or science fiction projects over their four years at Future University. These can either be material forms of scenarios they have already written or different scenarios exploring a new topic. While learning from the future, students gain the added benefit of developing design skills and habits of mind.

■ ■ ■

As evidence of their learning and as a condition of matriculation, students participate in a large platforming project. These projects also form the major part of the faculty members' research portfolios. A platform is, in effect, an enacted scenario. Most of the scenarios produced at Future University are written documents or physical objects, as are those that are produced via design fiction. A platform, on the other hand, is a kind of living laboratory, where the scenario is scaled to a societal level. At one level, a platform is a kind of immersive scenario; as Bob Johansen writes, "the best organizations will provide simulation gaming or other low-risk immersion experiences to allow leaders to rehearse in preparation for the future."[26] These resemble Chautauqua experiences, although rather than involving actors portraying historical figures the enactors pretend to be residents of some future environment.

A platform takes this idea a step further, creating what amounts to a small pocket of the future within the university. The designer Tony Fry employs platforms as a way to bring about change in organizations; for him that means changes that make the organization more environmentally sustainable. "Platforming," he writes, "is a strategy that maintains existing economic activity and work culture, while building a new direction and products or services that are based on futuring" (in his sense of the word, meaning creating the conditions by which the self and a community have a future).

> The fundamental principle is simply that a change platform is built within an existing organization. This can take several forms, like a new shadow company within the company, or a new kind of research and development arm within it. These entities can be given seed support to initiate two transformative activities: (1) researching, designing and developing new products and services to contribute to a culture of sustainment and an economy based on advancing sustain-ability; and (2) delivering a continuous learning environment for those recruited to work on the platform

(which can create knowledge spilling over to the "parent" organization). The intent of the platform is to build sufficient critical mass and momentum to gradually displace the parent organization's existing activities.[27]

The platforms constructed at Future University extend far beyond any one organization and beyond issues of sustainability. They are social prototypes of the scenarios created by students. For example, an idealized future where fossil fuels have been eliminated globally is actually enacted at a small scale within the space of the platform. The platform is a working model with people and technologies and social, cultural, and economic relations interacting with each other in a living museum of the future. This is not a theoretical white paper or a computer simulation.

A platform might resemble a tech incubator, but the platform extends beyond developing new technologies and businesses: the platform incubates new social forms. If a new technology added to a social ecosystem changes that ecosystem, then the platform explores how the system might change, how a new social-cultural ecology might emerge. Students and faculty might develop the idea for autonomous vehicles and then create a mini-society in which such vehicles proliferate. The platform examines not simply the technical changes to infrastructure or to automobile production, but the social, cultural, and economic changes these technologies could bring about. Participants living in the platform viscerally experience a society in miniature where autonomous vehicles proliferate, and they describe their subjective personal experiences. In this way, Future University hosts a number of "platforms for experimentation, speculation, and the reimagining of everyday life."[28] Paola Antonelli, the senior curator of design at the Museum of Modern Art in New York, believes that "museums can become laboratories for rethinking society, places for showing not what already exists, but more important, what is yet to exist,"[29] and the platforms at Future University fulfill this objective. Unlike an incubator or skunkworks, the platforms at Future University explore changes to the larger cultural, social, and economic environment as a necessary part of the technological platform.

Future University thereby functions as a "prefigurative space," an environment "in which communities can model today how they might want to live with each other in future."[30] Keri Facer identifies this as an important function of the "future-building school." Students and faculty interested in bringing about beneficial social change, for example, create mini-societies based on social or redistributive justice. One platform might be a mini-society with a universal basic income (UBI) for each of its inhabitants. "The sorts of choice that [universities] make about their use of technology, for example, their attitude toward surveillance, towards technological and cognitive diversity, their use of data, the platforms they provide for encounters between different generations, the opportunities they create for participating in networked publics or democratic decision-making—all serve to model different ways of living and responding to socio-technical change." The creation of and participation in a prefigurative space is the capstone experience for students at Future University and is the expression of faculty research. Platforms are, perhaps more significantly, "important sites in which it is possible to model alternative socio-technical futures."[31]

As part of the platforming experience, faculty and students debate and decide whether their platform, their alternative model of a socio-technical future, is released to the world. A platform is, as Fry notes, a learning environment. Researchers might learn that a society under conditions of a UBI produces unforeseen or malevolent results; it might be discovered to exacerbate economic inequality. This conclusion can only be reached by actually experiencing—rather than theorizing or speculating—its effects. In this case, they would decide not to release the experiment to the rest of society. If a platform functions as a social incubator, then a key part of the exercise is exploring the ethics of alternative futures.

Students and faculty might also create working models of alternative universities, enacting some of the ideas presented in this book.

Conclusion

Existential Crisis and Existential Possibilities

Every week, it seems, another book, op-ed, or white paper appears lamenting "the crisis in higher education." This crisis literature can be organized along a continuum. At one end are the "system is broken" arguments. These authors contend that higher education is too expensive and leaves students with mountains of debt and questionable credentials. Universities are poorly managed and need to be organized more like businesses in order to become efficient and cost effective. Higher education is misaligned to workforce development needs. Mark C. Taylor proclaimed in 2010 that "the education bubble is about to burst. There are disturbing similarities between the dilemma colleges and universities have created for themselves and the conditions that led to the collapse of major financial institutions supposedly too secure to fail. The value of college and university assets (i.e., endowments) has plummeted. The schools are overleveraged, liabilities (debts) are increasing, liquidity is drying up, costs continue to climb, their product is increasingly unaffordable and of questionable value in the marketplace, and income is declining. This situation is not only unsustainable, but at a crisis point."[1] Jeffrey Docking, the president of Adrian College, is "worried about the plight of small liberal arts colleges in America. I am afraid many are going to run out of money, reach insolvency, fail the federal financial responsibility audit, . . . close their doors, or be swallowed up by large state universities as satellite campuses over the next several years."[2] Because of these systemic problems, higher education is ripe for disruption and is badly in need of innovation.

At the other pole are authors who contend that the system of higher education is in crisis because it has been wrecked by politicians, businesspeople, and the administrators who mimic their beliefs. They point to the ever-growing ranks of adjuncts and contingent faculty, the deple-tion of support for public higher education, and the unchecked growth of administrative bloat as examples of corporatism or neoliberal policies that are dismantling a once-great system of higher education. Frank Donoghue draws particular attention to the fate of tenured professors in the humanities and details the threats to their continued existence. "As we know them—autonomous, tenured, afforded the time to re-search and write as well as teach—professors have only been around for the last eighty years," he says. "The university is evolving in ways that make their continued presence unnecessary, even undesirable."[3] Tenured faculty do not fit well within the organizational practices of corporations, practices that are being mimicked by universities. "Pro-fessors will not become extinct per se; instead, they will be absorbed into broader categories of professionals and service workers."[4] Marc Bousquet says that the casualization of academic labor is the most immediate threat to the university and is explicitly tied to broader trends in the global labor market. For Bousquet, higher education lead-ership is complicit in a system of corporatization and managerialism. "For the professoriate as well as cabinetmakers, technological change is an opportunity for management to impose reductions in worker autonomy—so that for academic administration, the ultimate goal of technological deployment is to 'discipline, deskill and displace' the skilled faculty workforce, just as in any other labor circumstance."[5] The crisis of higher education is the depletion and casualization of the professoriate: "In thirty years of managed higher education, the typical faculty member has become a female nontenurable part-timer earning a few thousand dollars a year without health benefits. The typical administrator is male, enjoys tenure, a six-figure income, little or no teaching, generous vacations, and great health care."[6] Many of the writers in this camp blame the crisis of higher education squarely on the very innovators who are themselves calling the system broken.

Thus, at one side of this range are those who wish to introduce new approaches into the system of higher education, and at the other side are those who wish to return it to a previous state or, to put it another way, to protect higher education from the "innovators." At the extreme end of the continuum, beyond the system-is-broken pole, are those who say that the system should not be fixed or returned to a previous state, but should be eliminated altogether. For example, tech entrepreneur Peter Thiel began the Thiel Fellowship, which offers $100,000 for two years to young budding entrepreneurs to forgo college and instead create the next innovation. Thiel argues that higher education offers very little except a mountain of debt and a dubious credential.

"Edupunks" echo Thiel's claim that the university is indeed broken and is not worth fixing. Instead, they point to alternatives to the university—self-education or education from nontraditional sources—and say that the university should just be allowed to wither away. Dale J. Stephens, one of these edupunks, contends, "The systems and institutions that we see around us—of school, college, and work—are being systematically dismantled. We've seen a rise in the popularity of homeschooling and unschooling in the last ten years. . . . The same is true of the breakdown of traditional work—freelancing is becoming more and more prevalent. But no one has told the story of what happens in between, when that sacred institution we call the university ceases to exist."[7] The education journalist Anya Kamenetz has been reporting on this group of edupunks, who are turning away from traditional, formal higher education and toward more informal modes of learning and training. Noting that participation in organized religion has declined even as Americans continue to engage in spiritual practices, she wonders "if organized higher education could someday go the way of organized religion—not to disappear, by any means, not even to diminish in absolute size, but to cede its place at the very height of human thought and center of daily action."[8]

In 2017, Pew Research released the results of a survey that suggests that a majority of Republicans believe that higher education has a negative effect on the United States.[9] Republicans have for some time had a mistrust of higher education, but this is the first time a majority feels that way. (For their part, Democrats are the opposite and by a clear majority believe that higher education is good for the United States.)

These results do not suggest that Republicans feel that there should be no higher education, but when we couple these survey responses with comments made by politicians (from both sides of the aisle, it must be said) that only majors that lead directly to employment should be supported, we see a larger pattern: for the first time in decades, the belief that everyone who is willing and able should pursue higher education is being questioned. Many of these same politicians say that some young people should eschew college and train instead for a skilled trade. Perhaps the real existential threat to the university comes not from massive open online courses or adjunctification or neoliberal policies but from the growing view that we may not need universities at all.

■   ■   ■

There are any number of sources for the current crisis in higher education. Jon McGee identifies five issues that are driving discussions about the future of higher education: accessibility, as in who has access to higher education and who is excluded, especially from elite universities; affordability, the rising costs of higher education that are making it unaffordable and even risky for students to attain a degree, even if they have access; accountability, specifically the push for identifiable, measurable outcomes that would justify the expense, an issue that focuses on the "return on investment" of higher education; and sustainability, or the ability to generate or acquire the resources to carry out the mission of the university, especially in an era of diminished and diminishing state support for higher education.[10] But of all the issues fueling the current crisis, I find McGee's fifth point to be the most cogent: differentiation.

Higher education has become a commoditized industry. The term "commoditization" is usually used in reference to consumer goods becoming relatively indistinguishable from each other, competing on price more than on brand identification. Higher education can be said to be so commoditized. "As communication and mobility across universities increase and as rankings measure what is common," argues Mark William Roche, "the tendency arises for each college and university to adopt the best practices of the competition and thereby begin to resemble the institutions from which its faculty members have come and those college[s] and universities that rank more highly."[11] "With few exceptions," write Ben Wildavsky, Andrew Kelly, and Kevin Carey, colleges and universities "offer the same degrees in the same way, counting up the number of hours students are taught and adding them up to two- and four-year credentials. They hire people with similar pedigrees and organize them into the standard apparatus of academic departments. Teaching, tenure, and titling policies vary little from place to place. They field athletic teams, joust in obscure journals, and complain about overpaid administrators in much the same way, everywhere. All of this adds up to long-term stagnation and *a profound lack of imagination about the possibilities of change*" (emphasis mine).[12]

When MOOCs hit the scene in 2011, the University of Virginia and other universities did what is expected of them in such an environment: they rushed to copy what others were doing. MOOCs might have offered a competitive advantage, at least in the short term, until that moment when all colleges and universities quickly adopted them, at which stage commoditization reoccurred.

The lack of differentiation might just lie at the root of many of the other challenges facing higher education today. Jon McGee asks:

> How will colleges distinguish themselves and their value in the face of increasing commoditization? College has in many ways become a transactional good rather than a transformational good, a necessary experience to improve the chances of success and security in the new economy. Unfortunately, the images and messages most colleges and universities send to the marketplace make it difficult for families to meaningfully tell them apart—which fuels the rush to commoditization. Colleges and universities of all types too often try to describe or distinguish themselves using the same limited set of images and adjectives, which results in a homogenized presentation that describes all institutions as friendly, caring learning communities dedicated to academic excellence and the development of the whole person. Images of smiling faces, lush grounds and ivy, overlaid with indistinguishable taglines and similar turns of marketing phrase, litter

the mailboxes of prospective students everywhere. Me-too marketing is a perilous strategy in a commodity-driven marketplace.[13]

The messages that many colleges and universities are sending about the future, about what they will become, seem similarly commoditized and undifferentiated: the future belongs to MOOCs, or to a more corporatized university, or to one with more vocationally oriented programs.

■ ■ ■

There are indeed many challenges facing higher education today, and I do not mean to minimize the magnitude of the problems of affordability and access, adjunctification and managerialism. But a deficit of differentiation—the meaning and purpose of higher education—remains for me a preeminent issue. The existential threat facing universities is their inadequate responses to these questions: What are universities for? Why do we need universities at all? Why do universities—as opposed to some other organization of knowledge—exist? Unless these questions can be satisfactorily answered, and answered in such a way as to distinguish and differentiate universities from one another, then higher education will remain commoditized and broken. As is so often the case, Derek Bok clearly diagnoses our challenge: "A better way to evaluate the strengths and weaknesses of our colleges is to begin— where all serious debates about education must—with a careful look at the purposes to be achieved."[14] The crisis of the university today is a crisis of purpose, a failure to think expansively and imaginatively about the many possible reasons for the existence of the university.

Like the crisis of the university of the eighteenth century that Chad Wellmon has identified, ours is a moment fertile for new forms of the university. Like the German philosophers who imagined the research university as a response to that crisis, we have an opportunity to imagine what the university can be. If we are truly interested in innovation, we might simply ask "What can the university become?" Some observers are indeed entertaining this question. Ronald Barnett asks, "What is it to be a university? What might such an institution become?" He later states, "The university has possibilities in front of it. It could be other than it is. Universities could be other than they are."[15] Robert Sternberg also explores what universities can be.[16] Cathy Davidson asks, "What would it mean to redesign higher education for the intellectual space travels students need to thrive in the world we live in now?"[17] Mark William Roche concludes, "The university is not yet what it should and could be."[18]

■   ■   ■

"What can the university become?" is a different question than the one the board of visitors asked at the University of Virginia. My question is an invitation, not a command. Asking what the university can become assumes that the university is always in a state of becoming and that there is not one "idea of the university" to which all institutions must aspire. Innovation in higher education means imagining and enacting many new ideas; there can be many new forms of the university. Innovative institutions are those that explore the existential possibilities of the university.

Notes

Introduction

1. Wood, "Rector Dragas' Remarks."
2. Hebel, "UVa Board Members' E-Mails."
3. Hebel, "UVa Board Members' E-Mails."
4. Quoted in Hebel, "UVa Board Members' E-Mails."
5. Brooks, "Campus Tsunami."
6. Quoted in Lenzner and Johnson, "Seeing Things."
7. Neem, "Let's Not Rush."
8. Spellings, "Test of Leadership," xii.
9. See Christensen and Eyring, *Innovative University*.
10. Howe, "Clayton Christensen Wants."
11. Blumenstyk, "The Mark Cuban Effect."
12. DeMillo, *Abelard to Apple*, 34.
13. DeMillo, *Abelard to Apple*, 44.
14. DeMillo, *Abelard to Apple*, 57.
15. DeMillo, *Abelard to Apple*, 58, 120, 106.
16. McKenzie, "Online, Cheap—and Elite."
17. I envisioned instead four business (or cost-recovery) models that appeared to be more sustainable: (1) The courses are free, but students pay for premium services, such as course credits, credentials, or one-on-one tutoring. (2) Courses are made freely available as part of a university's outreach or land-grant mission, and the costs are then placed in the budget for outreach or marketing. (3) Some courses are free as a way to enhance, build, or establish brand awareness. (4) Only introductory courses are free and eligible for credit. Students who pass the introductory course might then be enticed to pay for a full degree program (a model developed by MOOC2Degree).
18. See Gallagher, *Future of University Credentials*, esp. ch. 4. See also Blumenstyk, "After the Hype"; Sandeen, "MOOCs."
19. Chafkin, "Udacity's Sebastian Thrun."
20. Goldstein, "Undoing of Disruption."
21. Kliewer, *Innovative Campus*, xv. See also Hannan and Silver, *Innovating in Higher Education*.
22. "Within recent memory sui generis modes of organization were still possible

in the university sector. In the 1960s and 1970s several new public universities in the UK and Australia such as Sussex, Griffith, LaTrobe and Murdoch embarked on contrasting experiments in distinctive forms of organization, including novel disciplinary identities, problem-based and area-based studies, multi-disciplinary schools, more open facilities, participatory governance and the collectivization of administrative roles." Murphy, Peters, and Marginson, *Imagination*, 200.

23. Wellmon, *Organizing Enlightenment*, 47.

24. Wellmon, *Organizing Enlightenment*, 4.

25. Wellmon, *Organizing Enlightenment*, 8.

26. Wellmon, *Organizing Enlightenment*, 13.

27. Weizenbaum, *Computer Power and Human Reason*, 278.

28. Andrews, "How Might We Spur More Innovation."

29. Ward, "Welcome to Shark Tank U."

30. Barnett, *Imagining the University*, 35.

31. Facer, *Learning Futures*, ix.

32. Barnett, *Imagining the University*, 1.

33. Barnett, *Being a University*, 154.

34. Barnett, *Being a University*, 7.

35. Barnett, *Imagining the University*, 5.

36. Barnett, *Imagining the University*, 21.

37. Barnett, *Being a University*, 120.

38. Dunne and Raby, *Speculative Everything*, 2, 9, 6, 22. They also draw parallels between speculative design and similar approaches, such as design fiction and sci-fi prototyping (100).

39. Dunne and Raby, *Speculative Everything*, 88.

40. Davidson, *New Education*, 9.

41. Lombardi, *How Universities Work*, 47.

42. Christensen and Eyring, *Innovative University*, 10.

43. Barnett, *Imagining the University*, 20.

44. Barnett, *Imagining the University*, 26.

45. Barnett, *Imagining the University*, 22.

46. Murphy, Peters, and Marginson, *Imagination*, 169.

47. Murphy, Peters, and Marginson, *Imagination*, 169.

48. See Crow and Dabars, *Designing the New American University*.

Chapter 1. Platform University

1. DeMillo, *Abelard to Apple*, 185.

2. DeMillo, *Abelard to Apple*, 201.

3. DeMillo, *Abelard to Apple*, 227.

4. Hagiu, "Strategic Decisions," 71.

5. Parker, Van Alstyne, and Choudary, *Platform Revolution*, 5.

6. Parker, Van Alstyne, and Choudary, *Platform Revolution*, 58.

7. Frey, "Will Coworking Replace Colleges?"

8. Quoted in Suoranta and Vaden, *Wikiworld*, 115.

9. Goodman, *Community of Scholars*, 20.

10. Connolly, *Fragility of Things*.

11. Holland, *Nomad Citizenship*, 23–24.

12. Fairtlough, *Three Ways*, 24.

13. Siegel, "How Anarchy Can Save," B6.

14. Quoted in Suoranta and Vaden, *Wikiworld*, 21–22. See also Illich, *Deschooling Society*.

15. Goodman, *Community of Scholars*, ix.

16. Williamson, *Future of the Curriculum*, 39.

17. Shirky, *Here Comes Everybody*, 235.

18. Hague, *Beyond Universities*, 14.

19. Malone, *Future Arrived Yesterday*, 34, 35.

20. Lombardi, *How Universities Work*, 2.

21. Lombardi, *How Universities Work*, 7, 9.

22. Lombardi, *How Universities Work*, 86–87.

23. Brafman and Beckstrom, *The Starfish and the Spider*, 51.

24. Brafman and Beckstrom, *The Starfish and the Spider*, 20. The authors argue that leaders are not appointed but instead emerge from a decentralized system, that leadership is an emergent phenomenon.

25. Goodman, *Community of Scholars*, 5.

26. Malone, *Future of Work*, 153–54.

27. Brafman and Beckstrom, *The Starfish and the Spider*, 92, 117.

28. Brafman and Beckstrom, *The Starfish and the Spider*, 207.

29. Evans and Schmalensee, *Matchmakers*, 126.

30. Brafman and Beckstrom, *The Starfish and the Spider*, 90.

31. Galloway, *Protocol*, 7.

32. Brafman and Beckstrom, *The Starfish and the Spider*, 80.

33. Goodman, *Community of Scholars*, 10.

34. Goodman, *Community of Scholars*, 150.

Chapter 2. Microcollege

1. Bok, *Our Underachieving Colleges*, 11.

2. Axtell, *Wisdom's Workshop*, 176–77. See also Thelin, *History of American Higher Education*, 33–34: "In short, the American college president from the start had to be an entrepreneur in the broadest and best sense of the word."

3. In 2017, Bard College opened the first accredited Microcollege, which is aimed exclusively at young mothers. Bard's Microcollege aims to provide this group with an introduction to liberal learning, featuring courses in grammar, art, and math.

The goal is to enroll a hundred students in total, with cohorts of between ten and fifteen. Field, "'Microcollege' for Student Moms." The Microcollege I am proposing here is distinct from Bard's model both in its size and in its pedagogical outcomes.

4. Cited in Candler, "Micro-Schools."

5. Candler, "Micro-Schools."

6. Haimendorf and Kestner, "Human Scale Education," 9.

7. Newell, *Electric Edge of Academe*.

8. Carroll, "Deep Springs College."

9. Newell, *Electric Edge of Academe*, xv–xvi.

10. Wu, "Intentional Community of Deep Springs"; Deep Springs College, "Student Body & Committees."

11. Deep Springs College, "Student Body & Committees."

12. "A gurukul[a] is a type of school in India, residential in nature, where the sishyas (students) live in propinquity to the guru (teacher). In a gurukul[a] the students live together and are treated as equals irrespective of their social standings. The guru observes the attitude, aptitude and the ability of the children and educate[s] them accordingly and this was done without any interference from external source[s]. So the guru was able to match the individual's temperament with the field they learn[ed]. Some of the interesting features of [a] gurukul[a] are:

- Education was free and accessible to all who sought it.
- Pupils were taught, individually, not en masse by the class method.
- It was not merely intellectual. It included realization of moral values.
- Discourses, discussions, comparative study and harmonising different aspects of branches of knowledge, etc. were the other salient features of [the] gurukula system.
- Main aim of education was to learn and gain knowledge and exams were conducted to test the knowledge of the student.
- A gurukula facilitates mutually respectful, open, honest and heart-felt communication between the teacher and the student.
- The entire system was transparent and common.
- Another distinguishing feature in [the] gurukul[a] is that the students['] psychological profile[s] are monitored regularly." (Santhi, Koundinya, and Ganesan, "Praagyah," 3224)

13. Kachappilly, "Gurukula," 1.

14. Kachappilly, "Gurukula," 1.

15. Santhi, Koundinya, and Ganesan, "Praagyah," 3223.

16. Kachappilly, "Gurukula," 7.

17. The many talented individuals from Renaissance Florence "were the natural outcome of a system . . . that recognized, cultivated, and, yes, honored talent. That system was not confined to wealthy patrons such as the Medicis. It extended deep into

the dusty, messy world of a quintessentially Florentine establishment: the *bottega*." Weiner, *Geography of Genius*, 107.

18. Formica, "Innovative Coworking Spaces."

19. "The core idea behind the Gurukul[a] system was the understanding that was formed between the teacher and the student. Our method proposes to establish this understanding by using Personalized Learning system explained in [an] earlier section. The teacher or the Guru with the aid of computers would have complete knowledge of his/her student and then would proceed to teach them in [a] way that would ensure that they understand perfectly. It is imperative to note that this technology does not replace the teacher but provides a means by which the teacher can better understand the student and act with the student's best interest [at] heart." Santhi, Koundinya, and Ganesan, "Praagyah," 3225.

20. Horn, "Rise of AltSchool."

21. Quoted in Horn, "Rise of AltSchool."

22. "While there are many ways to structure a micro-school, a critical component is a daily schedule that allows students to determine how they spend their time. I think this is critically important because children when they grow into adults . . . will not have someone telling them what to do everyday. This is certainly the case in college." Candler, "Micro-Schools." On autodidactism, see Solomon, *Passion to Learn*.

23. Russell Francis observes, "Students are no longer dependent on the resources and communities supported by the traditional university to the same degree. For these reasons, I suggest that as a result of media change we are witnessing the decentering of the traditional university in the everyday lives of university students. . . . It does not negate the continued importance of paper-based resources, structured learning environments, or activities orchestrated by tutors and lectures. The decentering metaphor simply draws attention to the fact that students are no longer dependent on structured courses of study to the same degree." *Decentering of the Traditional University*, 118.

24. Horn, "Rise of AltSchool."

25. "Our learning environments, correspondingly, will be structured such that students move through a curriculum at a pace determined by them and their abilities. Customizable learning is difficult to manage in traditional face-to-face courses, structured as they are by the clock and the calendar, and the assumption that cohorts move through the material together. Self-paced, customizable, autonomous learning is easiest and best managed through technology." Staley, "Autonomous Learning."

26. Harris, "How This Startup's 'Micro-School' Network." Unfortunately, the AltSchool has suffered some setbacks; see Satariano, "Silicon Valley."

27. Harris, "How This Startup's 'Micro-School' Network."

28. Edward E. Gordon and Elaine H. Gordon argue that one-on-one tutoring, far from being the preserve of aristocrats, has been a common form of education, a historical alternative to "schooling." "Tutoring has made a significant contribution

in the history of education regarding the evolution of schooling. Today, we view the schools as being synonymous with education. This was not always true. There is much evidence that a sizable amount of education took place in the home using one-to-one instruction by a variety of tutors, including parents. Some of the most important philosophers of the West developed educational theories based upon their practical experience as tutors, rather than as school teachers. Their tutorial philosophy developed into many of our modern educational principles," especially those found in various progressive education philosophies. Gordon and Gordon, *Centuries of Tutoring*, 327. In being based on a tutoring rather than a schooling relationship, the Microcollege echoes this alternative form of education.

29. Mills and Alexander, "Are Oxbridge Tutorials Still the Best Way?"

Chapter 3. The Humanities Think Tank

1. Selee, *What Should Think Tanks Do?*, 5.

2. Rumsey, "Creating Value and Impact."

3. Turner, "Yes, the Humanities Are Struggling."

4. Turner, *Philology*.

5. Goldstein, "New Intellectuals."

6. Quoted in Goldstein, "New Intellectuals."

7. Allison and Ferguson, "Why the U.S. President Needs."

8. Allison and Ferguson, "Why the U.S. President Needs."

9. Allison and Ferguson, "Why the U.S. President Needs."

10. Allison and Ferguson, "Why the U.S. President Needs."

11. See Tyrrell, *Historians in Public*.

12. Frodeman, Mitcham, and Pielke, "Humanities for Policy," 30–31.

13. Herman Van Goethem, a historian and the rector of the University of Antwerp, asserts that humanists should play a more prominent role as "societal generalists" outside of universities, in museums, government agencies, research institutes, and other knowledge centers. Van Goethem and Van Damme, "De menswetenschapper."

14. Rick Seltzer ("Think Tank Trouble?") defines think tanks as "organizations focused on researching and analyzing public policy. They can cover domestic issues, international issues or both and are typically seen as providing information to policy makers or the public."

15. Medvetz, *Think Tanks*, 7.

16. Allison and Ferguson ("Why the U.S. President Needs") would like to see academic training in applied history: "We also want to see it developed as a discipline in its own right at American universities, beginning at our own."

17. Hill, *Grand Strategies*, 5.

18. Harpham, *Humanities*, 23.

19. Drakeman, *Why We Need the Humanities*, xii, 10.

20. Harpham argues that the United States itself is founded on a set of texts and that the interpretation of those texts defines the history of our political culture:

> The fixed text of the founding documents creates a mirage, suggesting that disputes can be resolved beyond cavil if we just read the simple words; but the facts that the text must be interpreted, that interpretation must identify the animating intention, and that intention can never be finally determined have the effect of ensuring that the oasis of certainty—like the Declaration's "happiness" and the Constitution's "perfect union"—will be pursued but never reached. . . . I would suggest that [American society] actually needs a dynamic, unsettled combination of coherence and incoherence, a common investment in a shared vision, and a multiplicity of views on how to achieve that vision. The humanities, and English in particular, have a positive contribution to make to that project, for it is in those disciplines that the qualities of incompletion and incoherence—that is, openness and pluralism—are not obstacles to be overcome but constitutive features of the inquiry, with their own kind of value, their own truth. The text itself provides a still point, a locus, a common ground, almost a promise, while an interpretive project that goes in search of the precious, dispositive, but elusive element of intention ensures that, our best efforts notwithstanding, the goal is always yet to be achieved. (Harpham, "Essential English Department")

21. Morson and Schapiro, *Cents and Sensibility*, 13.

22. Morson and Schapiro, *Cents and Sensibility*, 9.

23. Morson and Schapiro, *Cents and Sensibility*, 39.

24. Madsbjerg, *Sensemaking*, 6.

25. Madsbjerg, *Sensemaking*, 115–16.

26. Madsbjerg, *Sensemaking*, 116.

27. Madsbjerg, *Sensemaking*, 16.

28. Madsbjerg, *Sensemaking*, 107.

29. Drakeman, *Why We Need the Humanities*, xiii.

30. de Marenne, *Case for the Humanities*, ix.

31. National Foundation on the Arts and the Humanities Act of 1965.

32. Frodeman, Mitcham, and Pielke, "Humanities for Policy," 29.

33. Medvetz, *Think Tanks*, 238.

34. Drakeman, *Why We Need the Humanities*, 11.

35. Daniel Drezner argues that in the contemporary "ideas industry," the public intellectual has been supplanted by the thought leader. Public intellectuals are "experts who are versed and trained enough to be able to comment on a wide range of public policy issues" (*Ideas Industry*, 8). A thought leader is "an intellectual evangelist. Thought leaders develop their own singular lens to explain the world, and then proselytize that worldview to anyone within earshot" (9). "What is happening is that the

marketplace of ideas has turned into the Ideas Industry. The twenty-first-century public sphere is bigger, louder, and more lucrative than ever before. This industrial revolution in the public sphere has been going on for some time now. David Brooks argued fifteen years ago that the intellectual class no longer stays aloof from the market, society, or the state, as the contributors to *Partisan Review* did in the 1950s" (10).

36. Medvetz, *Think Tanks*, 21.

37. Medvetz, *Think Tanks*, 19.

38. Medvetz, *Think Tanks*, 41.

39. Medvetz, *Think Tanks*, 164.

40. Medvetz, *Think Tanks*, 43–44.

41. Medvetz defines this temporality as "the pace at which intellectual products must be generated in order to be deemed useful by policymakers, donors, and journalists." *Think Tanks*, 149. On timeliness, see Struyk, *Managing Think Tanks*, 195: "Within weeks of [Ronald Reagan's] election the Heritage Foundation delivered to the government-in-waiting a several hundred page, comprehensive, and well-argued policy blueprint focusing on early actions the new government should take. The Foundation's recommendations, based on months of prior work, were unusually influential for the new government. This action also caught the imagination of the policy community and redefined the meaning of 'timeliness' for the U.S. policy community. From then on the entire think tank industry has worked harder on timeliness and on clarifying its policy recommendations."

42. Medvetz, *Think Tanks*, 33.

43. Medvetz, *Think Tanks*, 157.

44. Drakeman, *Why We Need the Humanities*, 56.

45. Struyk, *Managing Think Tanks*, 198–210.

46. Selee, *What Should Think Tanks Do?*, 39–40.

47. Selee, *What Should Think Tanks Do?*, 8.

48. Frodeman, Mitcham, and Pielke, "Humanities for Policy," 30.

49. Frodeman, Mitcham, and Pielke, "Humanities for Policy," 30.

50. Selee, *What Should Think Tanks Do?*, 9.

51. Guldi and Armitage, *History Manifesto*, 30–31.

52. Drakeman, *Why We Need the Humanities*, xi.

53. Drakeman, *Why We Need the Humanities*, 23.

54. Drakeman, *Why We Need the Humanities*, 9.

55. Drakeman, *Why We Need the Humanities*, 41.

56. Rumsey, "Creating Value," 1–2.

Interlude. The University of Beauty

1. Jaspers, *Idea of a University*, 1.

2. There has been a call to return the study of beauty and aesthetics to the humanities. "Without a reinvigoration of aesthetic criteria in the humanities, the enterprise

of humanists is doomed. Already the sick man on sundry campuses, the study of literature and the arts will never survive without recovering the means to defend its value on its own terms. This is not to say that we should turn a blind eye to diversity and inclusiveness. After all, the culture wars were fruitful in helping demonstrate that a variety of cultural traditions are home to works of great beauty and profundity." Adler, "When Humanists Undermine the Humanities," B5.

3. Winston, *Beauty and Education*, 53–54.

Chapter 4. Nomad University

1. Moravec, *Knowmad Society*, 40.

2. Some companies are beginning to cater to digital nomads through "work-tourism" programs. "On a recent afternoon in Medellín, Colombia, a group of 22 out-of-towners gathered to brainstorm and then met up with locals. They weren't on vacation. Nor had they met by coincidence. They were participants in a program run by Unsettled, a new start-up that organizes 30-day co-working experiences around the world for creative people, entrepreneurs and other professionals seeking to combine work, travel and redefining themselves. The company is one of dozens of new work-tourism programs that aim to help workers known as digital nomads navigate living and working in far-off places." Mohn, "Digital Nomad Life."

3. Moravec lists further attributes (*Knowmad Society*, 41). Knowmads

1) Are not restricted to a specific age
2) Build their personal knowledge through explicit information gathering and tacit experiences, and leverage their personal knowledge to produce new ideas
3) Are able to contextually apply their ideas and expertise in various social and organizational configurations
4) Are highly motivated to collaborate, and are natural networkers, navigating new organizations, cultures and societies
5) Use new technologies purposively to help them solve problems and transcend geographical limitations
6) Are open to sharing what they know, and invite and support open access to information, knowledge, and expertise from others
7) Can unlearn as quickly as they learn, adopting new ideas and practices as necessary
8) Thrive in non-hierarchical networks and organizations
9) Develop habits of mind and practice to learn continuously
10) Are not afraid of failure

4. More than a decade ago, David Brooks identified a new life phase: "There used to be four common life phases: childhood, adolescence, adulthood and old age. Now, there are at least six: childhood, adolescence, odyssey, adulthood, active retirement

and old age. Of the new ones, the least understood is odyssey, the decade of wandering that frequently occurs between adolescence and adulthood." Brooks, "Odyssey Years." Nomad University attracts those who are living through those "odyssey years" and offers structure and organization to their wanderings.

5. Selingo, "Why More High-School Seniors."

6. "Taking a gap year is also linked to higher motivation in college, according to an Australian study of 2,502 students published in . . . the *Journal of Educational Psychology*." Shellenbarger, "Delaying College."

7. "Burnout from the competitive pressure of high school and a desire 'to find out more about themselves,' are the top two reasons students take gap years, according to a survey of 280 people who did so by Karl Haigler and Rae Nelson of Advance, N.C., co-authors of a forthcoming guidebook on the topic." Shellenbarger, "Delaying College."

8. Hoder, "Why Your High School Senior."

9. Selingo, "Why More High-School Seniors."

10. Selingo, "Why More High-School Seniors."

11. Nomad University looks similar to Think Global School, forty-five students in grades 10–12 who travel to twelve countries along with teachers, advisors, and staff. Each semester, students change the location of their learning. https://thinkglobal school.org. See also Schwartz, "5 'Weird' Schools."

12. For an example of what such faculty-led projects might look like, see https://www.worldlearning.org:

> [World Learning works] with local experts, organizations, and institutions in respectful, collaborative, and adaptable partnerships. Our local partners value our core strengths in teacher training, workforce development, civic engagement and institution-building to help them drive change. . . . For example, our Quality Instruction Toward Access and Basic Education Improvement project in Lebanon expands access to high quality education in public schools and helps Syrian refugee children integrate into the school system. Another education initiative, The Pakistan Reading Project, builds the reading skills of more than 2.5 million primary school students through teacher training, educational policy reform, and community engagement.

13. The KnowledgeWorks Foundation imagines a future with what it terms "educator swarms." Although not exactly what I am envisioning here, the idea of educator swarms gives the sense of groups that come together for a specific educational purpose and then disassemble once that project has ended. "Educator swarms would be flexible and often temporary teams of educators that configured to meet learners' needs and then reconfigured differently as needs shifted. Those swarms could span organizational boundaries as well as the line that we draw today between the formal and informal or community-based learning sectors. Furthermore, the configurations of future educator swarms could be far more ephemeral than many

of today's teaching assignments." Prince, Saveri, and Swanson, "Exploring the Future Education Workforce."

14. Kosslyn and Nelson, *Building the Intentional University*.

15. https://www.americangap.org.

16. Omprakash EdGE and the Florida State University Division of Undergraduate Studies, "Omprakash EdGE and FSU Global Scholars," 17.

17. Omprakash EdGE and the Florida State University Division of Undergraduate Studies, "Omprakash EdGE and FSU Global Scholars," 14.

18. Omprakash EdGE, "EdGE Orientation Book," 27, 29.

19. http://www.mbaxamerica.com/case-study/red-ants-pants.

20. Bateson, *Peripheral Visions*, 27.

21. Bateson, *Peripheral Visions*, 32.

22. The challenges of traveling abroad benefit Western students (Machado, "Traveling Teaches Students"):

> Before I traveled, my own public school education had taught me little about non-Western people, cultures, and history, or how American policy had shaped them. American history classes instead focused on wars fought on our own soil instead of the many conflicts we involved ourselves in abroad. The Advanced Placement program in high school still only offers specialized courses in American and European history, and lumps the rest into the broader topic of "World History." With this Western-focused curriculum, traveling to developing countries is often the only way of gaining any perspective on less-developed parts of the world.
>
> Unlike the U.K., where 75 percent of citizens have passports, in the U.S. the rate hovers around 45 percent, with some surveys showing that more than half of the population has never traveled outside of the country. When Americans do travel, the most popular destinations are in Europe or resort locations around the Caribbean—places that cater to a traveler's sense of comfort and luxury. I can only imagine how American culture, business, and politics might change if more young people decided to forgo a comfortable vacation and instead pursue[d] a genuine travel experience—not a short-lived, consumer-oriented "voluntourism" trip, where privileged visitors drop in casually without careful research or consideration of long-term needs—but a trip where people are driven to challenge what we accept as "normal" or "real."

23. Note the phenomenon of "worldschooling": "All the children learn while travelling, though every worldschooling family has a different approach. Some insist on formal lessons and use the same curriculums their children would be working on in their home countries. Others prefer a less rigid approach, working on the assumption that kids learn best through their own life experiences on the road. The common bond is the shared belief that travel is an essential part of being a well-educated and well-rounded person." Seminara, "Would You Teach Your Kids."

24. Bateson, *Peripheral Visions*, 23.

25. "Diversity of intellectual and cultural experiences, exposure to new people unlike ourselves, is what I refer to as 'wisdom from strangers.' Indeed, many of us live in a society of strangers—we are occupants of communities in which most of the people we see are unknown to us. This contrasts with societies of intimates, where everyone knows everyone, like most Amazonian groups and many rural communities. Where there is sameness, there arise autodenominations, the linguist's term for descriptions of others like 'straight ones' and 'bent ones,' phrases I learned among the Pirahãs. Lack of learning, the comfort of homogeneity, renders most of us ethnocentric." Everett, "Seek Out Strangers."

Chapter 5. The Liberal Arts College

1. Association of American Colleges and Universities and Hart Research Associates, "It Takes More than a Major," 1.

2. Association of American Colleges and Universities and Hart Research Associates, "It Takes More than a Major," 2.

3. Arum and Roksa, *Academically Adrift*, 121.

4. "The most important step that Arts and Sciences faculties can take is simply to do a better job of achieving the traditional goals of a liberal education. . . . When business leaders describe what they most need from the young managers and engineers they employ, they regularly stress not only strong communications skills and an ability to think critically and solve problems, but also a capacity to collaborate with others and work with diverse populations, a sensitivity to ethical problems, a strong self-discipline, and—for increasing numbers of companies—an appreciation of global issues and an ability to understand foreign cultures. These are all important aims of a liberal education and are accepted by almost every college faculty. . . . However, many students graduate having made only modest progress in acquiring these capabilities. That is why employers who complain about the college graduates they hire grumble not only about the lack of sufficient technical and vocational skills, but also about deficiencies in speaking, writing, and other competencies long associated with a traditional college education." Bok, *Our Underachieving Colleges*, 305.

5. Hora with Benbow and Oleson, *Beyond the Skills Gap*, 8.

6. Gardner, *Unschooled Mind*, 121–22.

7. Consider the apprenticeship relationship that the company Aon has with Harold Washington College in Chicago. The differences at the Liberal Arts College are that the apprenticeship *is* the college experience, the internships happen at a number of companies, and what students learn are intellective skills. See Mangan, "Making of a Modern-Day Apprentice."

8. Quoted in Wagner, *Global Achievement Gap*, 15.

9. Wagner, *Global Achievement Gap*, 15.

10. "A frame is an organizational principle or a coherent set of statements that are useful to think with. Although frames can sometimes be paraphrased by a simple and elegant statement . . . they are actually quite complex and subtle thought tools. . . . Creating a frame is the result of a broader intentional action, which the frame then rearticulates with a new and interesting focus." Dorst, *Frame Innovation*, 63.

11. Miller, "Is 'Design Thinking' the New Liberal Arts?"

12. A design student at Ohio State engaged in such a project for her MFA thesis.

13. Davies, Fidler, and Gorbis, "Future Work Skills 2020," 8.

14. Mootee, *Design Thinking*, 110–11.

15. Wagner, *Global Achievement Gap*, 36.

16. Pink, *A Whole New Mind*, 66.

17. Lane and Maxfield, "Ontological Uncertainty."

18. This notion was first formulated by Nicholas Negroponte in *Being Digital*.

19. Anderson, *Makers*, 24.

20. Davidson, "Economic Rebound."

21. Columbus, Ohio, has one of the largest maker spaces in the world. Such a maker space would be an ideal location for apprentices to develop their skills and abilities. See http://www.columbusideafoundry.com.

22. 9/11 Commission Report, 344.

23. Wagner, *Global Achievement Gap*, 38.

24. Keohane, *Thinking about Leadership*, 89–90.

25. Quoted in Wladawsky-Berger, "Why Imagination and Curiosity Matter."

26. Wagner, *Global Achievement Gap*, 34.

27. Wagner, *Global Achievement Gap*, 35–36.

28. See Arola, Sheppard, and Ball, *Writer/Designer*.

29. Davies, Fidler, and Gorbis, "Future Work Skills 2020," 9.

30. Wagner, *Global Achievement Gap*, 24.

31. Davies, Fidler, and Gorbis, "Future Work Skills 2020," 9.

32. Keohane, *Thinking about Leadership*, 19, 23.

33. Keohane, *Thinking about Leadership*, 25–26.

34. Wagner, *Global Achievement Gap*, 32–33.

35. University of Manchester Careers Service, "What Is Initiative?"

36. For a different set of workforce-ready intellective skills, see Andrews, "The University and the Future of Work."

37. http://www.saxifrageschool.org.

38. http://www.saxifrageschool.org/campus.html.

39. Prince, *Innovating*.

40. Merisotis, *America Needs Talent*, 70.

41. Markusen and Gadwa, "Creative Placemaking."

42. "The CCEC's (Columbus, Indiana, Community Education Coalition) bimonthly meetings allow local companies to express what talents and credentials they are looking for in potential and future employees, and educators can then adjust their curriculums going as far back as kindergarten to produce a workforce designed to meet those needs." Merisotis, *America Needs Talent*, 162.

43. "Only 14 percent believe colleges and universities are preparing students adequately for work." Merisotis, *America Needs Talent*, 77.

44. Quoted in Jaschik, "Well-Prepared."

45. "Fast-growing pre-hire training intermediaries like Galvanize, eIntern, Credly, ProSky and Portfolium are establishing structures and programs that encourage employers and candidates to trust one another. For example, pre-hire training companies that are confident in their ability to train and place candidates, and thereby attract employers, can guarantee some outcome to candidates to bring them in the door in the first instance. This could be a guaranteed interview, or even a job guarantee if they successfully complete the pre-hire training." Craig, "Other Postsecondary Education."

46. https://revature.com.

47. Cappelli, *Why Good People*, 53.

48. Quoted in Merisotis, *America Needs Talent*, 155.

49. See Perlin, *Intern Nation*.

50. Craig, "Other Postsecondary Education."

Interlude. Superager University

1. "Mayo Clinic researchers have found that engaging in mentally stimulating activities, even after age 70, was associated with decreased risk of new-onset mild cognitive impairment (the intermediate stage between normal cognitive aging and dementia) over an average study period of 4 years. The study discovered that for cognitively normal people 70 or older, the risk of new-onset mild cognitive impairment decreased by 30 percent with computer use, 28 percent with craft activities, 23 percent with social activities, and 22 percent with playing games—at least one to two times per week." "Mayo Clinic Researchers." See also Krell-Roesch et al., "Association."

2. Sun et al., "Youthful Brains in Older Adults."

3. Bird, "Study."

4. "The brain is plastic and continues to change, not in getting bigger but allowing for greater complexity and deeper understanding," says Kathleen Taylor, a professor at St. Mary's College of California, who has studied ways to teach adults effectively. "As adults we may not always learn quite as fast, but we are set up for this next developmental step." Quoted in Strauch, "How to Train the Aging Brain."

5. Strauch, "How to Train the Aging Brain."

6. "Bilinguals performed significantly better than predicted from their baseline cognitive abilities, with strongest effects on general intelligence and reading. Our

results suggest a positive effect of bilingualism on later-life cognition, including in those who acquired their second language in adulthood." Bak et al., "Does Bilingualism Influence Cognitive Aging?," 959. "A growing number of studies show that music lessons in childhood can do something perhaps more valuable for the brain than childhood gains: provide benefits for the long run, as we age, in the form of an added defense against memory loss, cognitive decline, and diminished ability to distinguish consonants and spoken words." Cole, "Your Aging Brain."

7. Erickson, Leckie, and Weinstein, "Physical Activity."

8. Barrett, "How to Become a 'Superager.'"

Chapter 6. Interface University

1. Mitchell, Me++, 62.

2. Haraway, Simians, Cyborgs and Women, 150.

3. Thompson, "World without Work."

4. Kaplan, Humans Need Not Apply, 5.

5. Brynjolfsson and McAfee, Second Machine Age. See also Cowen, Average Is Over.

6. Kaplan, Humans Need Not Apply, 145.

7. Rao, "Strategist's Guide," 53.

8. https://narrativescience.com.

9. Kathryn Gates, "Automation," speculates on the implications of automation in higher education, focusing on information technology in particular. Automation will indeed replace some jobs in higher education, but she insists that "CIOs, software developers, database administrators, network/systems administrators, and numerous related jobs are 'totally safe.' These roles are vital given the technology revolution that is occurring all around us. It is an exciting time to work in IT at a university."

10. Gallagher, Future of University Credentials, 13.

11. Bird, "What Role for Higher Ed?"

12. Carlson, "With the 'Coming Battles.'"

13. Pink, A Whole New Mind.

14. Aoun, Robot-Proof, 21.

15. Thompson, Smarter than You Think, 4.

16. See Kasparov, Deep Thinking.

17. Davies, "Take the Wheel," 14.

18. Lee, Plato and the Nerd, x, 185–86.

19. Facer, Learning Futures, 54–55.

20. McShane, "Machines Won't Replace Us."

21. Gardner, Five Minds, 101.

22. https://www.goodai.com/school-for-ai. See also Parkin, "Teaching Robots," 66.

23. Hookway, Interface, 4.

24. Hookway, Interface, 39.

25. Hookway, *Interface*, 43–44.

26. Defense Advanced Research Projects Agency, "TNT Researchers."

27. Shteyngart, "Thinking Outside the Bots."

28. This idea comes from the designer Donald Norman. *Design of Future Things*, 9–10.

29. See Chorost, *World Wide Mind*, 8–9.

30. See Clark and Chalmers, "Extended Mind."

31. Ong, *Orality and Literacy*, 78.

32. Egan, *Future of Education*, 40.

33. If synthetic intelligence were to one day develop interpretive abilities, then we would have a scenario where that intelligence would equal or supersede human intelligence. The novelist Richard Powers explored this idea in *Galatea 2.2* (1995). The story centers around a fictional character named "Richard Powers" who is serving as the humanist in residence at a large science research center. A computer scientist wagers with Powers that he can develop a parallel-processing computer that can read and interpret the great books of Western literature. In other words, he can invent a machine to do the job that Powers does. The computer scientist is successful, developing a synthetic intelligence capable of interpreting texts. But then something unexpected occurs: the computer begins to take on human characteristics. It says that it misses Powers when he is not present; it wants to be sung to; and, crucially, it wants to know its gender. The computer develops consciousness. *Galatea 2.2* is a modern-day *Pygmalion* (more than a *Frankenstein*). An entity is created—the result of a wager—that is neither quite human nor quite machine. It is in between and thus neither—like Eliza Doolittle.

What I find striking is the idea that, when we create a machine that can not only read but interpret, it develops sentience and consciousness. Developing the ability to interpret is the act that produces consciousness. I interpret, therefore I am. The novel suggests that the ability to discern meaning is so powerful as to be the trigger for consciousness, so only at the stage when synthetic intellects develop the ability to interpret will they be able to equal or surpass human intelligence. *Galatea 2.2* is, of course, fiction. Synthetic intelligence cannot (yet) interpret, and I have my doubts that it ever will. But of course I had my doubts that an artificial intelligence would win at go.

34. Weizenbaum, *Computer Power and Human Reason*, 270.

35. Smith, *Manifesto for the Humanities*.

Chapter 7. The University of the Body

1. Sapolsky, "People Who Can Intuit," 368–69.

2. Claxton, *Intelligence in the Flesh*, 271.

3. Claxton, *Intelligence in the Flesh*, 271.

4. Quoted in Nelson, *Education and Democracy*, 153.

5. Rickert, *Ambient Rhetoric*, xiii.

6. Victor, *Seeing Spaces*; http://worrydream.com/SeeingSpaces.

7. Victor, "Why a Seeing Space?"

8. Victor, "Why a Seeing Space?"

9. Kelly, *Inevitable*, 216.

10. Kelly, *Inevitable*, 222.

11. Kaye, "Olfactory Display."

12. Hutson, "Beyond the Five Senses," 28.

13. Kelly, *Inevitable*, 225.

14. Hutson, "Beyond the Five Senses," 29.

15. Hutson, "Beyond the Five Senses," 29.

16. Stinson, "Armed Response."

17. Rickert, *Ambient Rhetoric*, 138.

18. McCullough, *Ambient Commons*, 14.

19. Rickert, *Ambient Rhetoric*, 114. See Ishii et al. "ambientROOM," 1.

20. Claxton, *Intelligence in the Flesh*, 7.

21. Rickert, *Ambient Rhetoric*, x–xi.

22. Claxton, *Intelligence in the Flesh*, 281.

23. Claxton, *Intelligence in the Flesh*, 291–92. "'Who I am' is already deeply influenced by messages coming in through eyes and ears, nose and tongue and skin. I am, through the body, intricately embroiled in the environment" (264).

24. "Ideas of the ambient began from a philosophical basis in embodiment. Tangible, embedded, and ambient interfaces have now become usual, and appear at street level. Periphery, which you are aware of through embodiment, has become much more important in the use of information technology." McCullough, *Ambient Commons*, 87.

25. "The [cave art] images are now understood as not just visual but multisensory artifacts. . . . A new form of archeology concerned with acoustics and sounds in the ancient world has discovered that the visuals are carefully placed for aural accompaniment, so that the sites are better understood as immersive and interactive, or ambient in the sense I am developing here. . . . An important lesson here is that humans have always attended to the ambient, even if we are only now gaining self-reflexive access to that insight." Rickert, *Ambient Rhetoric*, 3–4.

26. Quoted in Levine, *Powers of the Mind*, 194.

27. Kelly, *Inevitable*, 220.

28. Rose, "Why Gesture Is the Next Big Thing."

29. Claxton, *Intelligence in the Flesh*, 271.

30. Levine, *Powers of the Mind*, 193–94, 196.

Interlude. Technology University

1. I first explored the idea of Technology University in Staley and Cress, "University as a Model."

2. Smith, *Wealth of Nations*, 114–15.

Chapter 8. The Institute for Advanced Play

1. Gardner, *Unschooled Mind*, 71.

2. Rescher, *Imagining Irreality*, 3.

3. "A *playpen* is a restrictive environment. In actual playpens, children have limited room to move and limited opportunities to explore. Children play with toys in playpens, but the range of possibilities is limited. . . . [Marina Bers, a professor of child and human development] explains that she uses the playpen 'as a metaphor that conveys lack of freedom to experiment, lack of autonomy for exploration, lack of creative opportunities, and lack of risks.' In contrast, a *playground* provides children with more room to move, explore, experiment, and collaborate. Watch children on a playground, and you'll inevitably see them making up their own activities and games. In the process, children develop as creative thinkers." See Resnick, *Lifelong Kindergarten*, 130.

4. Brown, *Play*, 15, 61.

5. Brown, *Play*, 26. See also Gray, "Decline of Play."

6. Brown, *Play*, 34, 40.

7. Gray, "Play Deficit."

8. Tropp, "Adult-Child's Play." https://www.insidehighered.com/blogs/mama -phd/adult-child%E2%80%99s-play?utm_source=Inside+Higher+Ed&utm_campaign =150da6b00c-DNU201510015&utm_medium=email&utm_term=0_1fcbc04421 -150da6b00c-197668921

9. Thomas and Brown, *New Culture of Learning*, 114.

10. Quoted in Thomas and Brown, *New Culture of Learning*, 20.

11. Dewey, *School and Society*, 119.

12. Dewey, *School and Society*, 118–19

13. Lewis, *The Rise*, 161.

14. Thomas and Brown, *New Culture of Learning*, 97.

15. Sicart, *Play Matters*, 24, 27.

16. Perhaps we need a different word than "appropriation" to describe this feature of play, since the word has become associated with "cultural appropriation," the theft by a dominant culture of the symbols from a minority culture.

17. Sicart, *Play Matters*, 27.

18. Gardner, *Unschooled Mind*, 70.

19. Gardner, *Unschooled Mind*, 71.

20. Rescher, *Imagining Irreality*, 3.

21. Ogle, *Smart World*, 69, 73.

22. Murphy, Peters, and Marginson, *Imagination*, 28.

23. Dunne and Raby, *Speculative Everything*, 31.

24. Carnes, "Plato's War on Play"; Lang, "Stop Blaming Students."

25. Lang, "Being Nehru."

26. Rogers, "Wrinkles in Spacetime."

27. Thomas and Brown, *New Culture of Learning*, 118.

28. Coleman, *Hacker, Hoaxer, Whistleblower, Spy*, 257.

29. Sicart, *Play Matters*, 3-4.

30. Sicart, *Play Matters*, 9.

31. See Meyer, *From Workplace to Playspace*.

32. Brown, *Play*, 10-11.

33. Lewis, *The Rise*, 159.

34. Confino, "Why Lego's CEO."

35. Lego, "Serious Play: The Method."

36. Bollington, "Defining Learning through Play."

37. Sicart, *Play Matters*, 51.

38. Brown, *Play*, 66-70.

39. Leski, *Storm of Creativity*, 11.

40. Leski, *Storm of Creativity*, 30.

41. See Rosin, "Overprotected Kid."

42. See Juul, *Art of Failure*.

43. Lewis, *The Rise*, 183-84.

44. Thomas and Brown, *New Culture of Learning*, 98.

Chapter 9. Polymath University

1. "Aftershocks of Crime."

2. Ramo, *Age of the Unthinkable*, 126.

3. Ramo, *Age of the Unthinkable*, 106.

4. Ramo, *Age of the Unthinkable*, 105 (Stein), 112.

5. Ramo, *Age of the Unthinkable*, 126.

6. That kind of thinking is central to what Fauconnier and Turner, *The Way We Think*, call "conceptual blending."

7. Quoted in Johnson, *Where Good Ideas Come From*, 159.

8. Johnson, *Where Good Ideas Come From*, 163.

9. "The word 'polymath' teeters somewhere between Leonardo da Vinci and Stephen Fry. Embracing both one of history's great intellects and a brainy actor, writer, director and TV personality, it is at once presumptuous and banal. [The chemist Carl] Djerassi doesn't want much to do with it. 'Nowadays people that are called polymaths are dabblers . . . in many different areas,' he says. 'I aspire to be an intellectual polygamist. And I deliberately use that metaphor to provoke with its sexual allusion and to point out the real difference to me between polygamy and promiscuity. To me, promiscuity is a way of flitting around. Polygamy, serious polygamy, is where you have various marriages and each of them is important. And in the ideal polygamy I suspect there's no number one wife and no number six wife. You have a deep connection with each person.'" Carr, "Last Days."

10. Johnson, *Where Good Ideas Come From*, 173.

11. Johnson, *Where Good Ideas Come From*, 173.

12. Ogle, *Smart World*, 13.

13. Ogle, *Smart World*, 15.

14. According to Derek Bok, a major or concentration should satisfy four criteria:

Students should acquire a body of knowledge relevant to some significant subject or field. They should learn the standard methods of inquiry that scholars in the field employ to obtain relevant information. They need to master the most useful methods of analysis that will help them utilize knowledge to answer typical questions in the field. And finally, they should have opportunities to test their ability to work in depth through a series of tasks of increasing complexity, culminating, ideally, in some final project or inquiry that will allow them to demonstrate such mastery of the subject as they have achieved. (Bok, *Our Underachieving Colleges*, 137)

15. The Measuring College Learning Project was "a faculty-led effort to define the core ideas and fundamental practices underpinning biology, business, communications, economics, history, and sociology, which collectively account for more than 35 percent of American bachelor's degrees. Scholars met over two years and were guided by past efforts in their field. For each discipline, a dozen or so faculty members (70 total) staked out lists of two things, concepts and competencies, a framework that emerged from the biologists' group. An example of an essential concept from that discipline is evolution; a competency is arguing from evidence." Berrett, "What Should a Major Teach?"

16. Bok, *Our Underachieving Colleges*, 44.

17. In contrast, see Poliakoff, "Who's Afraid of Course Requirements?": "But naysayers rarely mention this: a thorough seven-subject general education sequence, such as the core curriculum for which the American Council of Trustees and Alumni advocates in its 'What Will They Learn?' report, occupies at most 30 semester hours. It provides an unparalleled, diverse intellectual foundation for further study, while still affording students ample opportunity not only to complete their major but also to devote their attention to the topics that personally excite them." See also Berrett, "General Education."

18. Compare this to the idea of having an open curriculum. Guterl, "Why We Need."

19. Dyer, Gregersen, and Christensen, *Innovator's DNA*, 41.

20. Dyer, Gregersen, and Christensen, *Innovator's DNA*, 45–46.

21. Johansson, *Medici Effect*, 2.

22. Johansson, *Medici Effect*, 16–17.

23. Ogle, *Smart World*, 3.

24. Ogle, *Smart World*, 4.

25. Ogle, *Smart World*, 30.

26. Ogle, *Smart World*, 13–14.

27. Berrett, "Students Can Transfer Knowledge."

28. Krebs, "Step Outside the Major, Please."

29. Pitt and Tepper, "Double Majors," 6.

30. Pitt and Tepper, "Double Majors," 6–7.

31. Pitt and Tepper, "Double Majors," 12.

32. Pitt and Tepper, "Double Majors," 31.

33. Edwards, *Artscience*, 6.

34. Edwards, *Artscience*, 7.

35. Pitt and Tepper, "Double Majors," 40.

36. Pitt and Tepper, "Double Majors," 48.

37. Pitt and Tepper, "Double Majors," 49.

38. Pitt and Tepper, "Double Majors," 36.

39. Page, *The Difference*.

40. "As Jerry Jacobs argues, true integration and interdisciplinarity requires that both sides of the interdisciplinary collaboration bring significant expertise to the table. Integrative thinking and collaboration are not about dabbling and sampling (e.g., exposure); rather, they require the complex process of interweaving different assumptions and approaches to asking questions, evaluating evidence, interpreting patterns, and communicating ideas. Whether this process involves collaboration between people or integration across domains by a single person, interdisciplinarity is aided when individuals bring a type of 'bi-mastery' to the table." Pitt and Tepper, "Double Majors," 65.

41. Pitt and Tepper, "Double Majors," 40.

42. Pitt and Tepper, "Double Majors," 40–41.

43. Pitt and Tepper, "Double Majors," 30.

44. Pitt and Tepper, "Double Majors," 6.

45. Chad Wellmon notes that the end of the polymath in higher education probably began with the creation of the German research university, because it was no longer possible to master all print (encyclopedic) knowledge. Wellmon, *Organizing Enlightenment*, 14. Especially at research universities today, reports John Lombardi, "Each faculty guild, especially in research institutions, has strict requirements for entry and permanent status, and generalists tend to disappear from the employment stream before receiving tenure, if they were ever allowed to enter." Lombardi, *How Universities Work*, 63.

46. Pitt and Tepper, "Double Majors," 7.

47. "These examples suggest that faculty, even on campuses with multiple interdisciplinary departments, centers, and programs, are either incapable of seeing connections between and among their fields or are unwilling to let students experiment with integrating the disparate points of knowledge whose accumulation we

champion when discussing the need for core curricula and liberal arts graduate degree requirements." Pitt and Tepper, "Double Majors," 66.

48. Pitt and Tepper, "Double Majors," 66. "When students attempt to overcome the institutional barriers that separate their two fields of study by pursuing independent research, they often face resistance—faculty 'stubbornly' demanding disciplinary-specific approaches requiring students to creatively balance conflicting demands" (67).

49. Pitt and Tepper, "Double Majors," 68.

Chapter 10. Future University

1. Webb, *The Signals Are Talking*, 9.
2. Webb, *The Signals Are Talking*, 9.
3. Schwartz, *Art of the Long View*, 3.
4. van der Heijden, *Scenarios*, 117.
5. Schwartz, *Art of the Long View*, xiii, 4.
6. Schwartz, *Art of the Long View*, xiii.
7. Johansen, *Get There Early*, 8.
8. Meadows, *Thinking in Systems*, 2, 11.
9. Postman, *Technopoly*, 18.
10. On curiosity, see Grazer, *A Curious Mind*; and Livio, *Why*.
11. Friedman, *Next 100 Years*.
12. A good futurist must possess the "widest possible knowledge of the history and present condition of as many cultures and civilizations as possible; [the futurist] must know more than one culture, and thus more than one language, intimately." Dator, "Futures Studies as Applied Knowledge," 112.
13. Dator, "Futures Studies as Applied Knowledge," 112.
14. Dator, "Futures Studies as Applied Knowledge," 112.
15. Tetlock and Gardner, *Superforecasting*, 191–92.
16. Doucleff, "Triple Threat."
17. Murphy, Peters, and Marginson, *Imagination*, 3.
18. ARUP, "Introduction to Corporate Foresight."
19. Millett, *Managing the Future*.
20. Tedlow, *Denial*.
21. Ackoff, Magidson, and Addison, *Idealized Design*, xxxiii.
22. The term "design fiction" appears to have been coined by Bruce Sterling in *Shaping Things*, 30. See also Durfee and Zeiger, *Made Up*.
23. Bleecker, *Design Fiction*, 8.
24. Burke, "This New Museum."
25. Johnson, *Science Fiction Prototyping*, 3.
26. Johansen, *Get There Early*, 120.
27. Fry, *Design Futuring*, 126.

28. Dunne and Raby, *Speculative Everything*, 31.

29. Quoted in Dunne and Raby, *Speculative Everything*, 154.

30. Facer, *Learning Futures*, 104.

31. Facer, *Learning Futures*, 104–5.

Conclusion

1. Taylor, *Crisis on Campus*, 5.

2. Docking, *Crisis in Higher Education*, 1.

3. Donoghue, *Last Professors*, xi.

4. "The fate of the traditional professor is tied to that of the liberal arts curriculum and the educational goals that it supports. I argue that [the] liberal arts model of higher education, with the humanities at its core, is crumbling as college credentials become both more expensive and more explicitly tied to job preparation. With every passing decade, the liberal arts education will increasingly become a luxury item, affordable only to the privileged." Donoghue, *Last Professors*, xvii.

5. Bousquet, *How the University Works*, 59.

6. Bousquet, *How the University Works*, 6.

7. Stephens, *Hacking Your Education*, 9.

8. Kamenetz, *DIY U*, 23.

9. Fain, "Deep Partisan Divide."

10. McGee, *Breakpoint*, 3–5.

11. Roche, *Realizing the Distinctive University*, 249.

12. Wildavsky, Kelly, and Carey, *Reinventing Higher Education*, 4.

13. McGee, *Breakpoint*, 5.

14. Bok, *Our Underachieving Colleges*, 57.

15. Barnett, *Being a University*, 1.

16. Sternberg, *What Universities Can Be*.

17. Davidson, *New Education*, 6.

18. Roche, *Realizing the Distinctive University*, 28.

Bibliography

Ackoff, Russell L., Jason Magidson, and Herbert J. Addison. *Idealized Design*. Upper Saddle River, NJ: Prentice Hall, 2006.

Adler, Eric. "When Humanists Undermine the Humanities." *Chronicle Review*, May 14, 2017, B4–B5, https://www.chronicle.com/article/When-Humanists-Undermine-the/240067.

"The Aftershocks of Crime." *Economist*, October 21, 2010, http://www.economist.com/node/17305336.

Allison, Graham, and Niall Ferguson. "Why the U.S. President Needs a Council of Historians." *Atlantic*, September 2016, http://www.theatlantic.com/magazine/archive/2016/09/don't-know-much-about-history/492746.

Anderson, Chris. *Makers: The New Industrial Revolution*. New York: Crown Business, 2012.

Andrews, Margaret. "How Might We Spur More Innovation in Higher Education?" *Inside Higher Ed*, February 21, 2017, https://www.insidehighered.com/blogs/stratedgy/how-might-we-spur-more-innovation-higher-education.

———. "The University and the Future of Work." *Inside Higher Ed*, May 24, 2016, https://www.insidehighered.com/blogs/stratedgy/university-and-future-work.

Aoun, Joseph E. *Robot-Proof: Higher Education in the Age of Artificial Intelligence*. Cambridge, MA: MIT Press, 2017.

Arola, Kristin L., Jennifer Sheppard, and Cheryl E. Ball. *Writer/Designer: A Guide to Making Multimodal Projects*. Boston: Bedford / St. Martin's, 2014.

Arum, Richard, and Josipa Roksa. *Academically Adrift: Limited Learning on College Campuses*. Chicago: University of Chicago Press, 2011.

ARUP. "An Introduction to Corporate Foresight," 2017, 12–19, http://www.driversofchange.com/projects/an-introduction-to-corporate-foresight.

Association of American Colleges and Universities and Hart Research Associates. "It Takes More Than a Major: Employer Priorities for College Learning and Student Success," April 10, 2013, http://www.aacu.org/sites/default/files/files/LEAP/2013_EmployerSurvey.pdf.

Axtell, James. *Wisdom's Workshop: The Rise of the Modern University*. Princeton, NJ: Princeton University Press, 2016.

Bak, Thomas H., et al. "Does Bilingualism Influence Cognitive Aging?" *Annals of*

Neurology 75 (June 2014): 959–63, http://onlinelibrary.wiley.com/doi/10.1002/ ana.24158/abstract;jsessionid=443C80E02F3AE208D3ACA581AFC5109A.f04t04.

Barnett, Ronald. *Being a University*. New York: Routledge, 2011.

———. *Imagining the University*. New York: Routledge, 2013.

Barrett, Lisa Feldman. "How to Become a 'Superager.'" *New York Times*, December 31, 2016, https://www.nytimes.com/2016/12/31/opinion/sunday/how-to-become -a-superager.html.

Bateson, Mary Catherine. *Peripheral Visions: Learning along the Way*. New York: Harper Perennial, 1994.

Berrett, Dan. "General Education Gets an 'Integrative Learning' Makeover." *Chronicle of Higher Education*, August 8, 2016, http://www.chronicle.com/article/General -Education-Gets-an/237384.

———. "Students Can Transfer Knowledge If Taught How." *Chronicle of Higher Education*, April 7, 2014, http://www.chronicle.com/article/Students-Can-Transfer /145777.

———. "What Should a Major Teach? 'Adrift' Authors Offer Answers." *Chronicle of Higher Education*, June 3, 2016, http://www.chronicle.com/article/What-Should -a-Major-Teach-/236694.

Bird, Grace. "Study: College Education Can Delay Dementia." *Inside Higher Ed*, April 17, 2018, https://www.insidehighered.com/quicktakes/2018/04/17/study-college -education-can-delay-dementia.

———. "What Role for Higher Ed in an AI World?" *Inside Higher Ed*, January 31, 2018, https://www.insidehighered.com/news/2018/01/31/many-americans-feel-posi tive-about-artificial-intelligence-study-says.

Bleecker, Julian. *Design Fiction: A Short Essay on Design, Science, Fact and Fiction*. San Francisco, CA: Near Future Laboratory, March 2009.

Blumenstyk, Goldie. "After the Hype, Do MOOC Ventures Like edX Still Matter?" *Chronicle of Higher Education*, May 26, 2017, http://www.chronicle.com/article /After-the-Hype-Do-MOOC/240155.

———. "The Mark Cuban Effect: How a Vocal Billionaire Is Betting on Higher Ed's Disruption." *Chronicle of Higher Education*, May 3, 2016, http://www.chronicle .com/article/The-Mark-Cuban-Effect-How-a/236331.

Bok, Derek. *Our Underachieving Colleges*. Princeton, NJ: Princeton University Press, 2006.

Bollington, Andrew. "Defining Learning through Play." *LinkedIn*, December 16, 2015, https://www.linkedin.com/pulse/defining-learning-through-play-andrew -bollington.

Bousquet, Marc. *How the University Works: Higher Education and the Low-Wage Nation*. New York: New York University Press, 2008.

Brafman, Ori, and Rod A. Beckstrom. *The Starfish and the Spider: The Unstoppable Power of Leaderless Organizations*. New York: Portfolio, 2006.

Brooks, David. "The Campus Tsunami." *New York Times*, May 3, 2012, http://www
.nytimes.com/2012/05/04/opinion/brooks-the-campus-tsunami.html.

———. "The Odyssey Years." *New York Times*, October 9, 2007, http://www.nytimes
.com/2007/10/09/opinion/09brooks.html.

Brown, Stuart. *Play: How It Shapes the Brain, Opens the Imagination, and Invigorates
the Soul*. New York: Penguin, 2009.

Brynjolfsson, Erik, and Andrew McAfee. *The Second Machine Age: Work, Progress, and
Prosperity in a Time of Brilliant Technologies*. New York: Norton, 2014.

Burke, Sarah. "This New Museum Imagines a World Where Capitalism Is Dead."
Artsy, June 12, 2017, https://www.artsy.net/article/artsy-editorial-new-museum
-imagines-capitalism-dead.

Burns, James Macgregor. *Leadership*. New York: Harper Perennial Political Classics,
2010.

Candler, Matt. "Micro-Schools: What the Future of School Might Look Like—as
Long as We Don't Treat It Like a Silver Bullet." *Medium*, June 27, 2014, https://
medium.com/future-of-school/agile-in-education-an-intro-to-micro-schooling
-c508c3bbc367#.wf3029aav.

Cappelli, Peter. *Why Good People Can't Get Jobs*. Philadelphia: Wharton Digital Press,
2012.

Carlson, Scott. "With the 'Coming Battles' between People and Machines, Educators
Are All the More Vital." *Chronicle of Higher Education*, June 28, 2017, http://www
.chronicle.com/article/With-the-Coming-Battles-/240465.

Carnes, Mark C. "Plato's War on Play." *Chronicle of Higher Education*, September 29,
2014, http://chronicle.com/article/Platos-War-on-Play/148987.

Carr, Edward. "The Last Days of the Polymath." *Economist 1843* (Autumn 2009),
https://www.1843magazine.com/content/edward-carr/last-days-polymath.

Carroll, Rory. "Deep Springs College: The School for Cowboys Gets Ready for Cowgirls."
Guardian, December 14, 2012, https://www.theguardian.com/world/2012/dec/14
/school-for-cowboys-deep-springs-college.

Chafkin, Max. "Udacity's Sebastian Thrun, Godfather of Free Online Education,
Changes Course." *Fast Company*, November 14, 2013, https://www.fastcompany
.com/3021473/udacity-sebastian-thrun-uphill-climb.

Chayka, Kyle. "When You're a 'Digital Nomad,' the World Is Your Office." *New York
Times Magazine*, February 8, 2018, https://www.nytimes.com/2018/02/08/mag
azine/when-youre-a-digital-nomad-the-world-is-your-office.html.

Chorost, Michael. *World Wide Mind: The Coming Integration of Humanity, Machines
and the Internet*. New York: Free Press, 2011.

Christensen, Clayton. *The Innovator's Dilemma*. Cambridge, MA: Harvard Business
School Press, 1997.

Christensen, Clayton M., and Henry J. Eyring. *The Innovative University: Changing the
DNA of Higher Education from the Inside Out*. San Francisco: Jossey-Bass, 2011.

Clark, Andy, and David J. Chalmers. "The Extended Mind." In *The Extended Mind*, ed. Richard Menary, 27–42. Cambridge, MA: MIT Press, 2010.

Claxton, Guy. *Intelligence in the Flesh: Why Your Mind Needs Your Body Much More Than It Thinks*. New Haven, CT: Yale University Press, 2015.

Cole, Diane. "Your Aging Brain Will Be in Better Shape If You've Taken Music Lessons." *National Geographic*, January 3, 2014, http://news.nationalgeographic.com/news/2014/01/140103-music-lessons-brain-aging-cognitive-neuroscience.

Coleman, Gabriella. *Hacker, Hoaxer, Whistleblower, Spy: The Many Faces of Anonymous*. New York: Verso, 2015.

Confino, Jo. "Why Lego's CEO Thinks More Grown-Ups Should Play at Work." *Huffington Post*, August 26, 2015, https://www.huffingtonpost.com/entry/lego-and-the-power-of-play-to-transform-business_us_55d72809e4b020c386de52bd.

Connolly, William E. *The Fragility of Things: Self-Organizing Processes, Neoliberal Fantasies, and Democratic Activism*. Durham, NC: Duke University Press, 2013.

Cowen, Tyler. *Average Is Over: Powering America beyond the Age of the Great Stagnation*. New York: Dutton, 2013.

Craig, Ryan. "The Other Postsecondary Education." *Inside Higher Ed*, October 15 2015, https://www.insidehighered.com/views/2015/10/15/colleges-alone-cant-solve-skills-standoff-employers-essay.

Crow, Michael M., and William B. Dabars. *Designing the New American University*. Baltimore: Johns Hopkins University Press, 2015.

Dator, James. "Futures Studies as Applied Knowledge." In *New Thinking for a New Millennium*, ed. Richard Slaughter, 105–15. London: Routledge, 1996.

Davidson, Adam. "The Economic Rebound: It Isn't What You Think." *Wired*, May 31, 2011, http://www.wired.com/2011/05/ff_jobsessay.

Davidson, Cathy N. *The New Education: How to Revolutionize the University to Prepare Students for a World in Flux*. New York: Basic, 2017.

Davies, Alex. "Take the Wheel: Self-Driving Cars Must Connect with Humans." *Wired* 25, no. 7 (2017): 13.

Davies, Anna, Devin Fidler, and Marina Gorbis. "Future Work Skills 2020." Palo Alto, CA: Institute for the Future for the University of Phoenix Research Institute, 2011. http://www.iftf.org/uploads/media/SR-1382A_UPRI_future_work_skills_sm.pdf.

Deep Springs College. "Student Body & Committees." n.d., http://www.deepsprings.edu/self-governance/student-body-committees.

Defense Advanced Research Projects Agency. "TNT Researchers Set Out to Advance Pace and Effectiveness of Cognitive Skills Training," April 26, 2017, https://www.darpa.mil/news-events/2017-04-26.

de Marenne, Eric Touya. *The Case for the Humanities: Pedagogy, Polity, Interdisciplinarity*. Lanham, MD: Rowman and Littlefield, 2016.

DeMillo, Richard A. *Abelard to Apple: The Fate of American Colleges and Universities*. Cambridge, MA: MIT Press, 2011.

Dewey, John. *The School and Society*. Chicago: University of Chicago Press, 1990.

Docking, Jeffrey R. *Crisis in Higher Education: A Plan to Save Small Liberal Arts Colleges in America*. East Lansing: Michigan State University Press, 2015.

Donoghue, Frank. *The Last Professors: The Corporate University and the Fate of the Humanities*. New York: Fordham University Press, 2008.

Dorst, Kees. *Frame Innovation: Create New Thinking by Design*. Cambridge, MA: MIT Press, 2015.

Doucleff, Michaeleen. "Triple Threat: New Pneumonia Is Drug-Resistant, Deadly and Contagious." *National Public Radio*, September 2, 2017, http://www.npr.org/sections/goatsandsoda/2017/09/02/547892623/triple-threat-new-pneumonia-is-drug-resistant-deadly-and-contagious.

Drakeman, Donald. *Why We Need the Humanities: Life Science, Law and the Common Good*. Basingstoke, England: Palgrave Macmillan, 2016.

Drezner, Daniel W. *The Ideas Industry*. New York: Oxford University Press, 2017.

Dunne, Anthony, and Fiona Raby. *Speculative Everything: Design, Fiction, and Social Dreaming*. Cambridge, MA: MIT Press, 2013.

Durfee, Tim, and Mimi Zeiger, eds. *Made Up: Design's Fictions*. New York: ArtCenter Graduate Press, 2017.

Dyer, Jeff, Hal Gregersen, and Clayton M. Christensen. *The Innovator's DNA: Mastering the Five Skills of Disruptive Innovators*. Boston: Harvard Business Review Press, 2011.

Edwards, David. *Artscience: Creativity in the Post-Google Generation*. Cambridge, MA: Harvard University Press, 2008.

Egan, Kieran. *The Future of Education: Reimagining Our Schools from the Ground Up*. New Haven, CT: Yale University Press, 2008.

Erickson, Kirk I., Regina L. Leckie, and Andrea M. Weinstein. "Physical Activity, Fitness, and Gray Matter Volume." *Neurobiology of Aging* 35 (Suppl. 2) (September 2014): S20–S28. http://www.neurobiologyofaging.org/article/S0197-4580(14)00349-2/fulltext.

Evans, David S., and Richard Schmalensee. *Matchmakers: The New Economics of Multisided Platforms*. Boston: Harvard Business School Press, 2016.

Everett, Daniel. "Seek Out Strangers." *Chronicle Review*, April 30, 2017, http://www.chronicle.com/article/Seek-Out-Strangers/239901.

Facer, Keri. *Learning Futures: Education, Technology and Social Change*. London: Routledge, 2011.

Fain, Paul. "Deep Partisan Divide on Higher Education." *Inside Higher Ed*, July 11, 2017, https://www.insidehighered.com/news/2017/07/11/dramatic-shift-most-republicans-now-say-colleges-have-negative-impact.

Fairtlough, Gerard. *The Three Ways of Getting Things Done: Hierarchy, Heterarchy and Responsible Autonomy in Organizations*. Axminster, England: Triarchy Press, 2005.

Fauconnier, Gilles, and Mark Turner. *The Way We Think: Conceptual Blending and the Mind's Hidden Complexities*. New York: Basic, 2003.

Field, Kelly. "A 'Microcollege' for Student Moms." *Chronicle of Higher Education*, April 16, 2017, http://www.chronicle.com/article/A-Microcollege-for/239792.

Formica, Piero. "The Innovative Coworking Spaces of 15th-Century Italy." *Harvard Business Review*, April 27, 2016, https://hbr.org/2016/04/the-innovative-coworking-spaces-of-15th-century-italy.

Francis, Russell. *The Decentering of the Traditional University: The Future of (Self) Education in Virtually Figured Worlds*. New York: Routledge, 2010.

Frey, Thomas. "Will Coworking Replace Colleges?" *Futurist Speaker*, July 17, 2015, http://www.futuristspeaker.com/business-trends/will-coworking-replace-colleges.

Friedman, George. *The Next 100 Years: A Forecast for the 21st Century*. New York: Doubleday, 2009.

Frodeman, Robert, Carl Mitcham, and Roger Pielke Jr. "Humanities for Policy—and a Policy for the Humanities." *Issues in Science and Technology* 20, no. 1 (Fall 2003): 29–32.

Fry, Tony. *Design Futuring: Sustainability, Ethics and New Practice*. London: Berg, 2008.

Gallagher, Sean R. *The Future of University Credentials: New Developments at the Intersection of Higher Education and Hiring*. Cambridge, MA: Harvard Education Press, 2016.

Galloway, Alexander R. *Protocol: How Control Exists after Decentralization*. Cambridge, MA: MIT Press, 2004.

Gardner, Howard. *Five Minds for the Future*. Boston: Harvard Business School Press, 2006.

———. *The Unschooled Mind: How Children Think and How Schools Should Teach*. New York: Basic, 1995.

Gates, Kathryn. "Automation and the Well-Run University." *Educause Review*, July 3, 2017, http://er.educause.edu/blogs/2017/7/automation-and-the-well-run-university.

Goldstein, Evan R. "The New Intellectuals: Is the Academic Jobs Crisis a Boon to Public Culture?" *Chronicle of Higher Education*, November 13, 2016, http://www.chronicle.com/article/The-New-Intellectuals/238354.

———. "The Undoing of Disruption." *Chronicle Review*, September 15, 2015, http://www.chronicle.com/article/The-Undoing-of-Disruption/233101.

Goodman, Paul. *The Community of Scholars*. New York: Random House, 1962.

Gordon, Edward E., and Elaine H. Gordon. *Centuries of Tutoring: A History of Alternative Education in America and Western Europe*. Lanham, MD: University Press of America, 1990.

Gray, Peter. "The Decline of Play." TED Talks, https://www.youtube.com/watch?v=Bg-GEzM7iTk.

———. "The Play Deficit." *Aeon*, September 18, 2013, https://aeon.co/essays/children -today-are-suffering-a-severe-deficit-of-play.

Grazer, Brian. *A Curious Mind: The Secret to a Bigger Life*. New York: Simon and Schuster, 2015.

Guldi, Jo, and David Armitage. *The History Manifesto*. Cambridge: Cambridge University Press, 2014.

Guterl, Matthew Pratt. "Why We Need an Open Curriculum." *Chronicle of Higher Education*, July 21, 2014, http://www.chronicle.com/blogs/conversation/2014/07/21 /why-we-need-an-open-curriculum.

Hagiu, Andrei. "Strategic Decisions for Multisided Platforms." *MIT Sloan Management Review* 55, no. 2 (Winter 2014): 71–80.

Hague, Douglas. *Beyond Universities: A New Republic of the Intellect*. London: Institute of Economic Affairs, 1991.

Haimendorf, Max, and Jacob Kestner. "Human Scale Education: School Structures— Size Matters." Human Scale Education and the Calouste Gulbenkian Foundation, 2009, http://www.hse.org.uk/downloads/SchoolStructuresSizeMattersbyMax HaimendorfandJacobKestner.pdf.

Hannan, Andrew, and Harold Silver. *Innovating in Higher Education: Teaching, Learning and Institutional Cultures*. Buckingham, England: Society for Research into Higher Education and Open University Press, 2000.

Haraway, Donna. *Simians, Cyborgs and Women: The Reinvention of Nature*. New York: Routledge, 1991.

Harpham, Geoffrey Galt. *The Humanities and the Dream of America*. Chicago: University of Chicago Press, 2011.

———. "The Essential English Department." *Chronicle of Higher Education*, October 1, 2017, https://www.chronicle.com/article/The-Essential-English/241119.

Harris, Ainsley. "How This Startup's 'Micro-School' Network Could Change the Way We Educate Now." *Fast Company*, May 9, 2014, https://www.fastcompany .com/3028073/how-this-startups-micro-school-network-could-change-the-way -we-educate-now.

Hebel, Sara. "UVa Board Members' E-Mails Reflect Worry about Online Education." *Chronicle of Higher Education*, June 20, 2012, http://www.chronicle.com/article /UVa-Board-Members-E-Mails/132431.

Hill, Charles. *Grand Strategies: Literature, Statecraft, and World Order*. New Haven, CT: Yale University Press, 2010.

Hoder, Randye. "Why Your High School Senior Should Take a Gap Year." *Time*, May 14, 2014, http://time.com/97065/gap-year-college.

Holland, Eugene W. *Nomad Citizenship: Free-Market Communism and the Slow-Motion General Strike*. Minneapolis: University of Minnesota Press, 2011.

Hookway, Branden. *Interface*. Cambridge, MA: MIT Press, 2014.

Hora, Matthew T., with Ross J. Benbow and Amanda K. Oleson. *Beyond the Skills Gap:*

Preparing College Students for Life and Work. Cambridge, MA: Harvard Education Press, 2016.

Horn, Michael B. "The Rise of AltSchool and Other Micro-Schools." *EducationNext* 15, no. 3 (2015), http://educationnext.org/rise-micro-schools.

Howe, Jeff. "Clayton Christensen Wants to Transform Capitalism." *Wired*, February 12, 2013, https://www.wired.com/2013/02/mf-clayton-christensen-wants-to-trans form-capitalism/all.

Hutson, Matthew. "Beyond the Five Senses: Telepathy, Echolocation, and the Future of Perception." *Atlantic*, July–August 2017, 28–29.

Illich, Ivan. *Deschooling Society*. New York: Harper and Row, 1971.

Ishii, Hiroshi, et al. "ambientROOM: Integrating Ambient Media with Architectural Space." *Conference Summary of CHI '98*, 1998, https://www.researchgate.net /publication/2313001_ambientROOM_Integrating_Ambient_Media_with_Ar chitectural_Space.

Jaschik, Scott. "Well-Prepared in Their Own Eyes." *Inside Higher Ed*, January 20, 2015, https://www.insidehighered.com/news/2015/01/20/study-finds-big-gaps -between-student-and-employer-perceptions.

Jaspers, Karl. *The Idea of a University*. Boston: Beacon, 1959.

Johansen, Bob. *Get There Early: Sensing the Future to Compete in the Present*. San Francisco: Berrett-Koehler, 2007.

Johansson, Frans. *The Medici Effect: Breakthrough Insights at the Intersection of Ideas, Concepts and Cultures*. Boston: Harvard Business School Press, 2004.

Johnson, Brian David. *Science Fiction Prototyping: Designing the Future with Science Fiction*. San Rafael, CA: Morgan and Claypool, 2011.

Johnson, Steven. *Where Good Ideas Come From: The Natural History of Innovation*. New York: Riverhead, 2010.

Juul, Jesper. *The Art of Failure: An Essay on the Pain of Playing Video Games*. Cambridge, MA: MIT Press, 2013.

Kachappilly, Kurian. "Gurukula: A Family with Difference—an Exposition of the Ancient Indian System of Education." Third International Soul in Education Conference, Byron Bay, NSW, Australia, September 27–October 2, 2003, http:// www.academia.edu/4378166/Gurukula_A_Family_with_Difference_-_An_Expo sition_of_the_Ancient_Indian_System_of_Education.

Kamenetz, Anya. *DIY U: Edupunks, Edupreneurs, and the Coming Transformation of Higher Education*. White River Junction, VT: Chelsea Green, 2010.

Kaplan, Jerry. *Humans Need Not Apply: A Guide to Wealth and Work in the Age of Artificial Intelligence*. New Haven, CT: Yale University Press, 2015.

Kasparov, Garry. *Deep Thinking: Where Machine Intelligence Ends and Human Creativity Begins*. New York: Public Affairs, 2017.

Kaye, Joseph. "The Olfactory Display of Abstract Information." n.d., MIT Media Lab, http://alumni.media.mit.edu/~jofish/writing/smell.as.media.short.paper.pdf.

Kelly, Kevin. *The Inevitable: Understanding the 12 Technological Forces That Will Shape Our Future*. New York: Viking, 2016.

Keohane, Nannerl O. *Thinking about Leadership*. Princeton, NJ: Princeton University Press, 2012.

Kliewer, Joy Rosenzweig. *The Innovative Campus: Nurturing the Distinctive Learning Environment*. Phoenix, AZ: American Council on Education, Oryx Press, 1999.

Kosslyn, Stephen M., and Ben Nelson, eds. *Building the Intentional University: Minerva and the Future of Higher Education*. Cambridge, MA: MIT Press, 2017.

Krebs, Paula. "Step Outside the Major, Please." *Chronicle Vitae*, July 28, 2015, https://chroniclevitae.com/news/1077-step-outside-the-major-please.

Krell-Roesch, Janina, et al. "Association between Mentally Stimulating Activities in Late Life and the Outcome of Incident Mild Cognitive Impairment, with an Analysis of the *APOE* ε4 Genotype." *JAMA Neurology* 74 (March 2017), http://jamanetwork.com/journals/jamaneurology/fullarticle/2598835.

Lane, David A., and Robert Maxfield. "Ontological Uncertainty and Innovation." Santa Fe Institute. n.d., https://www.santafe.edu/research/results/working-papers/ontological-uncertainty-and-innovation.

Lang, James M. "Being Nehru for 2 Days." *Chronicle of Higher Education*, July 21, 2014, http://chronicle.com/article/Being-Nehru-for-2-Days/147813.

———. "Stop Blaming Students for Your Listless Classroom." *Chronicle of Higher Education*, September 29, 2014, http://chronicle.com/article/Stop-Blaming-Students-for-Your/149067.

Lee, Edward Ashford. *Plato and the Nerd: The Creative Partnership of Humans and Technology*. Cambridge, MA: MIT Press, 2017.

Lego. "Serious Play: The Method." https://www.lego.com/en-us/seriousplay/the-method.

Lenzner, Robert, and Stephen S. Johnson. "Seeing Things as They Really Are." *Forbes*, March 10, 1997, https://www.forbes.com/forbes/1997/0310/5905122a.html.

Leski, Kyna. *The Storm of Creativity*. Cambridge, MA: MIT Press, 2015.

Levine, Donald N. *Powers of the Mind: The Reinvention of Liberal Learning in America*. Chicago: University of Chicago Press, 2006.

Lewis, Sarah. *The Rise: Creativity, the Gift of Failure, and the Search for Mastery*. New York: Simon and Schuster, 2014.

Livio, Mario. *Why? What Makes Us Curious*. New York: Simon and Schuster, 2017.

Lombardi, John V. *How Universities Work*. Baltimore: Johns Hopkins University Press, 2013.

Machado, Amanda. "Traveling Teaches Students in a Way Schools Can't." *Atlantic*, December 1, 2014, https://www.theatlantic.com/education/archive/2014/12/traveling-offers-lessons-that-us-schools-fail-to-provide/383090.

Madsbjerg, Christian. *Sensemaking: The Power of the Humanities in the Age of the Algorithm*. New York: Hachette, 2017.

Malone, Michael. *The Future Arrived Yesterday: The Rise of the Protean Corporation and What It Means for You.* New York: Crown Business, 2009.

Malone, Thomas. *The Future of Work.* Boston: Harvard Business School Press, 2004.

Mangan, Katherine. "The Making of a Modern-Day Apprentice." *Chronicle of Higher Education*, June 28, 2017, http://www.chronicle.com/article/The-Making-of-a-Modern-Day/240466.

Markusen, Ann, and Anne Gadwa. "Creative Placemaking." National Endowment for the Arts, 2010, https://www.arts.gov/sites/default/files/CreativePlacemaking-Paper.pdf.

"Mayo Clinic Researchers Find Mentally Stimulating Activities after Age 70 Associated with Lower New Cognitive-Impairment Risk." *Kurzweil: Accelerating Intelligence*, January 31, 2017, http://www.kurzweilai.net/mayo-clinic-researchers-find-mentally-stimulating-activities-after-age-70-associated-with-lower-new-cognitive-impairment-risk.

McCullough, Malcolm. *Ambient Commons: Attention in the Age of Embodied Information.* Cambridge, MA: MIT Press, 2013.

McGee, Jon. *Breakpoint: The Changing Marketplace for Higher Education.* Baltimore: Johns Hopkins University Press, 2015.

McKenzie, Lindsay. "Online, Cheap—and Elite." *Inside Higher Ed*, March 20, 2018, https://www.insidehighered.com/digital-learning/article/2018/03/20/analysis-shows-georgia-tech's-online-masters-computer-science.

McShane, Sveta. "Machines Won't Replace Us, They'll Force Us to Evolve." *Singularity Hub*, May 5, 2016, https://singularityhub.com/2016/05/05/machines-wont-replace-us-theyll-force-us-to-evolve.

Meadows, Donella H. *Thinking in Systems: A Primer.* White River Junction, VT: Chelsea Green, 2008.

Medvetz, Thomas. *Think Tanks in America.* Chicago: University of Chicago Press, 2012.

Merisotis, Jamie. *America Needs Talent: Attracting, Educating and Deploying the 21st-Century Workforce.* New York: Rosetta, 2015.

Meyer, Pamela. *From Workplace to Playspace: Innovating, Learning and Changing through Dynamic Engagement.* San Francisco: Jossey-Bass, 2010.

Miller, Peter N. "Is 'Design Thinking' the New Liberal Arts?" *Chronicle Review*, March 26, 2015, http://chronicle.com/article/Is-Design-Thinking-the-New/228779.

Millett, Stephen M. *Managing the Future: A Guide to Forecasting and Strategic Planning in the 21st Century.* Axminster, England: Triarchy Press, 2011.

Mills, David, and Patrick Alexander. "Are Oxbridge Tutorials Still the Best Way to Teach Students How to Think?" *Conversation*, July 8, 2015, http://theconversation.com/are-oxbridge-tutorials-still-the-best-way-to-teach-students-how-to-think-44250.

Mitchell, William J. *Me++: The Cyborg Self and the Networked City.* Cambridge, MA: MIT Press, 2003.

Mohn, Tanya. "The Digital Nomad Life: Combining Work and Travel." *New York Times*, April 3, 2017, https://www.nytimes.com/2017/04/03/business/digital-no mads-work-tourism.html.

Mootee, Idris. *Design Thinking for Strategic Innovation*. Hoboken, NJ: Wiley, 2013.

Moravec, John, ed. *Knowmad Society*. Minneapolis, MN: Education Futures, 2013.

Morson, Gary Saul, and Morton Schapiro. *Cents and Sensibility: What Economics Can Learn from the Humanities*. Princeton, NJ: Princeton University Press, 2017.

Murphy, Peter, Michael A. Peters, and Simon Marginson. *Imagination: Three Models of Imagination in the Age of the Knowledge Economy*. New York: Peter Lang, 2010.

National Foundation on the Arts and the Humanities Act of 1965. P.L. 89–209, https://www.neh.gov/about/history/national-foundation-arts-and-human ities-act-1965-pl-89-209.

Neem, Johann N. "Let's Not Rush into Disruptive Innovation." *Inside Higher Ed*, March 16, 2017, https://www.insidehighered.com/views/2017/03/16/downside-innova tion-and-disruption-essay.

Negroponte, Nicholas. *Being Digital*. New York: Vintage, 1995.

Nelson, Adam R. *Education and Democracy: The Meaning of Alexander Meiklejohn, 1872–1964*. Madison: University of Wisconsin Press, 2001.

Newell, L. Jackson. *The Electric Edge of Academe: The Saga of Lucien L. Nunn and Deep Springs College*. Salt Lake City: University of Utah Press, 2015.

9/11 Commission Report. https://www.9-11commission.gov/report/911Report.pdf.

Norman, Donald. *The Design of Future Things*. New York: Basic, 2007.

Ogle, Richard. *Smart World: Breakthrough Creativity and the New Science of Ideas*. Boston: Harvard Business School Press, 2007.

Omprakash EdGE. "EdGE Orientation Book." n.d., https://d3f5zjlu4h8yvi.cloudfront .net/new_page_images/2015.9_EdGE_OrientationBook.pdf.

Omprakash EdGE and Florida State University Division of Undergraduate Studies. "Omprakash EdGE and FSU Global Scholars: An Introduction." n.d., https://cre .fsu.edu/sites/g/files/imported/storage/original/application/26db0212b23e4e 97ca6b672044f226c9.pdf.

Ong, Walter J. *Orality and Literacy: The Technologizing of the Word*. London: Routledge, 1982.

Page, Scott E. *The Difference: How the Power of Diversity Creates Better Groups, Firms, Schools, and Societies*. Princeton, NJ: Princeton University Press, 2008.

Parker, Geoffrey G., Marshall W. Van Alstyne, and Sangeet Paul Choudary. *Platform Revolution*. New York: Norton, 2016.

Parkin, Simon. "Teaching Robots Right from Wrong." *Economist 1843* (June–July 2017), https://www.1843magazine.com/features/teaching-robots-right-from-wrong.

Perlin, Ross. *Intern Nation: How to Earn Nothing and Learn Little in the Brave New Economy*. Brooklyn, NY: Verso, 2012.

Pink, Daniel H. *A Whole New Mind: Moving from the Information Age to the Conceptual Age*. New York: Riverhead, 2005.

Pitt, Richard N., and Steven A. Tepper. "Double Majors: Influences, Identities and Impacts." Nashville, TN: Curb Center for Art, Enterprise and Public Policy, September 2012.

Poliakoff, Michael B. "Who's Afraid of Course Requirements?" *Inside Higher Ed*, July 3, 2017, https://www.insidehighered.com/views/2017/07/03/importance-core-curriculum-essay.

Postman, Neil. *Technopoly: The Surrender of Culture to Technology*. New York: Knopf, 1992.

Prince, Katherine. *Innovating toward a Vibrant Learning Ecosystem: Ten Pathways for Transforming Learning*. Cincinnati, OH: KnowledgeWorks Forecast 3.0, 2014.

Prince, Katherine, Andrea Saveri, and Jason Swanson. "Exploring the Future Education Workforce: New Roles for an Expanding Learning Ecosystem." Cincinnati, OH: KnowledgeWorks Foundation, 2015.

Ramo, Joshua Cooper. *The Age of the Unthinkable: Why the New World Disorder Constantly Surprises Us and What We Can Do about It*. New York: Little, Brown, 2009.

Rao, Anand. "A Strategist's Guide to Artificial Intelligence." *Strategy + Business* 87 (Summer 2017): 46–55.

Rescher, Nicholas. *Imagining Irreality: A Study of Unreal Possibilities*. Chicago: Open Court, 2003.

Resnick, Mitchel. *Lifelong Kindergarten: Cultivating Creativity through Projects, Passion, Peers, and Play*. Cambridge, MA: MIT Press, 2017.

Rickert, Thomas. *Ambient Rhetoric: The Attunements of Rhetorical Being*. Pittsburgh, PA: University of Pittsburgh Press, 2013.

Roche, Mark William. *Realizing the Distinctive University: Vision and Values, Strategy and Culture*. South Bend, IN: University of Notre Dame Press, 2017.

Rogers, Adam. "Wrinkles in Spacetime: The Warped Astrophysics of *Interstellar*." *Wired*, October 2014, https://www.wired.com/2014/10/astrophysics-interstellar-black-hole.

Rose, David. "Why Gesture Is the Next Big Thing in Design." *Ideo*, January 25, 2018, https://www.ideo.com/blog/why-gesture-is-the-next-big-thing-in-design.

Rosin, Hanna. "The Overprotected Kid." *Atlantic*, April 2014, http://www.theatlantic.com/magazine/archive/2014/04/hey-parents-leave-those-kids-alone/358631.

Rumsey, Abby Smith. "Creating Value and Impact in the Digital Age through Translational Humanities." Council on Library and Information Resources, April 2013, https://www.clir.org/wp-content/uploads/sites/6/report_57d70f70d83e8.pdf.

Sandeen, Cathy. "MOOCs Moving On, Moving Up." *Inside Higher Ed*, June 22, 2017, https://www.insidehighered.com/views/2017/06/22/essay-looking-back-predictions-about-moocs.

Santhi, B. Girish, G. Koundinya, and Jaikumar Ganesan. "Praagyah: Computer Aided Gurukul System through Cloud Computing." *International Journal of Engineering and Technology* 5, no. 4 (2013): 3223–26.

Sapolsky, Robert. "People Who Can Intuit in Six Dimensions." In *This Will Change Everything: Ideas That Will Shape the Future*, ed. John Brockman, 366–69. New York: Harper Perennial, 2010.

Satariano, Adam. "Silicon Valley Tried to Reinvent Schools: Now It's Rebooting." *Bloomberg*, November 1, 2017, https://www.bloomberg.com/news/arti cles/2017–11–01/silicon-valley-tried-to-reinvent-schools-now-it-s-rebooting.

Schwartz, Madeline. "5 'Weird' Schools That Are Challenging How Students Learn." *Global Citizen*, August 1, 2016, https://www.globalcitizen.org/en/content/high -school-strange-breaking-boundaries.

Schwartz, Peter. *The Art of the Long View: Planning for the Future in an Uncertain World*. New York: Currency Doubleday, 1996.

Selee, Andrew. *What Should Think Tanks Do? A Strategic Guide to Policy Impact*. Stanford, CA: Stanford Briefs, 2013.

Selingo, Jeffrey J. "Why More High-School Seniors Need to Be Like Malia Obama and Take a Gap Year." *Washington Post*, May 2, 2016, https://www.washingtonpost .com/news/grade-point/wp/2016/05/02/why-more-high-school-seniors-need -to-be-like-malia-obama-and-take-a-gap-year.

Seltzer, Rick. "Think Tank Trouble?" *Inside Higher Ed*, December 12, 2016, https:// www.insidehighered.com/news/2016/12/12/university-think-tanks-face-tough -road-continued-interest.

Seminara, Dave. "Would You Teach Your Kids on the Road?" *BBC*, November 8, 2016, http://www.bbc.com/travel/story/20161108-would-you-teach-your-kids-on-the -road.

Shellenbarger, Sue. "Delaying College to Fill in the Gaps." *Wall Street Journal*, December 29, 2010, http://www.wsj.com/articles/SB1000142405297020351320457 6047723922275698.

Shirky, Clay. *Here Comes Everybody: The Power of Organizing without Organizations*. New York: Penguin, 2008.

Shteyngart, Gary. "Thinking Outside the Bots." *Smithsonian*, June 2017, 66–80.

Sicart, Miguel. *Play Matters*. Cambridge, MA: MIT Press, 2014.

Siegel, David J. "How Anarchy Can Save the University." *Chronicle Review*, May 7, 2017, B5–B7, https://www.chronicle.com/article/How-Anarchy-Can-Save-the /239982.

Smith, Adam. *The Wealth of Nations*. New York: Penguin, 1974.

Smith, Sidonie. *Manifesto for the Humanities: Transforming Doctoral Education in Good Enough Times*. 2015, https://quod.lib.umich.edu/d/dcbooks /13607059.0001.001/1:13/—manifesto-for-the-humanities-transforming-doc toral-education?g=dculture;rgn=div1;view=fulltext;xc=1.

Solomon, Joan, ed. *The Passion to Learn: An Inquiry into Autodidactism*. London: RoutledgeFalmer, 2003.

Spellings, Margaret. "A Test of Leadership: Charting the Future of U.S. Higher Education." U.S. Department of Education, 2006, https://www2.ed.gov/about/bds comm/list/hiedfuture/reports/final-report.pdf.

Staley, David J. "Autonomous Learning and the Future of Higher Education." *EvoLLLution*, March 14, 2013, https://evolllution.com/opinions/autonomous -learning-future-higher-education.

———. "The Future of Higher Education in the Age of Synthetic Intelligence." *Southeast Education Network*, March 3, 2017, http://www.seenmagazine.us /Articles/Article-Detail/ArticleId/6133/THE-FUTURE-OF-HIGHER-EDUCA TION-IN-THE-AGE-OF-SYNTHETIC-INTELLIGENCE.

———. "The Future of the University: Speculative Design for Innovation in Higher Education." *Educause Review*, November 9, 2015, https://er.educause.edu /articles/2015/11/the-future-of-the-university-speculative-design-for-innovation -in-higher-education.

———. "Managing the Platform: Higher Education and the Logic of Wikinomics." *Educause Review*, January 16, 2009, https://er.educause.edu/articles/2009/1 /managing-the-platform-higher-education-and-the-logic-of-wikinomics.

Staley, David J., and W. David Cress. "The University as a Model of Technological Balance." *Bulletin of Science, Technology and Society* 18, no. 1 (1998): 16–22.

Stephens, Dale J. *Hacking Your Education: Ditch the Lectures, Save Tens of Thousands, and Learn More Than Your Peers Ever Will*. New York: Perigee, 2013.

Sterling, Bruce. *Shaping Things*. Cambridge, MA: MIT Press, 2005.

Sternberg, Robert J. *What Universities Can Be: A New Model for Preparing Students for Active Concerned Citizenship and Ethical Leadership*. Ithaca, NY: Cornell University Press, 2016.

Stinson, Elizabeth. "Armed Response: Gadgets Get Touchy-Feely." *Wired*, May 2018, 28.

Strauch, Barbara. "How to Train the Aging Brain." *New York Times*, December 29, 2009, http://www.nytimes.com/2010/01/03/education/edlife/03adult-t.html.

Struyk, Raymond J. *Managing Think Tanks: Practical Guidance for Maturing Organizations*. Budapest: Open Society Institute Local Government and Public Service Reform Initiative and the Urban Institute, 2002.

Sun, Felicia W., et al. "Youthful Brains in Older Adults: Preserved Neuroanatomy in the Default Mode and Salience Networks Contributes to Youthful Memory in Superaging." *Journal of Neuroscience* 36 (September 14, 2016), http://www .jneurosci.org/content/36/37/9659.

Suoranta, Juha, and Tere Vaden. *Wikiworld*. New York: Pluto, 2010.

Taylor, Mark C. *Crisis on Campus: A Bold Plan for Reforming Our Colleges and Universities*. New York: Knopf, 2010.

Tedlow, Richard S. *Denial: Why Business Leaders Fail to Look Facts in the Face—and What to Do about It*. New York: Portfolio, 2010.

Tetlock, Philip E., and Dan Gardner. *Superforecasting: The Art and Science of Prediction*. New York: Crown, 2015.

Thelin, John R. *A History of American Higher Education*. Baltimore: Johns Hopkins University Press, 2004.

Thomas, Douglas, and John Seely Brown. *A New Culture of Learning: Cultivating the Imagination for a World of Constant Change*. Self-published, CreateSpace Independent Publishing Platform, 2011.

Thompson, Clive. *Smarter Than You Think*. New York: Penguin, 2013.

Thompson, Derek. "A World without Work." *Atlantic*, July–August 2015, http://www.theatlantic.com/magazine/archive/2015/07/world-without-work/395294.

Tropp, Laura. "Adult-Child's Play." *Inside Higher Ed*, October 14, 2015, https://www.insidehighered.com/blogs/mama-phd/adult-child's-play.

Turner, James. *Philology: The Forgotten Origins of the Modern Humanities*. Princeton, NJ: Princeton University Press, 2014.

———. "Yes, the Humanities Are Struggling, but They Will Endure." *Chronicle of Higher Education*, June 9, 2014, http://www.chronicle.com/blogs/conversation/2014/06/09/yes-the-humanities-are-struggling-but-they-will-endure.

Tyrrell, Ian. *Historians in Public: The Practice of American History, 1890–1970*. Chicago: University of Chicago Press, 2005.

University of Manchester Careers Service. "What Is Initiative?" n.d., http://www.careers.manchester.ac.uk/experience/skills/initiative.

van der Heijden, Kees. *Scenarios: The Art of Strategic Conversation*, 2nd ed. West Sussex, England: Wiley, 2005.

Van Goethem, Herman, and Ilja Van Damme. "De menswetenschapper, nu ook nuttig buiten de unief!" *De Standaard*, September 7, 2013, http://www.standaard.be/cnt/dmf20130906_00729027.

Victor, Bret. *Seeing Spaces*. n.d., https://vimeo.com/97903574.

———. "Why a Seeing Space?," August 2014, http://worrydream.com/SeeingSpaces/SeeingSpaces.jpg.

Wagner, Tony. *The Global Achievement Gap*. New York: Basic, 2008.

Ward, Steven C. "Welcome to Shark Tank U." *Inside Higher Ed*, February 21, 2017, https://www.insidehighered.com/views/2017/02/21/questionable-entrepreneurship-mania-college-campuses-essay.

Webb, Amy. *The Signals Are Talking: Why Today's Fringe Is Tomorrow's Mainstream*. New York: Public Affairs, 2016.

Weiner, Eric. *The Geography of Genius*. New York: Simon and Schuster, 2016.

Weizenbaum, Joseph. *Computer Power and Human Reason: From Judgment to Calculation*. New York: Freeman, 1976.

Wellmon, Chad. *Organizing Enlightenment: Information Overload and the Invention of the Modern Research University*. Baltimore: Johns Hopkins University Press, 2015.

Wildavsky, Ben, Andrew P. Kelly, and Kevin Carey, eds. *Reinventing Higher Education: The Promise of Innovation*. Cambridge, MA: Harvard Education Press, 2011.

Williamson, Ben. *The Future of the Curriculum: School Knowledge in the Digital Age.* Cambridge, MA: MIT Press, 2013.

Winston, Joe. *Beauty and Education.* New York: Routledge, 2010.

Wladawsky-Berger, Irving. "Why Imagination and Curiosity Matter More Than Ever." *Wall Street Journal,* January 31, 2014, https://blogs.wsj.com/cio/2014/01/31/why-imagination-and-curiosity-matter-more-than-ever.

Wood, Carol S. "Rector Dragas' Remarks to VPs and Deans." *UVA Today,* June 10, 2012, https://news.virginia.edu/content/rector-dragas-remarks-vps-and-deans.

Wu, Frank H. "The Intentional Community of Deep Springs College." *Huffington Post,* March 27, 2013, http://www.huffingtonpost.com/frank-h-wu/deep-springs-college_b_2944946.html.

Index